BROOKSIANA;

OR,

THE CONTROVERSY

BETWEEN

Senator Brooks and Archbishop Hughes,

GROWING OUT OF THE RECENTLY ENACTED
CHURCH PROPERTY BILL,

WITH AN INTRODUCTION

BY THE

MOST REV. ARCHBISHOP OF NEW YORK.

NEW YORK:
EDWARD DUNIGAN & BROTHER, 151 FULTON STREET.
1855.

INTRODUCTION.

Few questions of a comparatively local character have arisen in modern times to which circumstances have so much attracted public attention as the question of the late Church Property Bill, passed in the Legislature of New York, and the incidents antecedent to or growing out of its enactments. The writer would not have the slightest doubt as to the accuracy of public sentiment if the question were thoroughly understood. He has unbounded confidence in the justice and fairness which characterize the judgment of the American people in regard to any matter, the true merits of which have been brought under their notice. No doubt that under the impulse of generous feelings, they are sometimes liable to be led away by appearances. We have seen that in more than one instance political adventurers from other countries have succeeded in imposing upon them, and betraying them into proceedings far from creditable to their calmer judgments. But such delusions have been of very brief and transitory duration. The sober second thought soon replaces the sentiment of impulse and rectifies its errors. It will be so in regard to the question now under consideration. The American people, the living embodiment and practical administrator of the great and noble principles which are inscribed in our free constitutions, will never allow those sacred principles to be perverted or trampled under foot to gratify the spurious patriotism of a clique who are attempting to infuse religious strife into the very arteries of civil freedom, of social happiness and national strength.

This being now as it has ever been the deliberate judgment of the writer in regard to the character of the American people, he has deemed it but a respectful duty to them to furnish in this introduction such explanation of the true grounds of the question involved in the late act of the Legislature of New York, as will enable them to form their own just conclusions, according to the merit and evidence of the case submitted.

I.

It has been the supreme and sovereign will of the American people from the period of their independence, that all religious denominations residing within their borders should enjoy the same equality of rights and privileges under the Constitution and laws of the country. And although several of the States continued for many years to retain enactments preventing Catholics from the full enjoyment of these equal privileges, still the great predominant sentiment of the country induced those States one after another to abolish such enactments, so that at the present day they disgrace the statute book of no commonwealth in the whole Union, except that of New Hampshire. In this great principle of religious equality among the various denominations composing the powerful free empire of the American people, it was never intended that the State should prescribe for any denomination a code of discipline which should embarrass its members in carrying out the principles of their faith. It never was intended that the rules which might harmonize with the faith of one denomination, should be imposed unsolicited upon another whose religious belief was of an entirely different character. On the contrary, the principle hitherto adopted and universally acted upon, if we except the Church Property Bill as it is commonly called, has been that each denomination should either use a general enactment, such as the law of 1784 in this State, or solicit at the hands of the Legislature such special enactment as might enable them, consistently with the requirements of the Constitution, to manage the external affairs of their communion as a religious body according to their respective symbols of faith.

II.

The venerable Archbishop Carroll, who himself took part in the revolution by which American independence was won, wished to assimilate as far as possible the outward administration of Catholic Church property in a way that would harmonize with the democratic principles on which the new government was founded. With this view he authorized and instituted the system of lay trustees in Catholic congregations. Regarded *a priori*, no system could appear to be less objectionable, or more likely, both to secure advantages to those congregations, and at the same time to recommend the Catholic religion to the liberal consideration of the Protestant sentiment of the country. It would, he thought, relieve the priest from the necessity and painfulness of having to appeal from the altar on questions connected with money, touching either the means of his own support, repairs of the church, or other measures essential to the welfare of his congregation. It would at the same time secure the property by the protection of law for the perpetual uses to which it had been set apart and consecrated. It would be a bond of union between the priest and the people. It would be a shield to protect the minister of the altar, from the very suspicion of being a money-seeker, and at the same time a means to provide for his decent maintenance. All these were no doubt the considerations which moved the venerable and patriotic Archbishop to adopt and recommend the system of lay trustees. On paper and in theory that system was entirely unobjectionable. It was well calculated to gain the confidence of a mind so generous and so liberal as that of the first Archbishop of Baltimore. But in practice it became the bitter chalice of his old age. It led to violent strifes in Charleston and in Norfolk. It led to riots and bloodshed in Baltimore and Philadelphia. Archbishop Carroll, when there were but two churches in the city of Baltimore, was doomed to witness the congregation of one of them assembling at the house of Divine worship on Sunday with loaded muskets in their hands. He was doomed even during his own administration to see an excommunicated priest inaugurated by lay trustees in another church in Philadelphia; and to undergo a legal prosecution at the hands of lay trustees, in the Civil Court, for a simple act of Episcopal jurisdiction. It is impossible to tell what would have been the consequence of that prosecution had it not been for the high character which the good prelate had sustained, and for the high estimation in which he was held by the whole community of Philadelphia, Protestant as well as Catholic. After his death, similar results of lay-trusteeship followed in the church of St. Mary in Philadelphia. Whoever will turn to the press of that city in the years 1821, 1822, 1823, 1824, 1825, will see melancholy evidence of its workings in social strifes, religious enmities, schism, lawsuits, fearful riots and bloodshed.

The evils which manifested themselves in these churches on a grand scale, were witnessed in a minor degree in almost every congregation throughout the country, under the government of lay trustees. The churches of this city were by no means exempt from them; and some of our older Catholic inhabitants have witnessed, both in St. Peter's and in St. Patrick's, scenes of strife which they deplored, and which they would be ashamed to read in recorded detail.

III.

Such was the general condition of the Catholic people of the United States in the year 1829, when their Bishops were numerous enough to hold counsel together for the purpose of securing peace, promoting piety, and improving the moral and social condition of their respective flocks. In the fifth decree of this first council the following statute was agreed upon, and rendered applicable to each diocese except that of Charleston.

"Whereas lay trustees have frequently abused the right conceded to them by the State, to the great detriment of religion and scandal of the faithful, we desire earnestly that henceforth no church be erected or consecrated unless the title thereof, whenever it can be done, shall be assigned by a written document to the bishop of the diocese in which it is to be erected, for the purpose of divine worship, and the benefit of the faithful." In the fourth decree of the third council of Baltimore, held in 1837, both the clergy and laity are reminded of the heavy spiritual penalties decreed by the Council of Trent against all persons, whether lay or clerical, perverting from the sacred purpose to which it is appropriated any thing given by the faithful for religious or charitable uses. The fourth statute of the seventh Provincial Council of Baltimore, held in 1849, lays down the rule as follows:—

"The fathers have ordained that all churches and other ecclesiastical goods which have accrued from the gifts or offerings of the faithful, and which are to be employed for purposes of charity or religion, shall belong to the ordinary, unless it appear and is proven in writing, that they have been conceded to some religious order, or congregation of priests for their own use."

These are the only laws of discipline regarding church property which I find enacted in the Provincial Councils of Baltimore. This latter statute had reference more particularly to that kind of property which might have been given in a vague and indefinite way; and which it might happen that the priest, either in good faith or otherwise, might construe as having been given to himself for his personal use. But in no case has the idea ever been entertained of acquiring wealth or making the Church rich, or creating revenues which even a Bishop or Archbishop might be at liberty to use or abuse at his discretion.

IV.

It is hardly necessary to remind the Protestant reader that Catholics have their own mode of Church government, and that when they were admitted to equality of privileges, the same as other religious denominations, their mode of regulating questions of Church discipline, according to the principlesof their creed, was substantially recognized and guaranteed. This of course should be in harmony with those principles of the constitution and general laws of the State by which its own supreme sovereignty should be maintained, and its right of protection to all its inhabitants in the domain of civil legislation secured. Still, it was never intended that the Catholic idea regarding Church property should, through the operation of civil laws, be made conformable to those of any other denomination of Christians. This would be a contradiction. It would be taking from them by legislation a portion of what had been secured to them by the Constitution and the Bill of Rights.

It was under these convictions that the present Archbishop of New York enjoined upon the Catholics under his charge the obligation of regarding Church property in the light of their faith. Hence in his pastoral letter, published after the first diocesan synod in 1842, we find the following as the true Catholic idea, according to which Church property is to be regarded. The document was published at a time when the evil consequences of lay-trusteeship in the city of New York were beginning to manifest themselves.

"Now, ecclesiastical property is that, and all that, which the faithful contribute from religious motives and for religious purposes. It is the Church, the cemetery, and all estate thereto belonging. It is the pew rents;—the collections,—and all moneys derived from, or for the benefit of religion. It is the sacred furniture of the house of God. In a word, it is all that exists for ecclesiastical purposes. According to the laws of the Church and the usage of all nations, such property, though it must be protected by human laws, as other material property, yet, being once brought into existence in the form, and for the uses of religion, is considered as if it were the property of God; which cannot be violated, alienated, or wastefully squandered, without (besides ordinary injustice as if it were common property), the additional guilt of a kind of sacrilege. It is not considered, in the canon law, either the property of the Bishop, or the property of his clergy, or the property of the people ; but as the property of God,—for the religious uses of them all. Hence, it is the duty of all to preserve it, but to preserve it not with the care which would be sufficient in matters of a secular character, but under a sense of the awful responsibility involved in such administration. In the enactments of the canon law, the highest functionaries of the hierarchy itself were not allowed to undertake their administration, without having first taken an oath that they would administer, preserve, and transmit it, as above described."

This is the same pastoral letter which became a stumbling-block to the trustees of St. Louis' church, Buffalo. In their petition to the legislature they substitute an entire falsehood of their own invention, as the ground of their opposition to episcopal authority. They say that Bishop Hughes attempted to compel them (the trustees) to make over the title of their church to him. The spirit of this false statement was the foundation for the bill enacted in the last session of the Legislature. And when Senator Brooks asserted that among the property conveyed to the Archbishop of New York there were numerous transfers from trustees, there was especial malice blended with the falsehood of his assertions. It was intended by him to be understood, and it was so understood by those who heard or read his speech, that the Archbishop had abused his episcopal authority for the purpose of wresting from the hands of lay trustees the property which the law of the State had authorized them to hold and administer. But thanks to Almighty God the writer of this has been providentially forearmed, if not forewarned, against such unfounded calumnies as Mr. Brooks has seen fit to invent and publish in the Senate chamber of the State of New York. On pages 11 and 12 of that same pastoral letter, published in 1842, we find the following statement, showing how grossly Mr. Senator Brooks has at once misrepresented the state of facts and the purity of motives. Referring to the discipline of the Catholic Church, as laid down in the Provincial Councils at Baltimore, the Archbishop says:

"One of the first and most explicit decrees of the Provincial Council in Baltimore, directed and enjoined on the Bishops of this province, that they should not, thenceforward, consecrate any church therein, unless the deed had been previously made, in trust, to the Bishop thereof. This rule has hitherto been followed strictly by the great majority of the episcopal body; and wherever it has been followed, the faithful are exempted from many of the evils to which we have already referred. Religion progresses—the clergy are freed from annoyances—their ministry is respected—their influence with the people obtains large and numerous contributions, for the erection or improvement of churches, and the danger of seeing those sold for debt, and given over to profanation, is alike removed from the apprehensions of pastor and people. In proportion to their numbers, the multiplication of churches has been as great among them, as in this diocese, and yet their churches are almost, if not entirely, out of debt.

"Notwithstanding the feelings that must arise from the contrast of their situation with ours, *we have, for what appeared weighty reasons, hitherto declined executing the statutes of the decrees of the Baltimore councils on this subject.* In the first place, the system existed here, more, perhaps, than in any other diocese. Secondly, it was intimated that the laws rendered the tenure in trust, of Church property by the ordinary, uncertain, if not insecure. Besides, if it could be avoided, without injury to religion and the ecclesiastical property, we should be glad to see the Bishop freed from the solicitude inseparable from its guardianship. These considerations, which might be much enlarged, have induced us to hope that the present system of lay trustees might be so modified, as to secure some benefit, and exclude many of the evils which have resulted from the irresponsible exercise of its powers.

V.

About this period the bankruptcy of our lay trustees commenced. Churches, also, began to rise, in which the people did not desire their services. And so earnest was the Bishop in taking precautions against maladministration in the new system, and against the dangers of reproach or even suspicion in regard to their administration by the pastors, that he published the following rules:—

RULES

FOR THE ADMINISTRATION OF CHURCHES WHICH HAVE NO TRUSTEES.

"Inasmuch as the temporal affairs of any church may fall into disorder from the absence of a regular system for the management of the same; and inasmuch as the responsibility, and perhaps the reproach of maladministration would rest upon the clergyman, it is deemed essential, both for the regulation of the temporal concerns of each congregation, and for the protection of the pastoral character, that certain general rules, as nearly uniform as possible, should be adopted. It is hoped that the following simple rules will be found sufficient for the purpose.

"1*st.* The income of our churches arises from two sources, viz.: Pew-rents and Sunday collections. The Pastor is required to keep in a book of his own a regular account of the collections taken up on Sundays and Festivals—he is also required to keep a similar regular account of the Pew-rents as paid in by the Collector; he is required to appoint at least *two* confidential and pious members of his congregation, competent for such a task, by their own good sense and experience—the one to be Treasurer of Church revenues, the other Secretary, for keeping regular records of such transactions, appertaining to the affairs of the Church, as are to be recorded—both to be his assistants in managing his temporal concerns, and in aiding him with their knowledge of affairs and advice in every matter which requires reflection, and is of any importance.

"2d. All moneys arising from the sources of income already mentioned, shall be deposited in the hands of the Treasurer. The Collector shall make a double report of the sums, receiving credit in his book, as he deposits them with the Treasurer, and entering each transaction on the book kept by the Pastor; so that one book shall be exactly correspondent with the other. Neither the Secretary nor Treasurer shall appropriate or expend any of this money, except by virtue of a written order from the Pastor in each case, which order shall be the Treasurer's voucher. The Pastor is required, in the expenditure of this income, for which he shall be responsible, to conform strictly to the rules of the Diocese, with regard to the manner, and the amount and limitation of such expenditure.

"Under the head of expenditure, is included the necessary expense of supporting public worship—the salaries given to persons employed in the Church, or for the congregation—as Organist, Sexton, or Collector. These, the Pastor will regulate with due regard to the propriety of the selection and the circumstances of his Church. Under the same head will come, the amount necessary for the maintenance of the Pastor, and of his Assistant, when there is more than one Clergyman. It is the Bishop's wish, that so far as the fixed sum necessary for the support of the Pastor is concerned, it should be the same in all Churches throughout the Diocese, viz.: Six Hundred Dollars for the Pastor, and Four Hundred Dollars for the Assistant, with the understanding that the Assistant shall bear half the expenses of the house, receiving half the perquisites, and, if he should prefer paying a weekly sum for board, he shall receive one-third of the perquisites.

"In case it happen, that either for the convenience of the congregation, or as a means of living, some clergyman, incapable of rendering other missionary service than that of celebrating Mass, should be engaged, the sum to be allowed shall in no case exceed Three Hundred Dollars. If such Clergyman shall in process of time become capable of performing certain other duties of the mission, this sum will be increased, at the discretion of the Pastor, with the knowledge and approbation of the Bishop.

"*3d.* Wherever there is a parsonage attached to the Church and belonging to the congregation, it shall be for the use of the Pastor and such other Clergymen as may officiate in such Church—in such case, too, at least for the time to come, the congregation should provide the residence of the Clergy with a sufficient and decent supply of furniture, and having once furnished such supply, it is to be kept up ever afterwards as church property, at the expense of the pastor for the time being.

"No article of church service, such as sacred vessels, vestments, paintings or other things of this kind, for which the congregation shall have contributed, either by direct contribution or through the medium of the Church income, shall belong to the Pastor; but every such article shall belong to the Church and congregation, for its use and benefit.

"In cases in which there is no parsonage owned by the congregation, for the Pastor's residence, it will be lawful for him to receive $100 per annum, additional, for the purpose of defraying house rent; but it is earnestly recommended that wherever there is a permanent congregation, they and their Pastor together take measures to erect a suitable dwelling for his residence.

"*4th.* It is further required, that every six months a strict report of the condition, the income, and the expenditure, regularly audited, shall be forwarded to the Bishop, for the purpose of being recorded in a Registry, to be kept at his house for that purpose. A copy also of such report shall be published and distributed among the congregation.

"The circumstances in which some of the Churches in this extended Diocese vary from others, will probably prevent these rules from being equally applied to them all, but it is considered that they are entirely applicable to all the larger congregations, in which the Divine service is regularly kept on all Sundays and Festivals. It is hoped also that many congregations of recent origin, and limited resources, will grow up in a short time, by their prudence in managing their affairs and the increase of their numbers, to the measure of being able to comply with these requirements.

"✠ JOHN HUGHES, Archbishop of New York.

"New York, *July*, 1853."

First published in 1843, and re-published July, 1853.

VI.

It was by no act of the bishop that the trustee system of New York broke down within a year or two after the publication of this document. All the Catholic churches of this city had been under the management of lay trustees. They were at that period eight in number. Of these five boards of as many churches, namely, St. James's Transfiguration, St. Paul's at Harlem, St. Peter's in Barclay street, and St. John's at the corner of 50th street and Fifth avenue, all became bankrupt,—their last official act having been to pass the churches severally either to assignees or to be sold by the sheriff for the benefit of creditors. Two other churches, namely, St. Joseph's and St. Mary's, permitted their trustees to retire from office, and thus saved their property from the fate of the other churches. The church of St. Nicholas, in 2d street, was then under trustees, and has still continued to be administered by them without the slightest hindrance on the part of the bishop. St. Patrick's church has also continued under similar administration. They proposed more than once to resign, but the bishop would not consent to it, inasmuch as their trusts were more important, and as they were disposed at all times to discharge them in a manner conformable to the principles of the Catholic faith, and at the same time in accordance with the law of their charter derived from the State.

Here, then, we have five churches thrown into market to be alienated from Catholic worship, through the unfortunate administration of lay trustees. Were they to be sold as so many insolvent theatres? Their trustees had contracted debts in the name of the Catholic community—were their creditors to be cheated out of money which they had loaned in good faith? Were the Catholics to be not only deprived of their altars, but also to incur the disgrace of non-payment of debts which their trustees had lawfully contracted in their name? These were the questions which the bishop, and the clergy, and the people of New York had to decide. It was agreed that the bishop should purchase these churches, and if possible preserve them for the sacred purposes to which they had been dedicated. But they were indebted for more than double the amount for which they were sold. And these melancholy legacies of debt thrown upon the bishop and the Catholic people constitute the greater part of the pretended wealth which Senator Brooks ascribed to the bishop. They were indeed entered on the records as the bishop's property, but the acquisition, burdened as it was to an amount more than double its value, instead of making a poor man rich, would be calculated to make a rich man poor.

It would be tiresome to go into a detail of the embarrassments in which the mismanagement of lay trustees had contrived to involve these churches. Let it suffice to state in general that by a determination which does immortal honor to the Catholic community of New York, every claim against them in law and in equity, has been honorably met and discharged or provided for. No man, Catholic or Protestant, Jew or Gentile, is able to say that he was defrauded or that he lost so much as one penny by the insolvency of these churches, at the period of the bankruptcy of their trustees. But it may be instructive as regards both the past and the future, to give a brief history of the workings of the trustee system, as contrasted with the present mode of administration in one of these churches. That of St. Peter's in Barclay street, shall be taken as a sample of the condition of the others.

St. Peter's is the oldest Catholic church in the city. It was for twenty-five years the only one. Its congregation was the wealthiest until within a recent period. It had always been under the management of lay trustees. When the former St. Peter's was found too small and it was determined to replace it by a new church, the board then existing had the ground free of debt, the materials of the old edifice, ten thousand dollars, it is said, in their treasury, as well as whatever may have been realized from voluntary contributions for the construction of the present church. This, one would suppose to indicate an auspicious commencement of the work. When the church was completed as it now stands, and a pastoral residence built on ground which they had leased from the corporation of Trinity church, the trustees, besides whatever money was in hand at the commencement of the work, found themselves indebted to the amount of $116,444 23. They continued their administration of the church from April, 1837, to May, 1844, and in this interval, instead of diminishing the debt they increased it by the sum of $18, 500 77, making the whole debt when they became bankrupt and made an assignment of the church for the benefit of creditors, $134,945. When this property was sold at the Exchange it was knocked down at the highest bid, which was $46,000. It was purchased by one of the congregation to be transferred to the bishop. Here then is one of those entries of a property valued at $46,000, but with a moral obligation incumbent on the purchaser to provide for its debts to the amount of $134,945. And this is quoted by Senator Brooks as evidence of the immense wealth of the Archbishop. Another entry which he quotes as evidence of property acquired is the unexpired term of the lease from Trinity Church of the ground on which the pastoral residence of St. Peter's Church is built. The Archbishop had to assume the payment of arrears of ground rent, with interest on the same, to the amount of $2,200. There were but three years of the term of that lease unexpired, and yet Senator Brooks, concealing all this, cites the transfer from the assignees as an evidence of the immense wealth which the Archbishop was gathering into his possession.

It may be matter of surprise that the trustees should have been able to accumulate such an amount of borrowed money on a property which sold in the Exchange for less than one third of its indebtedness. This is to be explained as follows:—Soon after the erection of the church was commenced, the trustees induced the pastor of the church to proclaim from the pulpit, that the poor who had money, even in small sums, might with perfect safety give the use of it to the Board of Trustees—that they should allow the same interest that was allowed on deposits in the Savings Banks,—that it would be perfectly safe; and that, without loss to themselves, the depositors would be aiding the church and promoting religion. When these announcements were made I am quite persuaded that all parties acted in good faith, and had entire confidence in their future ability to return these sums, whenever they should be called for. Accordingly, an indefinite number of certificates, handsomely engraved, and fortified by the corporate seal of the Board, were given in due form to the depositors who came to offer their money. In this way they found their treasury replenished and overflowing. Time went on—they struggled during a period of seven years to pay their interest, but the capital of their debt increased during the same time from $116,000 to $135,000. Their charter required that the Bishop of the diocese should be invited to attend their meetings, but no such invitation was ever sent to the present Archbishop. On the contrary, they regarded him as one having no confidence in their system,—in short, as one opposed to trustees. Neither shall I conceal a fact which it is no pleasure to me to have to record. And it is this, that finding themselves and their church sinking irretrievably, they waited on the Bishop a short time before the assignment, intimated to him their financial condition, but with a gilding of confidence in which he could not participate, desired he would authorize them to increase their mortgage to a sum of $40,000 instead of $19,000, out of which they should pay off the old mortgage, and from the balance discharge certain other pressing debts. They acknowledged at the same time that the trustee system was by no means the best, and proposed with the greatest simplicity to transfer the whole property to the Bishop, which he respectfully but absolutely declined. The

Bishop also admonished them, that as honest men they could not allow the claims of a new and enlarged mortgage on their property to come in against the rights of the note-holders. That the church, according to their own acknowledgment, was bankrupt, and consequently belonged in right and in justice equally pro-rata to all their creditors. They seemed to acquiesce in this just view of the case. But it came to the knowledge of the Bishop within a few days afterwards, that they were actually negotiating for a loan of $40,000 at an insurance office in Wall street. The Bishop then wrote a note, addressed to their Board, warning them against proceeding in the matter of that loan, and stating that if they did proceed he should publish a copy of that note, both for his own vindication, and to their discredit. They proceeded notwithstanding. They paid off their old mortgage, and applied the balance of the new one to the payment of such debts as they thought proper to discharge before making their assignment. When reproached afterwards for having disregarded the advice of the Bishop, it was alleged that his communication had been mislaid among their papers, and had escaped notice until the whole transaction was completed.

Finally, the assignment was made September 14th, 1844, in which the trustee system bequeathed to any purchaser the ecclesiastical property of St. Peter's Church, which was sold according to law in the Exchange of New York for $46,000. By this transaction the Catholic community were pledged for a surplus debt over and above the amount which the church brought of $88,945. This was the legacy which lay trusteeism bequeathed to a betrayed community. This was its last will and testament, if we except a codicil resulting from the assignment, and the sale of the property.

VII.

Previous to the assignment by the bankrupt trustees, some of the note-holders had taken legal measures for the recovery of their claim. These persons, under legal advice, disputed the validity of the sale, and hence the whole question was referred to the courts of law, and remained undecided until the 1st of November, 1849,—that is, five years, one month, and sixteen days. During this period the officers of the law,—namely, the assignees, and those employed by them, were for the time being not only administrators, but proprietors of the Church of St. Peter. At the commencement of their administration, the Bishop was assured that inasmuch as the law whilst the case was in chancery would not allow any interest to be paid except that of the bond and mortgage, there would be an accumulation from the income of the church of three or four thousand dollars per annum. This would have made some eighteen thousand dollars of a fund for the payment of note-holders at the expiration of the suit. Instead of this, however, the surplus income, if there was any, has never been accounted for. Even the annual interest on the bond and mortgage was not fully paid. The church went in arrears on the item of interest alone, during these five years, four thousand and sixty-four dollars, and eighty-one cents. It went in arrears on the ground-rent of the priest's residence, due to the corporation of Trinity Church, two thousand two hundred dollars; thus making an arrearage during these five years of six thousand two hundred and sixty-four dollars, and eighty-one cents. From this is to be taken one thousand two hundred and thirty-three dollars, and eighty-seven cents, paid to note-holders from the revenues of the church, and leaving the arrearage of interest on its debt five thousand and thirty dollars, and ninety-four cents. From all which we present the following results. When the trustees of St. Peter's commenced the building of their present church, the ground on which it stands was free of debt. They had, it is commonly said, in their possession, besides contributions, which are not counted, and besides the materials of the old edifice, which are not counted, the sum of $10,000 00

When the church was completed in 1837, they were indebted 116,444 23

During their administration from 1837 to 1844, they increased this debt by the amount of . 18,500 77

After the assignment, when they got the State of New York to play the part of sexton and administrator, they increased this debt still further to the amount of	5,030,94
Making in all	$149,975,94

The Catholics of the State of New York ought to be grateful to the excommunicated trustees of St. Louis Church, the Hon. Mr. Putnam, and the Hon. Mr. Brooks, for the success of their joint labors in fastening upon them a system of lay-trusteeship, of the workings of which the history of St. Peter's Church in Barclay street furnishes a specimen. Neither has it been simply in the unaccountable increase of debt that the administration of that church has entailed evil upon the Catholic community. During a great portion of the time, but especially during the period of the assignment, nothing was left undone to bring disgrace and infamy on the Catholic name in New York. The assignees were the pastors of the church. The senior pastor was through ill health, for the most part, confined to his room, and unable to attend with proper diligence to the duties which the law had imposed on him. The junior assignee took but little interest in the subject, partly because he was the junior, and partly because his natural force of character, especially when a stern duty was to be performed, would range somewhere between the positive and the negative of whatever question would come up. The consequence was, that, under legal advice, a third party was introduced, and constituted a plenipotentiary in the administration of the affairs of St. Peter's. He was supposed at the time to be a Catholic. When he entered on the duties of his office his pecuniary condition was but a few degrees above that of a pauper. He was said to be a good bookkeeper, and the writer would not endorse that sentiment, whilst he is willing to acknowledge that he kept his books well—although even in this respect there are items on his books which appear to have never been accounted for. This man was treasurer, secretary, trustee—in fact, every thing in St. Peter's Church. He employed subordinates at his will, dismissed them when he chose; received all moneys for pew-rents; counted Sunday collections; made his entries of income and expenditure just as he thought proper. After some time, the Archbishop learned with regret that the promised accumulation of surplus income was not to be expected. He urged that every practicable economy should be resorted to; inquired into the items of expenditure which might be reduced, and found as the only result, that this administrator of the law had but one item of economy, which was indignantly spurned by the Archbishop; and this was, a suggestion to withhold from the senior pastor the sum allowed to him, but which his broken health did not permit him to earn by actual labor. This may show the delicate scrupulosity of an agent of the law in administering the temporal affairs of a Catholic church. In the mean time, the unfortunate note-holders, whose money had been received by the trustees of St. Peter's, rendered the Bishop's life a daily martyrdom by their wailings and lamentations at the loss of the little earnings which their industry had accumulated, and which now, that age and poverty, and ill-health had overtaken them, were no longer within their reach. He could not come to their aid, but he could not, on the other hand, drive them from his door harshly. He was doomed to listen to their tales of distress. If he told them that they must address themselves to the assignees, their answer was that they had applied; that the assignees referred them to the agent of the law, who received all the moneys of St. Peter's Church;—that when they applied to him he swore at them, and threatened to kick them out of his office.

This species of daily torture continued during the whole period of the assignment. And as time went on, one could read in such newspapers as were liable to be imposed upon, a series of scurrilous articles against the Archbishop, and against St. Patrick's Cathedral, for not coming to the relief of the poor note-holders of St. Peter's. Whence those articles proceeded was by no means a secret. The last edition of them has appeared in the New York Express. And if any editor thinks that he can annoy Archbishop Hughes with a republication of the scurrilities which emanated from under the assignment of St. Peter's Church, he will easily find the man to furnish them.

The Catholic reader would not have a full idea of the abominations connected with this legal administration of St. Peter's Church, if we were to withhold from him the following statements. We have seen that the legal administrator was a plenipotentiary in all respects. He allowed arrears to accumulate on the interest of bond and mortgage. He allowed arrearages to accumulate on the ground-rent of the pastoral residence. Death had removed the senior pastor. Other clergymen were sent to aid in discharging the spiritual duties of the sacred ministry. They were men who feared God, and did not fear powers of attorney. Their presence became disagreeable to our plenipotentiary; and, in order to scatter the priests from his neighborhood, he made known that the corporation of Trinity Church, inasmuch as their ground-rent had not been paid, wished to re-enter and take possession of their property. He placed a bill accordingly on their house, "TO LET." Some of the priests were already frightened away—others had their books packed up—but in the mean time, and by the merest accident, it came to the knowledge of the Archbishop that the corporation of Trinity Church had no wish to drive out the priests of St. Peter's on account of arrearage, but that they acceded to the proposition, under the advice of the legal plenipotentiary, who had stated to them that the interests of the church required a larger revenue, and that the only means to effect it were to dispossess the priests of their abode and rent the house. Under these circumstances the Archbishop sent word that he would become their tenant, and see that the arrearage should be duly paid. At this stage of the proceedings, patience and endurance had become exhausted. The Archbishop directed that a meeting should be called of the congregation on the following Sunday evening. This broke somewhat unexpectedly on the ears of our plenipotentiary. But he was conscious of the powers which the law gave him within the sacred precincts of St. Peter's Church, and he remarked in the most calm and philosophical way imaginable to one of the congregation—"The Bishop is coming here this evening: I hope he will behave well. If he does, we shall treat him with respect, but if he does not, I shall say to him, 'Bishop, there's the door for you.'"

This meeting took place, however, and the Bishop behaved well. But he brought this man up, and placed his conduct and administration before his eyes in such a light that without being told to quit his office, he sought the door and relinquished it—that is, ceased to render any further services, but claimed and obtained his salary according to law for the unexpired portion of his engagement.

If the Catholics of St. Peter's desire to go through another experience like this, they are at liberty to organize lay trustees when they will, and the Archbishop will have no hesitation in passing to a new Board the title of the property which is now recorded in his name—which he has been instrumental in saving for them and for religion, and in restoring their reputation for honesty, which would have been sacrificed if it had not been for his interference.

VIII.

The condition of St. Peter's Church was at the lowest mark on the night of the meeting just alluded to, from which the plenipotentiary of the law made his final exit. The legality of the sale under the assignment was confirmed by the proper tribunal. The Church began to be administered under the present system. The legacy from lay trusteeship at this period, was, omitting the $10,000 which they had in hand at the commencement of the building, $139,975 94, and the assets which they bequeathed as value for this, were the walls and the roof of St. Peter's as it stands. The law of the land would have been satisfied if the Catholics had paid only the $46,000 for which the church was sold under the assignment. But everlasting justice is an older and a higher law than is written on the statute books of men. And although the Catholic community had been betrayed into this false position by lay-trusteeism, still the sense of the higher law would not permit them to have recourse to repudiation of just debts. Measures were accordingly taken. The Archbishop brought together a number of the leading members of the church as a committee. They began nobly by subscribing themselves large amounts for the immediate relief of the note-holders who were most in need. Other measures were adopted and put in a train of execution. The consequence has been, that under the present system of management, within the period of five years, from the first of November 1849, to November 1854, the income of the church was $63,563 08, instead of $43,481 19, during a similar period of five years under the assignment—that the note-holders received during this time $22,674 72, instead of $1,233 87—that the arrears on interest and on ground-rent have been paid up—that, in short, every dollar of debt contracted by the abominable system of lay-trusteeship has been actually paid, or securely provided for.

As a memorial of this change, and a portion of the Catholic history of New York, we cannot do better than insert here, as taken from the Freeman's Journal, the proceedings of a meeting held in St. Peter's Church on the last Sunday evening of the year 1852:—

From the FREEMAN'S JOURNAL, *January* 1, 1853.

REDEMPTION OF ST. PETER'S CHURCH.

The discourse of the Most Rev. Archbishop, on last Sunday Evening, at St. Peter's Church, Barclay street, of which we have the pleasure of presenting the substance to our readers, will show that the work of redeeming that Church from its desperate financial embarrassments has already been accomplished, or is on the eve of being so. This result, joyful to every true Catholic in America, is one that could with difficulty have been conceived of as possible at the time the Archbishop, three years ago, took that Church into his hands to rescue it from the deplorable condition to which the "law" administration of the parish had reduced it.

In November, 1849, the Statement published in the *Freeman* respecting the debts accumulated, and till then increasing, upon the Church, made the work of rescuing it look like a tedious and dispiriting task, to be handed down from one faithful administration to its successor. How great then is the debt of gratitude due to the Archbishop, to the Rev. Mr. Quinn, who at that time consented to take charge of the parish, to the Rev. Mr. Bayley, who, with Mr. Jas. B. Nicholson, has spent so much time and labor in disentangling and regulating the confusion of affairs, and to all the fervent and devoted Catholics who have contributed their exertions to this good and glorious work! Catholics need no longer avoid Barclay street, nor blush, if they come in sight of St. Peter's, at the disgrace of which it stood out the bulky and only monument in the financial history of Catholic Churches.

The style of architecture of St. Peter's does not admit of the carvings we have seen on the outer faces of the walls of some old Gothic Churches in Europe, where figures were chiselled representing the spirits of evil driven forth, with hideous grimaces, from within the Temple; but their places might on this building be supplied by cutting on the granite tablets of its portico, in truthful figures of arithmetic, the history of its Boards of Trustees, and uncanonical manœuvres. While, within the Church, we think it might be a pious and edifying counterpart to engrave on a tablet of pure white—

"A LONG DESOLATION,
AND A SHAME GROWN OLD,
THREE YEARS OF CANONICAL OBEDIENCE AND CATHOLIC DEVOTION
HAVE SUFFICED TO REPAIR.
A. D., 1852."

The Church was very tastefully decorated, and the Altar was magnificently dressed, for this joyful occasion. The Church was densely crowded by an audience as intelligent and respectable as could well be assembled in any one place. At the close of the Archbishop's address the Congregation, who entered deeply into the jubilant spirit of the evening, rose, while the Choir, which always performs good music at St. Peter's, chanted the TE DEUM LAUDAMUS, as arranged by Romberg.

But we are too long detaining our readers from the words of the Archbishop, which were pretty nearly as follows :—"It is a little over three years since I had occasion, impelled by the duties of my office, to come here and call your attention to the situation of the temporal affairs of this Church. What had past, if not under my eyes, at least within the range of my knowledge, for some years previously, had filled me with apprehension that unless I interfered, with or without permission, not even the wreck of the hopes of the creditors of this Church would have been preserved; and on that occasion, you will remember, I had no words of kindness; but my language was of censure, and censure almost indiscriminately applied. Now, thanks be to Almighty God, I have no occasion to use the language of censure, but rather to congratulate you and the Catholic Church in this city, and in this country, upon the improvement in the condition of the temporal affairs of St. Peter's Church during the interval. The story of this Church has gone abroad to the world wherever the English language is spoken and known, and it has been deplored as a calamity by those who have never seen the country; because, in fact, if the result which was obvious, but a short time ago, had occurred, it would have left a permanent blemish upon the Catholic name, and it would have been the first time in the annals of the Catholic Church that men placing their confidence in the faith of that Church, especially where the sacred temple was concerned, had ever been known to have suffered or to have lost thereby. If you read Ecclesiastical history, you will not find another instance of a Catholic Church in the same circumstances in which St. Peter's was but three years ago; and, although I may not say that it is entirely released from that condition, nvertheless, I consider it so much so, that henceforward we need not hang our heads when the name of St. Peter's, as a specimen of Catholic honesty, is brought under our notice.

"Before referring to the actual condition of the Church at this moment, I will invite you to review with me briefly the history and events which have brought about this result. It pleased our ancestors in the faith, when they were yet few in this city, when they were poor and had much to struggle against, to conform their mode of administering temporal property connected with their religion, to the mode prevalent among their Protestant fellow-citizens. It was supposed to be *republican*, *enlightened*, and *advantageous*, and hence, instead of governing the Church property according to the rules—the ancient and safe rules of the Catholic Church—they received a patent and authority from the State for the management of the same. They got themselves incorporated, and a few individuals, selected by themselves from their number, became a body perfect in law, with all the prerogatives that are usually attached, and also the responsibilities to that special designation. And so they continued. I will not pretend to enlarge upon the advantages or disadvantages of this system in its relations to matters not now before us. I will not pretend to say whether it was in harmony with the spirit of the Catholic Church, or whether it did not tend to create a species of congregational feeling which is not Catholic. In all its relations to Catholic discipline, and to that unanimous harmony of feeling which ought to belong to the Catholic Church in social and religious relations, as a community of faith and charity—in all these regards, I will pass over the advantages or disadvantages of that system; but I have one heavy charge to bring against it in the relation that most interests us at present, and it is this—that it gave power to the body corporate for the time being, to contract debts to any amount that public credit would reach, strengthened in those days by the known fidelity of the Catholics in connection with their Church, to meet all their obligations. And what made this still more objectionable was, that these trustees did not continue from year to year the same individuals; for then, as a consequence, their operations would accumulate, and the same individuals could be held accountable for them, or at least would be in a situation to explain how they occurred, and to take measures to prevent them from becoming unmanageable; but this trustee system changed its members every two or three years, so that every new set coming in had the power to contract debts, and had also, especially as the time went on, to manage the obligations contracted by their predecessors, who had departed from the body corporate, and were lost and unknown in the multitude at large. They could say, we did not contract these debts, for we found them contracted; they have been entailed upon us, and we must bear with them. But, at the same time, when circumstances seemed to require it, they had the same power to contract new debts, and thus passing from one succession to another of trustees, the body corporate became but a fiction. Hence this Church—the very cradle of Catholicity, the very spot upon which the altar was permanently erected for the first time in the State of New York—this Church, the oldest and the most endeared by every fond recollection of the oldest families, became, at the period of its completion, and as it now is, indebted to the amount of $135,789; and this debt was contracted, not to those persons whose province it is to loan money with perfect sense as to the security and responsibility, but this money had been borrowed, upon the faith of a corporate seal, from the poor and the industrious mechanic, who had economized and laid up some of his earnings for the day of his need. It was borrowed from persons in the humbler departments of life, and the reason this debt is so sacred upon us is because they, in lending their money, and taking this seal of a corporate body as a sufficient guarantee, imagined in their own minds that they were loaning to the Catholic Church of God—the same Church which we speak of in the Apostles' Creed, where it is said, "I believe in the Catholic Church." They imagined that they were loaning to our Divine Saviour, and it was the fact of the Church, the creed of the Church, that constituted their security, and not the figment of a corporate right with the high seal of a sovereign State upon it.

This was the condition in which the church was at that period. I need not say that, while I was made aware, as Bishop of the diocese, of the condition of things here, I never was admitted to the confidence or the secrets of that civil corporation. Its requirements imposed upon its members the obligation of inviting me to their meetings; but the invitation I never received, nor did they ever pay to the Bishop of the Diocese that respect of consulting him in regard to matters involving such consequences, until the period when they came to make known that they were bankrupts, as a corporation, and proposed to pass over to me the church, with all its income, and all its responsibilities. I must do myself the justice to say, that upon that occasion I told them that they could not, in conscience, borrow one farthing more; and that they could not, in conscience, increase the amount of their bond and mortgage, because I conceived that the whole of their property was not equivalent to the several obligations of notes of hand which they had distributed among the poor; and that, therefore, the property, in justice, was no longer theirs, but was the property, and the only value, for those notes which they had given to persons who had claims; and that the effect of a mortgage would be to cut out some of those claims, or, at least, to leave them until after the claims of the mortgage should be paid. If, upon that occasion, my advice had been taken, all would have been sold without hesitation, because I do not look upon the value of a temple, even if it were of marble and gold, as any thing to be compared with the value of Catholic integrity in matters of religion. It was, however, overruled, and I do not regret it. The next thing was an assignment, which was to have taken place; but the parties who were the creditors, and who supposed they had a right to step in, caused an injunction (the full meaning of which I really am not able to explain, or even to comprehend) to be imposed, so that, up to 1844, the church was governed by law, in the name of a charter, and afterwards, it was governed by law, under another aspect, and in such a way that even the sacred officers of religion seemed to be, to a certain extent, regulated by the requirements of the ordinances of law. At this period, the church was indebted $134,381. That continued under assignees from November, 1844, until the period to which I have already referred, when I came here with a determination, and conscious of my own rights as a Bishop, and in my interpretation of my duties, to break up the whole system, no matter what should be the consequences, for it had gone on long enough. I had been induced to acquiesce in the arrangement at first by the promise, that during that interval, inasmuch as the law had put a stop to certain payments of interest, there would be an accumulation of $4,000 or $5,000 a year, to the benefit of the poor creditors. This reconciled me to it; yet after the four or five years were up, we found that not only was there no accumulation for the benefit of creditors, but the church had actually increased its debt, for up to the period of 1844 interest had been paid by the trustees, but from that period until November, 1849, except upon the mortgage, and not all upon that, no interest had been paid; and yet we find at this period that the debt was $135,789, showing an increase of debt, during those five years, of $1,408. Upon that occasion, you will recollect, I invited the congregation to rally around me, and see what could be done; and immediately after, measures were taken, by collection, by appealing to the generous members of the congregation, and by every means that could be suggested, to get something to pay the more needy and the more numerous class of the poor who were hovering about, and craving for the sums which they had deposited, or at least for some part of them. A society was formed, and, under the constancy and devotion of that society, guided by the zeal and incessant watchfulness of the Reverend Pastor of the church, much has been done since: for I find now, that within these three years, the debt has not increased, but, on the contrary, has been reduced by the sum of $19,706 92, and of this amount, $9,156 18 was paid to note-holders, in cash, on account, and the balance was paid to the assignees, for the same class of creditors. Besides this, during the same three years, in which the church has not been under the management of legal agents, there have been paid, for improvements and extra expenses, $2,742, making, in all, paid within the last three years, over and above current expenses, $22,448 72. You recollect that all this has been the gratuitous efforts of parties who had no individual concern in contracting the debts which have so long been impending upon this church. Their moneys have been gratuitous offerings to ransom the good faith of the Catholic church, and latterly there has been, in addition, an opportunity of disposing of the interest which this church had in certain lots in Fiftieth street, between the Fourth and Fifth avenues. I must take occasion here to remark, that these lots, and others, to the same extent, had been originally held by the Cathedral and St. Peter's conjointly, and that previous to the sale, there was a meeting of the trustees of the Cathedral called, at which I was present, and at which, with the good will of the people, and in accordance with my strong recommendation, it was resolved that the grounds belonging to St. Peter's should be bid up by them at any price whatever, not exceeding the whole debt upon this church. Why was this resolution adopted? It was because if they should sell for double their value; the money was to go to a part of the Catholic community, to whom it was honestly due. It was because the money with which that purchase should be paid belonged to the Catholic community, and because the idea of a Catholic community is, that there should be no selfishness or sectarianism in their dealings whenever their affairs are conducted according to the principles, and the views, and the salutary discipline of their own Church. By this means, the property was enhanced in value at least one fourth, and if occasion had required, it would have been bid up to a still greater amount. And now, what is the summary of all this? It is that you divide the payment of the debts of St. Peter's church between the security which the law has guaranteed, either in consequence of the acts of the trustees, or the duties of the assignees, and the supplement which has been made up by the generous feelings which have pervaded the breasts of all those who have taken part in adding to what the law furnished as a supplement, reaching to the whole estate. This constitutes the two elements; and whereas the present debt of the church is $115,000; and whereas there is secured as one item, to which note-holders have no claim—in which they have no interest—the mortgage of $40,000—the balance would be some $86,000 due; and on this amount the sale of real estate, by law, and personal property—for every thing has been sold, even to the vestments and organ—the result would be, if I can use the language employed elsewhere, a dividend of probably sixty-five or seventy per cent. to those poor note-holders. This is what the law simply would secure to them; but it is much to your credit, my dear brethren—you, the congregation of St. Peter's—that you have made up over and above what the law provides, and in such a manner, that I am here authorized to say, that before the first day of May next, every dollar and every cent that is due on the face of these notes shall be paid to their holders, without the diminution of one farthing.

The Archbishop then went on to detail the various applications made to him, through actual necessity, by the poorer class of subscribers to the church, and at the same time exonerated the Corporation of Trinity Church, in their capacity of lessors, from all blame on account of the too notorious move of ejectment, which sent some of the clergy away from the building used as a Presbytery. He alluded to them in the following expressions: "I return my thanks now to that corporation, for the kindness and forbearance with which they treated the clergy of St. Peter's Church upon that occasion, for they made the observation, that for a sum so trifling they would not be willing to see the clergy of any denomination dispossessed, and turned out from their lodgings and places of usual residence. What is the whole result of this review, my dear brethren? It is that I congratulate you for the constancy and the liberality with which you have entered into our plans, and contributed at the door on Sunday, without being fatigued during these three years, your offerings towards the full payment of the poor note-holders of this church. I congratulate your pastor, who, by his prudence and his devotion and unceasing energy, has been your representative, encouraging you, and accomplishing the wonderful things which he has accomplished, when you find that within three years, besides the ordinary expenses of this church, he has paid, or you have enabled him to pay, twenty-two thousand dollars to the poor note-holders. I congratulate St. Peter's Church that they have borne their own burthens, and called for no aid from other quarters. I congratulate and return my thanks to those gentlemen who first met me at the residence of the clergy, on the very night on which that downward system was broken up, when they, with a liberality for which, individually, they had been known in other circumstances, contributed their hundred, and even some of them five hundred dollars, towards the redemption of this temple, and towards wiping away the stain which its circumstances were calculated to leave upon the Catholic Church. Nor can I avoid returning thanks to the present assignees, the Rev. Mr. Bayley and Mr. James B. Nicholson, for I am well aware of the labors, the assiduity, the patience, the loss of time, and the trouble which these gentlemen have taken at all times to execute in the most perfect manner the trusts committed to their charge. And now, dearly beloved brethren, is this dear-bought experience to be lost upon the Catholic body? Is this fact, extending over more than fifteen years, and perplexing the efforts of the Catholic body in this entire city, bearing down their credit, and sending abroad the watchword of distrust against those dealing with the church—is all this to pass away, without impressing upon our minds some useful lesson? I trust not. I trust it will be a lesson to this congregation and this city, and to the Catholic Church throughout the entire United States. It is an experience, and an experience going to show that wherever, in the management even of their temporal affairs, the Catholic people have deserted the rules laid down in their Church, that God has not manifested His blessing in their operations. It will be a lesson which ought not to be lost on trustees, or bishops, or priests, or laymen, viz: that they have no right to turn into bankers, even though the poor should have full confidence in making them the depositories of money. It is a treacherous business. It was an unfortunate day on which the practice was introduced, because it steals upon men; and while I may seem to speak in a manner which would imply censure upon the motives or integrity of those who have been concerned in the administration of this church as trustees, I beg leave to say that I have never known any individual among them in whom I could not place the utmost confidence; but the system itself, the system of borrowing, I entirely deprecate. It is a dangerous system, and certainly as long as Almighty God permits me to be at the head of this diocese, no priest of mine, or. Catholic layman, shall ever have authority, in the name of religion, to receive one penny in the form of deposit. This is the lesson with the experience we have had should teach us, and another lesson is one of benefit, as well as warning, and it is this: It is now very difficult for Catholics, as such, to borrow money, for our reputation has been injured; and so far as we are a religious body, I rejoice that it is so, and I trust that the difficulty of borrowing money, except in cases of absolute necessity, will be so increased, that we shall learn to find within ourselves all the resources for the healthy continuation and extension of our Church. In this sense it will be a benefit; and, dearly beloved brethren, I cannot but rejoice, that during these three brief years, every thing which was so dark in the future, and almost hopeless, God, by his providence, and by inspiring you with those feelings which truly become your faith, to repair the blunders in which you had become involved by acting under different authorities, has changed to that point that I am able and authorized now to say, that every dollar of the money for which notes have been given by the trustees of this church, shall be paid. I must, however, make a distinction. I must say, that where these notes have passed for a very small sum in the days of need, from the hands of the original owners to persons who have purchased them, in all such cases the purchaser of the note, if he presents it, shall be entitled to what the law allows him, and this will be more than he paid for it. In the second place, there is no idea or pretence of paying interest upon these notes. In my recollection, most of the holders whom I saw would have been willing to give the notes for one fifth of their value: and the Catholics all—I may say all, for I conceive that in the purchase of the ground all have been represented—have taxed themselves and paid over and above what the law required to make up Catholic equity, instead of civil law. They have made this sacrifice, and if they are able to pay the poor Catholics, it is but just that the latter should, too, feel a small portion of the sacrifice; and I hope that there is no man or woman, calling himself or herself a Catholic, who will have the courage to speak, after this sacrifice, of claiming interest. Yet, I must make one exception. It has come to my knowledge, during my intercourse with a gentleman having charge of this matter, that, in some cases, the poor servants of families took their money, either if they had it by them, or in some instances from the Savings Bank, and brought it here, and that instances are known in which the companion of the Catholic, who was not herself a Catholic, but a Protestant, was nevertheless induced to invest the money as if she were a Catholic; and it would be very cruel, indeed, if persons not belonging to the Church at all, but yet having shown such a confidence in the Church, should not receive their money; and for this reason, I take it upon myself to say, not only that they shall receive their principal, but every farthing of interest to the present day; so that those who are not Catholics, and have deposited their money, are, under the circumstances, such as shall be entitled to their interest as well as principal; and whether the resources within our reach will be sufficient to meet this or not, I pledge my word, and take it upon myself, that in every such instance, these persons shall be paid both principal and interest. As far as the Catholics are concerned, they must not pretend to speak of interest. I am astonished to hear some persons, who only a year ago would have been thankful if they could have got half their capital, begin to speak as if they were in the market of usury, when they know how much their brethren have done. I will now conclude. It is the last Sunday evening of the year 1852. The next Sunday will be another year; and it has been in Catholic times a practice, always at the close of the year to return thanks to Almighty God, with prayer and solemn music, for the blessings which he has bestowed upon his people during the season that has just passed away. In addition to this I think you have other reasons. We have all other reasons to thank Almighty God, and on that account I shall say, both as commemorating the total dispersion of that black cloud which has so long impended over this church, that in both thanksgiving for that and the blessings that God has bestowed on us in this result, we shall unite in asking that there shall be offered to-day a solemn Te Deum in thanksgiving for all these blessings and benefits.

The Te Deum Laudamus was then sung by the choir, the entire congregation standing.

IX.

Enough has been said to give an idea of the results of lay-trusteeship as exemplified in a single church. Circumstances rendered the condition of the other four bankrupt churches, to which allusion has already been made, only less desperate than that of St. Peter's. The other ten churches that have been erected for as many new congregations, are still heavily in debt. But inasmuch as they cannot be irretrievably mortgaged without the knowledge of the Archbishop, and inasmuch as he will never suffer them to be so mortgaged, the danger of their being alienated from Catholic worship is remote and impossible. All these fifteen churches, the titles of which are nominally vested in the Archbishop, but which, in reality, belong to the several congregations, constitute the basis of that supposed wealth which Senator Brooks estimated at a little short of $5,000,000. We have the authority of Messrs. Glover and Wetmore for stating that after the payment of their debts, their value, allowing the average of the ground on which they stand at the very high sum of $5,000 each lot, would amount to the sum of $139,000, or thereabouts. Besides the nominal ownership of ground on which these churches stand, Archbishop Hughes is not the proprietor of a single square inch of land on Manhattan Island.

X.

It is not for us to determine by what right a Senator may be authorized to involve a private citizen (for neither the Constitution nor the laws of this country recognize any ecclesiastic in any different capacity) in the necessity of taking the trouble and going to the expense which a refutation of Mr. Brooks's falsehoods has imposed upon Archbishop Hughes. Certainly no man is a criminal on account of the amount of property which may be recorded in his name, provided it has been honestly acquired or honestly preserved for the purposes to which it is set apart. And if the acquisition of wealth by religious denominations is sufficient to excite the jealousy of the State, the investigation should extend to all denominations, and not be exceptionally restricted to one. At all events, if the legislature of New York is disposed to take an inventory of the ecclesiastical wealth of each denomination in the State, they should begin with those who by original rights or the prescription of time, have come into the management of really immense property. In that way the Episcopalians, the Dutch Reformed Church, the Presbyterians, the Methodists and Baptists would, by the immense preponderance of their ecclesiastical property, claim precedence over the Catholics, who are but of comparatively recent origin in this city, and even yet in the condition of pure struggle to provide places of worship for their increasing numbers. The writer of this entertains no jealousy towards any denomination on account of their ecclesiastical wealth. It is to be assumed that they came into its possession by honest and honorable means. And were it twice or ten times as large as it is, we would still say that the State has no right to interfere with it, at least in the sense of contingent confiscation, contemplated and provided for in Senator Putnam's Bill against Catholics.

XI.

Neither have we the slightest objection to the system of lay-trusteeship which the same bill would force upon Catholics, that is, so far as other denominations may have found it suitable to their interests and in harmony with their doctrines. It has so happened, however, as a historical fact, that the Episcopalians Dutch Reformed Church, Presbyterians, Methodists, Quakers, and probably some other denominations, have sought exemption and obtained it from the crude enactments of the law of 1784, which Senator Putnam has revived against Catholics. We say candidly, that this system is entirely out of keeping with the principles of religious belief and of ecclesiastical discipline peculiar to our faith. Nor do we know any denomination, except the Congregationalists, to whom it is applicable or by whom it is desired. Neither is it of much consequence to Catholics, that wherever it has existed some of the clergymen of other denominations have complained of it bitterly, as authorizing a despotism of the laity controlling their freedom in the "ministration of the Word," if not of the sacraments. Neither is it our business to complain that Protestant lay-trustees have not only in some instances brought their churches into market by their mismanagement, allowed some of them to be sold even to Catholics, but also, if report can be relied on, have failed to pay the debts which they had contracted in the name of the religious community to which they belonged—whether the sufferers were, as in some cases, those who had loaned them money on bond and mortgage, or cases more cruel still in which mechanics, laborers, and others were ultimately cheated out of the wages of their hard labor. All these are questions which our Protestant fellow-citizens have a right to decide for themselves, and if they are entirely satisfied as for themselves, with this system, certainly Catholics have no right to prevent their approval and adoption of it. We speak for Catholics only.

XII.

This may perhaps be the proper place in which to introduce a few explanatory remarks regarding some points alluded to by Senator Brooks, which, without explanation, the uncatholic reader would be liable to misunderstand. It has been stated in various ways that Catholics regard Church property, when once dedicated to religious purposes, as the property of God. The meaning, in the minds of Catholics is, that no matter in whom the title of such property is vested, its use is the common right of all; that the Bishop has no right to exclude the congregation, nor the congregation to exclude the Bishop; in short, that it is to be used for the purposes of Catholic worship. It has happened, and it may happen again, that some portions of property of this kind have been sold. Thus arises the question, very silly in itself, "How can the property of God be sold?" Two instances have been alluded to during this discussion. One was the old Transfiguration Church, in Chambers street. The Church edifice was exceedingly rickety. Improvement in the neighborhood required that great expense should be undergone to shore it up. And improvement demanded that the ground on which it stood should be occupied for warehouses, rather than as a place of worship. It was accordingly sold, and the money which it brought was used partly to pay its debts, and partly to purchase the present Transfiguration Church, formerly Protestant Episcopalian "Zion," corner of Mott and Cross streets. It may be remarked, by the way, that the old Transfiguration Church had *never been consecrated or dedicated* by any Catholic religious rites. The amount of debt from the beginning was such, that neither Bishop Dubois, nor Archbishop Hughes would consecrate a temple so likely to pass away from religious to secular uses. Something similar occurred in regard to what was called St. Stephen's Church, on the corner of 27th street and Madison avenue. Ground had been purchased there by the congregation with the sanction of the Bishop; a temporary building was erected, but never consecrated, inasmuch as it was only temporary and to be occupied as a school-house after the church should have been erected. In the mean time the Harlem R. R. Company became the proprietors of the rest of the block in which this building was situated. The character of that occupancy rendered it inexpedient to build the contemplated church on that ground. Whilst, on the other hand, the Harlem R. R. Company desired the possession of the whole square. It was accordingly sold to them, and the purchase money employed in buying lots and building St. Stephen's Church in a more suitable place. It was in relation to this property that Senator Brooks placed on record one of the most palpable falsehoods of which he has been guilty. He describes the sale of this property and its transfer to the Harlem R. R. Company. Of course, then, he was aware that it had passed out of the Archbishop's possession. And he must have known that he was perpetrating falsehood when he enumerated this same property as being still in the Archbishop's possession.

XIII.

It has been said that the Archbishop should not have applied terms of opprobrium to a Senator of the State of New York,—and some papers have gone so far as to say that he has applied the word liar, scoundrel, villain, &c., to Senator Brooks. This is entirely untrue. Whether Mr. Brooks deserves those epithets or not is purely a matter of inference in the mind of each reader. But the Archbishop has not applied them. Mr. Brooks in this respect has been his own worst enemy. In his Speech in the Senate of New York, he made statements which were entirely and absolutely false. Admonished as to their falsehood, he undertook to prove them, and in this attempt perpetrated many additional falsehoods. Thus the issue of veracity between him and the Archbishop became vital,—and if Mr. Brooks has gone to the wall on that issue, it has been by his own procurement. He became the centre of a triangular testimony. At one angle were his own statements,—at a second, those of Messrs. Glover and Wetmore, whose veracity no man will venture to call in question; and at the third point of the triangle were the records of the Register's office. Mr. Brooks had falsified these records. That fact is attested both by their own text, and by the testimony of the two gentlemen above named. If Mr. Brooks therefore has any complaint to make as to the charge of falsehood, let him blame not the Archbishop, but his own tongue and his own pen. In the speech in Albany he said there were *fifty-eight* entries of property then held by the Archbishop. When he came to examine them he found NOT *fifty-eight*, but *forty-six*. And when truthful men came to examine his special report, they found neither *fifty-eight*, nor *forty-six*, but only THIRTY TWO.

Let no one then be offended or scandalized if the Archbishop has applied to such statements of Senator Brooks the only term in our language which characterizes them according to what they are, namely, falsehoods. These they are—neither more nor less. And they would be just what they are, if by a ridiculous affectation of spurious politeness, the Archbishop had treated them as mere typographical errors. The only object of education in this life is to distinguish, in all departments of human knowledge, the line which separates truth from falsehood. If it were not in the hope of becoming able to make this distinction, the labors of the student would become purposeless, and education would be a mere toil without the prospect of a recompense. To apply the term falsehood to a deliberate statement made by any one claiming the immunities of social decency, must necessarily appear harsh, and is in fact a humiliating necessity on the part of him who employs it. But when there is no alternative left—when you have to deal with a man so unscrupulous as to leave you no choice, except to put him into the pit which he had dug for you, then in that case things must be called by their proper names—truth must be called truth, and falsehood, falsehood—it is for the author of either to be responsible both to God and men.

XIV.

It is said by many that the late controversy between Senator Brooks and myself will have made a great man of him. I doubt much whether that is possible. But if the event should verify the prediction, it will not awaken in my breast a single feeling of regret. I have no objection that Senator Brooks should succeed in any avocation of life to which he may devote himself. The late controversy between him and me has brought out for the admiration of his countrymen, if they choose to admire it, the special department of talent in which his forte lies. If they deem it worthy of recompense, let them reward it by making Senator Brooks Mayor of the city, Governor of the State, or President of the Union, in case they can find no fitter man. As for the writer of this, he has only to complain of the injustice done him by Senator Brooks in the speech which he delivered in the Senate, at Albany, on the 6th of last March. In that speech the Senator held up Archbishop Hughes to the odium and suspicion of his countrymen. And this he did, not by a statement of facts, but by a statement of silly and absurd falsehoods.

It may be as well to conclude this introduction with a re-statement of that portion of Mr. Brooks's speech, which has given rise to the late controversy between the Senator and the Archbishop of New York. The passage referred to is as follows :—

"I HAVE HAD OCCASION DURING A VISIT OF A DAY IN NEW YORK TO SECURE REFERENCES, TAKEN FROM THE REGISTER'S OFFICE THERE, OF THE AMOUNT OF PROPERTY HELD BY JOHN HUGHES IN THAT CITY. I SUPPOSE ITS VALUE TO BE, IN NEW YORK ALONE, NOT MUCH SHORT OF five millions of dollars. SO FAR FROM THIS PROPERTY BEING HELD, WHEN IN CHURCHES, BY TRUSTEES, THERE ARE NUMEROUS TRANSFERS FROM TRUSTEES TO JOHN HUGHES! BEGINNING WITH FEBRUARY, 1842, AND CONTINUING THROUGH 1854, A FRIEND OF MINE COPIED *fifty-eight entries of as many distinct parcels of* property made in the name of land for John Hughes, ALL IN THE SPACE OF TWELVE YEARS!—NOT TO JOHN HUGHES, BISHOP, NOR TO JOHN HUGHES, ARCH†BISHOP, NOR TO JOHN HUGHES, AS TRUSTEE FOR THE GREAT ROMAN CATHOLIC CHURCH, BUT TO PLAIN JOHN HUGHES, IN HIS OWN propria personæ. SOME OF THESE PARCELS COVER WHOLE SQUARES OF LAND, AND NEARLY ALL OF THEM ARE OF GREAT VALUE. THE RULE OF

THAT CHURCH IS NEVER TO PART WITH PROPERTY, AND TO RECEIVE ALL THAT CAN BE PURCHASED. WHAT IS TRUE OF NEW YORK CITY IS TRUE OF THE STATE, AND FIFTEEN OR TWENTY CASES OF PROPERTY ASSIGNED TO BISHOP JOHN TIMON WERE NAMED BY THE SENATOR FROM MONROE.

["To those who were curious in such matters, Mr. BROOKS exhibited to the Senate, the number, book and page of those several entries in the City of New York, in behalf of John Hughes."]

PETITION OF THE TRUSTEES OF ST. LOUIS' CHURCH, BUFFALO.

[*From the* N. Y. FREEMAN'S JOURNAL AND CATHOLIC REGISTER, *March* 31*st*, 1855.]

Mr. PUTNAM presented the following petition, which, as he said, in view of its great importance, should be printed. He accordingly made a motion to that effect, which was adopted.

To the Senate and Assembly :—

The undersigned, trustees and ex-trustees of the St. Louis Church, situate in Buffalo, beg to lay before the Legislature the following statement of facts, in the hope that some legislative action may be devised to remedy the evils of which they complain:—

In the year 1829, an estimable citizen of Buffalo, the late Louis Le Couteulx, Esq., conveyed two valuable lots on Main and Delaware streets, in that city, to the then Bishop in New York, Dubois, in trust for the use of the Catholic church, to be thereafter organized. Subsequently, and about the year 1838, St. Louis Church was duly organized under the act of 1813, under seven trustees, and has so continued from that time till the present, said congregation from time to time electing their trustees according to the requirements of said statute. This organization was effected with the hearty concurrence of the worthy Bishop, and of the liberal donor of the land. A church was erected by the congregation, and dedicated by the Bishop, and the Society continued in harmony and prosperity until the death of Bishop Dubois, about 1840, and the death of Mr. Couteulx, in 1842.

Shortly after these events Bishop Hughes attempted to compel the trustees to convey the title of this church property to him. The trustees resisted firmly. With a view to coerce compliance with his demands the Bishop withdrew the Priest and suspended the ordinances in St. Louis Church. The trustees declined to yield, and sent one of their number, Wm. B. Le Couteulx, Esq, to Europe, for the purpose of preventing this arbitrary and, as was claimed, this illegal action of the Bishop, through the intervention of Cardinal Fornari, the Pope's Nuncio at Paris. Mr. Le C. succeeded in his mission. No further efforts were made at the time by Bishop Hughes to disturb the title to the church, and its members fondly hoped that peace was permanently restored. Subsequently the diocese was divided, and those of Albany and Buffalo were erected. Bishop Timon became the head of the latter. He was installed into his holy office in this Church of St. Louis, the title of which then vested in said trustees. In process of time Bishop Timon renewed the effort to compel the trustees to surrender to him the title of said church. They again resisted resolutely. This procured various annoyances to the congregation, among which was the withdrawal of all Priests from that church. Deprived of all spiritual guides, the congregation were accustomed to meet at their church on the Sabbath and make their prayers in common. The case was at length presented to the Holy Father and the College of Propaganda, at Rome; the result of which was that in 1852, a special Envoy, Father Bedini, was sent to the United States to correct these abuses. The Prelate, yielding to the unfortunate influences which surrounded, early took sides against us, and our remonstrances were totally disregarded.

High-handed measures were then taken against us. For refusing to comply with what we regarded as the illegal and unjust demands of the Bishop to surrender property thus committed to our charge, as the legally constituted trustees of said church, the Bishop was pleased to issue against us a decree of excommunication. During the last three years the church itself has been, in effect, closed against the admission of her clergymen, and the ordinances and sacraments of the Catholic religion were withheld from the members of that Society.

Such are the unvarnished facts, to which we earnestly solicit your attention. The embarrassments and inconveniences resulting from this action of its Bishop, have been to us painful and oppressive. * * * For no higher offence than simply refusing to violate the Trust Law of our State, we have been subjected to the pains of excommunication, and our names held up to infamy and reproach. For this cause, too, have the entire congregation been placed under ban. To our members the holy rites of baptism and of burial have been denied. The marriage sacrament is refused. The Priest is forbidden to minister at our altars. In sickness, and at the hour of death, the holy consolations of religion are withheld. To the Catholic churchman it is scarcely possible to exaggerate the magnitude of such deprivations.

We yield to none in attachment to our religion, and cheerfully render to our Bishop that obedience, in spiritual matters, which the just interpretation of our faith may require; but, in respect to the temporalities of our Church, we claim the right of obeying the laws of the State whose protection we enjoy.

We would respectfully suggest that we are not unmindful of the fact that the American policy, which has been generally adopted, requiring church property to be vested in Trustees, who shall be elected by the members of their respective congregations, was instituted for the purpose of retaining these extensive ecclesiastical estates in the hands of those whose interests are linked to, and identified with the principles and fortunes of our beloved country. And with regret and mortification have we observed that the recent attempts to change these salutary laws respecting the tenure of church property, have excited jealousies, and have brought odium and reproach upon the Church to which we belong. Could, however, the untrammelled judgment of reflecting and intelligent Catholics, on this point, be ascertained, we feel assured that their voice would be decidedly in opposition to this effort of the Bishop to monopolize the temporalities of the church.

Until within the last twelve or fifteen years those temporalities have been held by trustees, according to existing statutes, and during that earlier period the American Catholic Church was blessed with eminent prosperity and success. While many churches throughout the State have, for the sake of peace, reluctantly submitted to the demands of the Bishops in this respect, a large portion of the several congregations in every locality have regarded this project as alike unjust and impolitic.

We feel confident that, by proper legislation, an end can for ever be put to these controversies and difficulties. We, therefore, ask for the passage of a law enforcing, under sufficient penalties, a faithful compliance with existing statutes, respecting the tenure of church property. To the true Catholic it is painful to be brought in antagonism with his Bishop and spiritual guide. Such a law will prevent this unpleasant condition of affairs. By no portion of our community will the rigid enforcement of such a statute be hailed with greater satisfaction than by intelligent and faithful Catholics.

And your petitioners will ever pray.

(*Signed*) George Fisher,
Michael Hesmer,
W. B. Le Couteulx,
George Londrack,
And seventeen others.

EXTRACT FROM LAWS OF NEW YORK.

CHAPTER 230.—AN ACT IN RELATION TO CONVEYANCES AND DEVICES OF PERSONAL AND REAL ESTATE FOR RELIGIOUS PURPOSES.

Passed April 9, 1855.

The People of the State of New York, represented in the Senate and Assembly, do enact as follows:—

SECTION 1. No grant, conveyance, devise or lease of personal or real estate to, nor any trust of such personal or real estate for the benefit of, any person and his successor or successors in any ecclesiastical office, shall vest any estate or interest in such person or in his successor, and no such grant, conveyance, devise or lease to, or for any such person by the designation of any such office shall vest any estate or interest in any successor of such person. But this section shall not be deemed to admit the validity of any such grant, conveyance, devise or lease, heretofore made.

§ 2. No future grant, conveyance, devise, or lease of any real estate consecrated, dedicated or appropriated, or intended to be consecrated, dedicated or appropriated, to the purposes of religious worship, for the use of any congregation or society, shall vest any right, title or interest in any person or persons to whom such grant, conveyance, devise or lease may be made, unless the same shall be made to a corporation organized according to the provisions of the laws of this State, under the act entitled "An Act for the incorporation of religious societies," and the acts amendatory thereof, or under the act entitled "An Act for the incorporation of societies to establish free churches,' passed April 13, 1854. But nothing herein contained shall prevent any such corporation from conveying such property on a bona fide sale thereof, under the direction of a court of competent jurisdiction to confer such authority, according to the laws of this State.

§ 3. Any real estate of the description named in section second of this act, and which has been heretofore granted, devised or demised, to any person or persons in any ecclesiastical office, or orders, by the designation of such office or orders, or otherwise, shall be deemed to be held in trust for the benefit of the congregation or society using the same, and shall, unless previously conveyed to a corporation, as provided in the last preceding section, upon the death of the person or persons in whom the legal title shall be vested at the time of the passage of this act, vest in the religious corporation formed by the congregation of religious society occupying or enjoying such real estate as aforesaid, provided such a corporation, organized according to the laws of this State, shall be in existence at the time of the decease of the person or persons holding the title thereto.

§ 4. In the event such congregation or society shall not be incorporated as aforesaid, then, and in that case, the title of such real estate shall vest in the people of the State of New York, in the same manner and with the same effect as if the person holding the legal title thereto had died intestate and without heirs capable of inheriting such real estate.

§ 5. Whenever title to any real estate shall vest in the people of the State of New York, under and by virtue of the last preceding section, it shall be under the charge of the commissioners of the land office of the State of New York, and it shall be their duty, and they are hereby authorized, upon their being satisfied that the congregation or society which had used, occupied or enjoyed such real estate for purposes of religious worship, prior to the death of the person or persons on whose decease the title thereto vested in this State, has been duly incorporated, under and according to the provisions of the act first named in the second section of this act, and upon the production to him of a certified copy of the recorded certificate of incorporation, under the hand of an official seal of the clerk of the county in whose office the same is recorded, to grant and convey such real estate, and all the right, title, and interest of the people of the State of New York, therein and thereto, to said corporation, which shall thereupon be vested with all the right, title, and interest, which became vested in the State by virtue of the provisions of this act.

§ 6. This act shall not be construed as repealing or in any way affecting chapter one hundred and eighty-four, passed April 17, 1839, entitled "An Act in relation to trusts for the benefit of the meetings of the religious Society of Friends," provided that nothing in this provision or in said chapter one hundred and eighty-four, shall authorize the vesting of the title of property appropriated or dedicated to religious worship and belonging to the Society of Friends in other than lay trustees.

§ 7. This act shall take effect immediately.

State of New York, Secretary's Office. } I have compared the preceding with the original law on file in this office, and do certify that the same is a correct transcript therefrom and of the whole of the said original.

ELIAS W. LEAVENWORTH, Secretary of State.

LETTER FROM ARCHBISHOP HUGHES,

In relation to the Petition of the Trustees of St. Louis' Church, Buffalo,—and to Mr. Putnam's Anti-Catholic Church Property Bill.

NEW YORK, *March* 28, 1855.

To the Editor of the New York Freeman's Journal:

Having arrived by the Atlantic yesterday, I have had barely time to read the foregoing strange documents. I proceed to make the following hasty observations in regard to them, inasmuch as Catholics, and others, perhaps, are anxious to know my opinions.

I do not think there is any real ground for the alarm and apprehension which I understand is now prevalent among the Catholics of this city, and no doubt of the entire State, as to the effects of a law, which is now under discussion in the Legislature at Albany, regarding ecclesiastical property. No doubt it is in its spirit and in its object an anti-Catholic enactment, although it professes to embrace all denominations except the Society of Friends. Should it pass, it may reach other religious communities, and strike deeper into their ecclesiastical organizations than its framers would wish. On the other hand, they felt themselves obliged to give it the form and appearance of a general law, instead of calling it by its true title, "a penal enactment, requiring Roman Catholics of the State of New York to be governed, in the enjoyment and use of their own property set apart for ecclesiastical purposes, not by the discipline of the religion which they profess, but by the statute of the Legislature." This would be the true title of the bill as it has now passed the Senate. But even should it become a law, we can hardly think that our

Protestant fellow-citizens would take any pleasure in executing upon us the annoyances and injuries, for the infliction of which, it has so ingeniously provided. It would impose such intricate, onerous, and sometimes odious duties on the officers who should be appointed to see it executed that, unless ample fees were provided, they would become disgusted with its requirements.

It would certainly inflict very great injury on us in our rights of conscience, and in our rights of property, and this without producing any benefit to any class of our fellow-citizens. Still, should it pass, we shall not sink under it. We have borne up under weightier discouragements. I should not be surprised if its results would be beneficial, rather than otherwise, to the real interests of the Catholic Church and people. The very fact that we have been singled out and fettered in the enjoyment of religious immunities, by civil enactments, will, in all probability, excite that sympathy which is natural to the American breast in favor of those who suffer under the reality, or even under the appearance of persecution, whether that persecution be legal or not. It will have the effect to brace many who have hitherto been lukewarm Catholics, to a higher, a deeper, and a holier appreciation of that religion which is thought to require civil enactments for the crippling of its progress. It will withdraw many from the too ardent pursuit of political ends, and political objects, by which their minds were led away and wasted on mere transitory and temporal concerns. It will insinuate to Catholics that, in the mind of their fellow-citizens, they, because of their religion, are hardly qualified to take part in the political strifes by which the country is perpetually agitated. And the more they withdraw from such agitations, whether by their own choice or by such legislative rebukes as the enactment under consideration contemplates, the more their hearts and their minds will turn to other considerations affecting their future being and the religion by means of which they are to secure ultimately the end of their creation. In this view it is probable that the law, now before the Legislature at Albany, will prove in its results rather beneficial than otherwise to the Catholic body at large. The

Legislature does not propose to confiscate their church property, but only to take the management of it out of their hands. It proposes to furnish them, and to force upon them, a wiser, juster, and therefore better code of ecclesiastical discipline for the management of their church property, than their Church has provided for them. But still it does not go the length of confiscation. It appears to be a foregone conclusion, in the minds of the framers, that the law will accomplish in practice the results which are outlined in its theory. This is not so certain. Professional gentlemen may discover some defect in the framing and wording of the enactment which will render it inapplicable. But even if this should not be the case, it will only produce, in the minds of Catholics, the very feelings and purposes which it aims to overthrow or prevent.

The Catholic laity, in my opinion, will reason with themselves thus: "The Legislature wishes to prevent our doing with our own property what we think proper; it wishes us to give nothing by devise, conveyance, gift, or any other form of transfer, to our Bishops and clergy, for the purpose of promoting or supporting our religion, except as *it* sees fit to direct. Now, in this it seems to meddle with our religious, as well as civil rights; and we shall find twenty ways outside the intricate web of its prohibitions for doing, and doing more largely still, the very things which it wishes us not to do. In these matters which invade our religious as well as civil rights, we shall take the liberty of doing what is right, in our own way."

It does not follow from all this, that I should witness the passage of the act in question with pleasure or satisfaction. But I look upon it in anticipation of its worst consequences; and in order to allay the apprehensions which prevail, I point out its probable consequences.

Under any circumstances, we must maintain our confidence in the justice and wisdom of the State, to which it is our pride to belong. If experience should make it apparent hereafter that the working out of this law is partial and oppressive upon *one* denomination, and only one, of the community, another future

Legislature, better informed of the true state of the case, will either amend its defects, or repeal it altogether, in case it should be found not amendable.

I have said that I could not, nor can any Catholic, approve of it, or witness its passing into a law with any feeling of pleasure or satisfaction. But, on the other hand, it is a matter of congratulation to the Catholics, that they have not had recourse to any thing like public meetings or remonstrances, such as are usually had recourse to, to prevent the passing of an iniquitous or injurious enactment. There have been times when it might have been their duty thus to meet, pass resolutions, and forward numerously signed remonstrances. But in an hour so pregnant with excitement, when it would be so easy to engender feelings that ought to be guarded against, they have acted wisely in leaving the matter entirely in the hands of those who are appointed legislators to represent the sovereign will of this sovereign State. No remonstrance shall go forth from me against the contemplated legislation, nor shall I encourage any thing of the kind in others. The matter is in the hands of the Senate and Assembly of New York. They are entirely, or nearly all, Protestants; and Protestants have always boasted that they were in favor of the most unbounded civil and religious liberty. If it be their good pleasure in this instance to refute their professions by their acts, be it so; but the glory or dishonor shall be theirs alone.

I think, however, that the chances for right legislation in this matter would be greater, if the Legislature of New York were better informed of the true state of the case—of the facts, and their bearings involved in the groundwork of the act of legislation to which we have referred. It is hardly possible that they should be acquainted by personal knowledge with the religious discipline peculiar to the various denominations of the community. So, also, in regard to the specific facts involved in the so-called ecclesiastical property question among Catholics. Their tutors appear to have been the lay trustees of St. Louis's Church, in Buffalo. What these gentlemen have said, whether orally or in the form of petition, has been regarded as Catholic testimony, and consequently the testimony of men who could not be suspected of wishing injury to that denomination to which they profess to belong. When one reads their petition, and the act now under deliberation, he is struck with how nicely they fit into each other. The petition of George Fisher, Michael Hesmer, William B. Le Couteulx, George Landrack, and seventeen others, is the foundation,—the bill before the House, the superstructure to be reared upon it. Now, wise legislation should rest upon a sound and solid basis. That which is presented to the Legislature by the gentlemen from Buffalo, is neither sound nor solid, and with this part of the question I propose to deal at some length,—the more so that they have introduced my name into their petition. I begin by declaring, as a man of honor and veracity, that the petition of the self-styled Catholics of St. Louis's church, so far as it alleges grievances to be redressed or provided against, is a compound of fiction in all its material parts, with a small sprinkling of truth in portions which are not material, from beginning to end. It begins with the following statement:

> "Shortly after these events, Bishop Hughes attempted to compel the trustees to convey the title of this church (St. Louis') to him. The trustees resisted firmly."

The whole burden of the petition rests upon the accuracy or the inaccuracy of this statement, at least so far as Bishop Hughes is concerned. I proclaim in the face of the signers of the petition, and of the Legislature, and of the whole world, that in the extract just quoted there is not a sentence, nor a word, nor a syllable, nor a letter of truth.

Having premised so much, it may be proper for me to give a brief history of the origin and nature of the difficulties between myself and the trustees of St. Louis's church, in Buffalo. In order to make the matter more intelligible, it is necessary that I should revert to the bearings of the question, as it affected the Catholic people of the diocese of New York at the period referred to.

When the undersigned was appointed to the government of the Diocese in 1839, he found every church therein under the management, so far as related to what was called temporalities, of lay trustees. He found the congregations of those churches generally divided among themselves into contending parties, having no mutual sympathies, one with the other. He found them involved in debt, more than equal to the value of the property. In the city of New York there were at that period six Catholic churches. Of these, three were barely able to meet the interest on their debts as they became due, whilst the other three were involved apparently beyond any prospect of extrication. These three latter churches, or rather the trustees representing them, became bankrupt in their corporate capacity. The real and personal property passed into the hands of assignees, and were disposed of in the ordinary course of law, just the same as if they had been bankrupt theatres. The price which they brought would not have paid more than thirty cents on the dollar to their creditors. And, on the other hand, it would have been a stigma on the Catholic body at large, and not on the trustees as individuals, if their debts, whether recoverable by law, or acknowledged to be due in justice, should not be paid to the last farthing.

Now, here was a result that startled and alarmed the Catholics. From the time of their origin in the city of New York, they had been in the habit of contributing generously by voluntary subscription, as well as by high pew-rents; and after a continuance of such contributions during a period of more than half a century, they made the melancholy discovery that the churches which they had built, and supposed themselves to own, were sunk in debt far more than they were worth, and belonged both in law and in equity to their creditors. All the money they had contributed for religious purposes, over and above current expenses for the maintenance of divine worship, was gone—gone; and with it their honor as a trustworthy religious community! The present Archbishop of New York was the purchaser of those churches when they were sold respectively; that is, he was the highest bidder, and accordingly they passed into his hands for the time being, not in the form of a trust for him and his successors, but by a legal title in fee simple. From that moment, the confidence and hopes of the Catholic people began to revive. They rallied around their Bishop, and around the clergymen respectively appointed by him to take charge of those churches. By an effort, which has continued for years, they paid off or provided for their debts, as determined by the legal price for which they were sold. But they did more than pay their legal debts. They retrieved their own honor as a religious denomination, by paying also those debts for the recovery of which there was no law. They wiped out every stigma which the bad management of lay trustees had brought upon their otherwise untarnished name.

I would not be understood here as imputing moral delinquency to the several Boards of Trustees then in existence, or to their predecessors. But experience has proved in our own country, as well as elsewhere, that there is a subtle element of deceptiveness lurking and inherent in the nature of corporate bodies. The members of such bodies are seldom conscious of the presence of this element, which, as long as things go on well, philosophy has been baffled in her attempts to define or identify. It is only when the community is stunned by some explosion or mismanagement of public trusts by corporate bodies, that the fact itself becomes palpable and undeniable. But even then, except in some startling case of fraud, the astonishment settles down into that benevolent humanity which winds up a catastrophe on a railroad, with the considerate verdict that blame is not to be attached to any one in particular.

I have never known an instance of fraud or peculation among the lay trustees of the unfortunate churches to which I have referred. In other respects, they were not exempt from those self-illusions to which corporate bodies, even in seasons of apparent prosperity, are so frequently liable. This was proved by the result of their long labors. After an administration of the temporal affairs of the Catholics during a period of fifty years, they and the community were astonished at discovering that the Church property under their management was still in debt, to an amount more than its entire value. Thus it was ascertained that, except in the mere use of the edifices for religious purposes, the condition of the Catholics of New York was worse than if they had never owned any Church property whatever. It was not surprising, therefore, that the Catholic community, clergy and laity, under such circumstances, should turn away, as they did, in disgust, from a system which had wrought out such unexpected, and, for the honor of their fame as a religious community, such discreditable results.

On the other hand, since the management of Church property by lay trustees has been set aside, or, rather, has died out, their reputation has been retrieved and restored. They have seen paid off not only their legal debts, but the debts of honor bequeathed to them by the defunct system. They have seen those older churches recovered from ruin, and new churches springing up on every side. They have seen an end put to divisions, bickerings and strifes in the several congregations of the diocese, and a spirit of union, harmony, and above all, charity, extending itself over their whole community.

With this experience fresh in their memory, nothing less than absolute coercion will induce them to return to a system, from the effects of which they have escaped at the expense of so many and such noble sacrifices.

I am, however, far from being satisfied with the mode in which Church property is generally held at the present time. It has involved the bishop in many cares, anxieties and responsibilities, which it would be for him a great and most desirable relief to be rid of. And I should hail with delight any legislative measure by which, on the one side, the dangers that have resulted from the former mismanagement of lay trustees might be securely guarded against; and, on the other side, the inconveniences of the present system remedied; the rights of the laity as well as of the clergy provided for; and the Church property legally secured to the sacred ends and purposes for which it was created and intended.

In the petition which Mr. Putnam presented to the legislature on behalf of the trustees of St. Louis' church, it is insinuated, if not asserted, that the system of lay trustees was set aside by the improper exercise of episcopal authority in the diocese of New York. This is entirely untrue. When that system was set aside there was no Catholic Bishop in the State of New York, except myself, and I know that I never used my episcopal authority whether properly or improperly, for the purpose of displacing lay trustees in any church in my diocese. It is quite true that when appealed to I have recommended, in a few instances, that they should resign, as the best means of putting an end to strifes among themselves, or of saving the church under their management from being sold for its debts. This, however, was always in the form of friendly advice; but in no case have I ever asked them to resign their office as an act of obedience to episcopal authority. In no case have I asked them, or any of them, to make over the title of their church property to me. I never recognized in them the right of ownership, and I should as soon have thought of asking the Corporation of Buffalo to make over to me their city property, as of asking the trustees of St. Louis' to make over the title of their church. It was not theirs in such a sense or for such a purpose. They could not do it if they would; and if they did attempt it, it would be as faithless agents, attempting to betray the confidence of their principals, in giving a worthless deed of property which was not theirs. Consequently, whilst the statement alluded to in the petition of the trustees, and seventeen others, is utterly empty of truth, it is filled and overflowing with absurdity and nonsense.

The authority of a Bishop in the Catholic Church is a spiritual authority. It is the same in a Church that has trustees, as in one that has none. All Catholics acknoweldge and are subject to that authority. I may add also what is indeed obvious, that that authority extends to outward things which are set apart and appropriated for purposes of religion; and that, consequently, when the faithful have contributed for the purposes of Catholic worship, it is of the jurisdiction, of the right, and duty of the Bishop, to see that property so contributed, and for such a purpose, shall not be misappropriated, squandered, or perverted from its use.

In the Statutes of our Synod, held in 1842, certain rules were laid down by which lay trustees should be thenceforward guided in administering the ecclesiastical property, which the Catholic people had contributed for the purpose of religion. The following extract from our Pastoral Letter, published on that occasion, contains the only rules which could in the least trench on the prerogatives of lay trustees which had been so long enjoyed for ruin, with impunity :—

"We have, therefore, directed and ordained, by the statutes of the Diocese, that, henceforward, no body of lay trustees, or lay persons, by whatever name called, shall be admitted to appoint, retain, or dismiss, any person connected with the Church—such as sexton, organist, singers, teachers, or other persons employed in connection with religion or public worship, against the will of the pastor, subject to the ultimate decision of the ordinary. We have ordained, likewise, that the expenses necessary for the maintenance of the pastors, and the support of religion, shall, in no case, be withheld or denied, if the congregation are able to afford them. It shall not be lawful for any Board of Trustees, or other lay persons, to make use of the church, chapel, basement, or other portions of ground, or edifices consecrated to religion, for any meeting, having a secular, or even an ecclesiastical object, without the approval, previously had, of the pastor, who shall be accountable to the Bishop for his decision. And, with a view to arrest the evils of the trustee system in expending inconsiderably, or otherwise, the property of the faithful, it has been ordained as a statute of the Diocese, that no Board of Trustees shall be at liberty to vote, expend, or appropriate for contracts, or under any pretext, any portion of the property which they are appointed to administer, (excepting the current expenses as above alluded to) without the express approval and approbation of the pastor, in every case. And it is further ordained, that even thus, the trustees of the churches, with the approbation of the pastor, shall not be at liberty to expend an amount larger than the sum of one hundred dollars in any one year, without the consent of the Bishop approving or permitting such expenditure."

I am sure that no member of the Legislature, not even Mr. Putnam, will be able to discover, in these regulations, any thing unjust, unwise, or oppressive. They took from the Boards of Trustees the power of contracting debts *ad libitum* and bequeathing to their successors in office the less pleasant duty of making payment. They took from lay trustees the right of employing church property for the payment of persons connected with religion, against whose fitness or moral character the pastor of the church might have strong and well-founded objections. In these regulations will be found the only grounds that ever existed for the resistance to episcopal authority, which the trustees of St. Louis's Church, Buffalo, were pleased to inaugurate.

All the other Boards of Trustees in the Diocese acquiesced in them, and the Catholics at large saw in them a prudent measure and a wise precaution. The only exception was the trustees of St. Louis's Church. They would be Catholics after their own fashion, and they have reaped the consequences. Not understanding the English language well, they caused the Pastoral to be translated into German. Then, in their corporate capacity as lay trustees, they took it into "mature and respectful" consideration, and reviewed it paragraph by paragraph. They were kind enough to approve of some parts, whilst in the most polite language, which a French gentleman knows so well how to employ, they signified to me that other portions of the document did not meet their approbation. Their objections were chiefly, I may say exclusively, against the regulations contained in the above extract from the Pastoral Letter. They would not allow either Bishop or Priest to examine their church books, or their treasurer's accounts. They would not allow the Pastor to have any thing to do with the approval or disapproval of persons whom they might think fit to employ in connection with the services of the Church. Thus, by implication, they would reserve to themselves the right to employ an infidel to teach catechism to the children of the congregation —the right to employ a Jew to serve the Priest at Mass, and a scoffer at all religion to play the organ on Sunday, or chant the praises of God in his holy temple. Their refusal to acquiesce in the above regulations of the Pastoral Letter was communicated to me accompanied by polite expressions of profound respect for episcopal authority. In reply, I expressed to them briefly my regret at the course which they thought proper to adopt, intimated that the duties of my office required that I should be the Bishop, and that in the government of the Diocese they should be content with their condition as laymen,—that under no circumstances would I quarrel or have any controversy with them,—that if they thought proper to persevere in their resolutions, we should part company in peace,—that Bishops and Priests, and religion itself, were quite as free in this country as were lay trustees.

In the Pastoral Letter it had been made known that at the period of six months from its promulgation, the Priest should be withdrawn from every church whose trustees should refuse to comply with the above regulations. The trustees of St. Louis's Church alone persevered in their refusal. The Priest, however, was not withdrawn by me, but was actually compelled by the ill-treatment he received from the trustees and their adherents to quit his post and return to his native country. From the time he left I did not send another Priest, nor was another Priest permitted to officiate in their church. But as the Catholic people whose interests these men had so mismanaged, whose peace they had destroyed, whom they had deprived of religious consolation so far as depended on them, were still a precious portion of my Catholic flock, I sent two other Priests, not indeed to be under the ignorant tyranny of lay trustees in St. Louis's Church, but to be free ministers of God, freely discharging their duties towards all the people.

The Almighty gave a blessing to their ministry and labors. A new temple was soon commenced, and this church of St. Louis remained, an altarless pile, which its owners might have disposed of as they thought proper. On my second episcopal visitation one or two years afterwards, the trustees then in office addressed me a note soliciting me to receive them for the purpose of an interview in regard to its condition. I informed them in reply that unless they were prepared to acquiesce in the requirements of the Pastoral Letter, and thus come back to the starting point of their schism, an interview would be useless, and could not be granted. They came, notwithstanding, at the hour which they indicated in their note. They asked me to explain the meaning of certain passages in the extract of the Pastoral as quoted above. This was readily given, and at its close they alleged as an apology for their schismatical course up to that time, that they were unacquainted with the value of English words, that Mr. Wm. B. Le Couteulx had been their interpreter—and that he had always assured them that the Bishop was endeavoring to get possession of their church property, in order to give it to the Irish! In short, they stated (that is, some of them stated and the rest remained silent) that if my interpretation of the Pastoral Letter was correct, Mr. Le Couteulx had been deceiving them from the beginning, and that now they were prepared to submit in all things to the general discipline of the Diocese as set forth in the Pastoral Letter. Their submission was complete and unconditional,—it was spontaneous, for, I neither argued with them nor suffered them to argue with me. I congratulated them, intimating at the same time that their acknowledged and causeless obstinacy had given great scandal, which, as good Christians, they were bound to repair as far as possible. This they admitted, and were prepared to ask pardon of God and of their Bishop for the scandals they had given. They besought the Bishop, however, to open their church and preach in it on the following day, which was Sunday. I replied that before I opened their church they should make the *amende honorable* to their fellow Catholics of the Diocese and of the world, which they did in the afternoon papers by a public expression of their regret for the course they had hitherto pursued. Here the matter ended, as between the Bishop of New York and the trustees of St. Louis's Church. A new pastor was appointed, and things went on peacefully till the Diocese was divided.

With the details of the subsequent history of this controversy I am unacquainted, but I am quite persuaded that the trustees of St. Louis's Church have had as little reason to complain of their present zealous and devoted Bishop as they had to complain of me.

Whether in view of the foregoing facts the Legislature can do any thing to relieve those gentlemen from the laws of the religious denomination to which they profess to belong, it will remain for Mr. Putnam and his colleagues to determine.

Their petition states as follows, viz:

"The trustees sent one of their number, Wm. B. Le Couteulx, Esq., to Europe for the purpose of preventing this arbitrary, and as was claimed, this illegal action of the Bishop, through the intervention of Cardinal Fornari, the Pope's Nuncio in Paris. Mr. L. C. succeeded in his mission. No further efforts were made at the time by Bishop Hughes to disturb the title to the Church, and its members fondly hoped that peace was permanently restored."

Here is a strange jumble of fact and fiction. It is quite true that Mr. Le Couteulx went to Europe,—it is quite false that he succeeded in his mission. Bishop Hughes had many conversations with Cardinal Fornari in Paris after Mr. Le C.'s visit, and the Nuncio never so much as alluded either to Mr. Le Couteulx or to the St. Louis's Church in Buffalo. Peace, then, was not restored in consequence of any authority in the Catholic Church, for neither Bishop, nor Cardinal, nor Pope, ever spoke or wrote to Bishop Hughes on the subject. But peace was restored in consequence of the trustees having, in the interview above alluded to, voluntarily and unconditionally submitted to the requirements of the Pastoral Letter;—in consequence of their having expressed sorrow for their scandalous conduct;—and in consequence of their having promised, if the Bishop would only grant them a Priest, to conform thenceforward in their administration as lay trustees to the rules of the Diocese.

Such is the plain, simple history of facts involved in the so-called controversy between the trustees of St. Louis's Church and myself, up to the period when the Diocese was divided. Let no one suppose that this statement of facts is untrue or incorrect in any of its parts. I had some correspondence, but no controversy with the trustees. I had much conversation also, especially with their spokesman; and I defy him to show that in writing, in speech, or by any act or sign, I have ever made the proposition, or exhibited the desire, to meddle, directly or indirectly, with the title of their church.

This is a true and simple, though hastily written statement, of the whole question between St. Louis Church and the undersigned.

✠ JOHN, Archbishop of New York.

[*From the* BUFFALO COMMERCIAL ADVERTISER, *April* 5.]

THE ST. LOUIS CHURCH DIFFICULTY.

To the RIGHT REV. JOHN HUGHES, *Archbishop of New York.*

RIGHT REVEREND SIR:—The letter which you have been pleased to publish in the New York *Freeman's Journal*, under date of the 28th of last March, has just been read by me; and since you have thought fit to make such a free use of my name, you will permit me to take the liberty to answer you "*in that polite language which a French gentleman knows so well how to employ.*"

As it would no doubt be as tedious to you as to the public, were I to follow you in your appreciation of the merits of the Hon. Senator Putnam's bill, I will come at once to what concerns the Church of St. Louis, of Buffalo, and my poor self.

It is true, sir, that you never demanded—that is to say, in express words—the title to our church property; but after reading your pastoral letter of 1842 or 1843, of which you give a copy in your last letter, imposing upon the Catholic congregations of your diocese, as a condition *sine qua non*, to obey your requirements, under pain of being deprived of pastors in their churches, I leave it to any one to decide if we, of the St. Louis church, were wrong in asserting that you demanded their property; for it is plain that if we had submitted to your requirements, our charter of incorporation would have been annulled, consequently our right to our temporal administration and to our church property; for the whole would have passed under your absolute control and dominion! But, sir, if this argument of mine on your pastoral letter is not conclusive, what are we to think of the decree adopted in the Synod of Baltimore in 1849, the fourth article being worded as follows:

Article IV. *The Fathers ordain*—that is, you and the other Bishops—*that all Churches, and all other ecclesiastical property, which have been acquired by donations, or the offerings of the Faithful, for religious or charitable use, belong to the Bishop of the Diocese, unless it shall be made to appear, and be confirmed by writings, that it was granted to some religious order of monks, or to some congregation of priests for their use.*

Is not that article conclusive? Does it not show plainly that you and Bishop Timon demanded our church property? Our resistance to your demands was the only cause of all your accusations,—particularly against the "spokesman"—and of your branding us in the public prints as infidels and liars! which is not very Christian, coming from an Archbishop! As to that part of your letter concerning the submission of the trustees of the St. Louis church, on your second yearly Episcopal visitation to Buffalo, "*and which was complete and unconditional, and who apologized for the schismatical course they had adopted, attributing it to their being unacquainted with the value of English words, and to the deceptions of* Mr. WILLIAM B. LE COUTEULX, *who was their interpreter of the Pastoral Letter, and who assured them that the Bishop was endeavoring to get possession of their church property, in order to give it to the Irish. That they could now easily see that said* W. B. LE COUTEULX *had been deceiving them from the beginning.*"

It requires, indeed, sir, all those feelings of a gentleman who respects his religion, and the rank which you occupy in our church, not to resent in the strongest terms the above assertions; but I have promised to be polite, and I will do it. My answer to said assertions will be limited to the following declaration, duly acknowledged before a Commissioner of Deeds, the original of which is in my hands, ready to be shown to any one wishing to see it:

We, the undersigned, surviving Trustees of the St. Louis Church, of Buffalo, present at the interview with the Right Reverend John Hughes, Bishop of the Diocese of New York, which took place in 1842 or 1843, on his second Episcopal visit in this city, declare by these presents, that the assertions of the Right Reverend Bishop, contained in his letter of the 28th of March of the present year, and published in the New York *Freeman's Journal*, concerning what we should have said about Mr. William D. Le Couteulx, is entirely and altogether incorrect, not having even the remembrance that his name was once pronounced during said interview.

BUFFALO, April 3, 1855.

(Signed,) MARTIN FISHER,
JOSEPH HABERSTRO,
N. HAAS,
B. RINCK.

STATE OF NEW YORK, *City of Buffalo, Erie Co.* } On this 3d day of April, in the year 1855, before me personally came Martin Fisher, Joseph Haberstro, Nicholas Haas, and Bartholomew Rinck, known to me to be the persons described in, and who executed the foregoing certificate, and each separately acknowledged that they have executed the same, for the purposes above mentioned.

(Signed,) NICHOLAS OTTENOT,
Com. of Deeds.

As to the card, which at the time you caused to be published by the trustees in the *Commercial Advertiser* of this city, "*as an amende honorable*," it was worded and even written by you, as a condition to your restoring a pastor in the St. Louis Church.

Your denial, sir, of Cardinal Fornari's interference with you to try to settle our difficulties, can never be conclusive for me, for I know too well the worth of that most learned, amiable, and benevolent prelate, not to believe him incapable of making a promise and not to keep it. It was him who dissuaded me to go to Rome to seek redress, telling me that he was sure to be able to settle our matters with you. And it was him also, who prevailed upon me to return to America, and made me promise to see you on my arrival, to try once more to settle our difficulties personally with you, asking me to inform him of the result of the interview. I did as he bade me, saw you, and the next day a letter, rendering him a faithful account of what had taken place between us, was on the way to Europe.

There is a coincidence, sir, which rather turns against that denial of yours, in the fact *that two months after the departure of my letter for Europe, just the necessary time for you to receive one from the Worthy Cardinal,* you came to Buffalo and settled every thing with the trustees, upon the publication of a card, showing that you was right and they wrong! I will drop this contest, and leave it as you will have it, "a strange jumble of fact and fiction."

As to Rev. Mr. Pax, Pastor of the St. Louis church, whom you would represent as a martyr of the trustees, "who had actually been compelled, through ill-treatment from them and their adherents, to quit his post and return to his native country," I will affirm, upon my honor, that I never knew but of one difficulty between them, and that it came from the impossibility of said trustees to reimburse him the sum of *six hundred dollars*, immediately upon his demand, and which he had prevailed upon them to borrow of him, for some work to be done to the church. However, he was soon paid by a collection made in the congregation.

That pastor, whom I knew well, was of a morose disposition, constantly regretting his native country, and expressing his intention to leave us as soon as he would have acquired the means to make his mother comfortable. He came to us very poor, and through our liberality, in less than four years, went away to see his mother with *six thousand dollars*, which is a pretty fair compensation for so short a time of martyrdom!

I will abstain from saying any thing about the paternal administration of Buffalo, since you pretend to know nothing about it; but I cannot help remarking how strange is that declaration from an Archbishop, speaking of the administrator of a diocese belonging to his Archbishopric!

Now, sir, that I have answered the different parts of your letter containing accusations and denials, permit me to tell you how easily I can conceive your displeasure on finding that some Catholics had been so bold as to seek at the hands of their Legislature the maintenance of some temporal rights which they had enjoyed for many years, sanctioned by the civil laws of the country, and which you wanted to wrest from them, in virtue of a decree of Baltimore! I can as easily conceive your wrath against the "spokesman" of the trustees of the St. Louis church, for his having dared to tender them that assistance which their situation needed. But, sir, that "*spokesman*," possessing a pure conscience and a firm mind, can bear, without fear, your displeasure, your attacks, and all your efforts to injure a reputation which he has acquired by the rectitude of his conduct, his manners, and his kind and upright disposition.

It is my firm belief, sir, although very few will dare to express it, that the great majority of the Catholics in this country will rejoice if Hon. Senator Putnam's bill becomes a law! And I would not be at all surprised were some of the pastors also to rejoice, *but in peto*, as the greatest part of their earnings go towards helping the payment for the property bought by their bishops, or the building of their cathedrals and other establishments, and some of them are in a most precarious situation, almost bordering on starvation.

That law, compared with the evil which you set forth, "of a few congregations getting into debt," will be of greater advantage in giving to the Bishops more time to devote to their spiritual duties, by not being any more obliged to go to foreign countries there to seek for the means to face their engagements at home for their purchases of real estate, &c., &c., giving the sad spectacle of their seeming more in quest of wealth than of souls. That law would also, in my opinion, have the advantage to destroy those reports about the influence of the Bishops in the elections, and be the means of putting an end to that jealousy and frequent strife between the Catholics and those of another religion.

Permit me to express to you here, in conclusion, my sincere regret to have been once more under the obligation to answer you, and that I would have preferred to have been left alone, which was so very easy for you to do. Still believe me to remain respectfully,

Right Reverend Sir, your obedient servant,

W. B. LE COUTEULX.

THE CHURCH QUESTION.—MORE OF THE DIFFICULTIES OF THE ST. LOUIS CHURCH, BUFFALO.

REPLY OF ARCHBISHOP HUGHES TO WM. B. LE COUTEULX, ESQ.

To the Editor of the New York Daily Times:

Mr. Wm. B. Le Couteulx's letter, addressed to me, and published in the Buffalo Commercial Advertiser of the 5th inst., and copied into your paper of this date, requires some notice at my hands. I shall have no direct controversy with Mr. Wm. B. Le Couteulx. But I must begin by disclaiming any intention to injure "a reputation which he has acquired by the rectitude of his conduct, his manners, and his kind and upright disposition." This is the character which he claims for himself, and with which I have nothing to do. It would be well for him if he had economized his reputation and spared it as much as I have done. I have no unkind feelings towards him or towards any human being. But his own acts determine that he is without the slightest necessity for an imputation against it on my part. Besides, if he looks at the testimonies of certain journals, he will be satisfied that he never stood so high as he does at present in the estimation of the enemies of the Catholic Church, for the accomplishment of whose purposes, he and his colleagues have made themselves voluntarily and gratuitously the efficient implements.

Mr. Le Couteulx assumes that I have branded him and his colleagues in the public prints as infidels and liars. I must beg leave to decline the authorship of such vulgar language. But if Mr. Le Couteulx adopts such epithets and applies them to himself and his associates, I cannot deny him the superior advantage of knowing whether they are truly applicable or not. I only disclaim having used or applied such terms, and throw back their authorship upon Mr. Wm. B. Le Couteulx. But I thank that gentleman for aiding me in establishing the triumph of truth over falsehood touching the difficulties between St. Louis's Church and myself.

In the petition presented to the Legislature of New York, it is stated, shortly after these events Bishop Hughes attempted to compel the Trustees to convey the title of their property to him. The Trustees resisted firmly." To this statement the name of Mr. Le Couteulx is signed among others as a veracious witness. In the letter now before me I find the following statement: "It is true, sir, that you (Bishop Hughes) never demanded, that is to say, in express words, the title to our Church property." This is signed as a veracious statement by Wm. B. Le Couteulx. These two statements from the same author contradict each other, and I choose to believe the statement in the letter, inasmuch as it is a substantial endorsement of what I had previously written—namely, that in the statement of the petition there was not a sentence, or a word, or a syllable, or a letter of truth. In this Mr. Le Couteulx substantially agrees, when he says that I never demanded the title to the Church property. But he goes on to say that, if he and the Trustees had acquiesced in the requirements of my Pastoral Letter, the whole of their property would have passed under my absolute control and dominion. This consequenee was altogether a *non sequitur*. Other congregations acquiesced in those regulations, and yet continued in the undisturbed possession of their property, just as before. And I may as well observe here, that from the day on which the Pastoral Letter was published until the present hour, I have never asked, I have never accepted, I have never received, one inch of Church property from Trustees, of any description. If Mr. Le Couteulx and his colleagues are so incapable of reasoning as to suppose that their compliance with a regulation of discipline, not touching on their vested rights in the least, was a transfer of their property, it furnishes an evidence of stupidity entirely unbecoming men of pretensions like theirs. But Mr. Le Couteulx himself has no confidence in this subterfuge, for he says: "If this argument of mine on your Pastoral Letter is not conclusive, what are we to think of the decree adopted in the Synod of Baltimore in 1849?" of which he gives the words of the fourth article. Alas, how Mr. Le Couteulx must feel himself lowered down when he is obliged to quote as a pretext for the schismatical course which he and his colleagues thought proper to adopt in 1842, any event which took place seven years afterwards. And this warrants him in asking "Is not that article conclusive? Does it not show plainly that you and Bishop Timon demanded our property? How manifestly it shows no such thing. First, because I (that is Bishop Hughes) had nothing to do with the St. Louis's Church in Buffalo when that article was written in 1849. Secondly, because that article had no reference to any vested title in Church property already existing, whether in Trustees or otherwise. Thirdly, because Mr. Le Couteulx, or whoever translated the fourth statute, has perverted the meaning and falsified the text. The words of the statute, as it stands in Latin, are as follows, viz: "*Statuerunt Patres Ecclesias omnes, ceteraque bona Ecclesiastica, quæ vel dono, vel Fidelium oblationibus acquisita, in charitatis vel religionis operibus sunt impendenda, ad ordinarium pertinere; nisi appareat, scriptoque constet illa ordini alicui Regulari, vel Sacerdotum Congregationi in ipsorum, usum tradita fuisse.*" The translation of which is simply this: "The Fathers have directed or ordained that all churches and other eclesiastical goods acquired by donation, or by the offerings of the faithful to be expended or employed in works of charity or of religion, belong to the ordinary, unless it appear and is made evident in writing that such property has been given to some religious order or community of Priests." The words which are suppressed in Mr. Le Couteulx's translation, and which show that this statute had a prospective and not a retrospective bearing are the words, "*Sunt impendenda*"—*to be* expended." It is singular how the translator should have omitted *by mistake* the only two words in the article which refute his interpretation of its meaning. Consequently, therefore, Mr. Le Couteulx is just as unfortunate in quoting this article as he is in making an event of the year 1849 a groundwork for what he and his colleagues had done in 1842. Mr. Le Couteulx now proceeds to controvert my statement with regard to the unqualified and spontaneous submission of the

Trustees on my Episcopal visit to Buffalo. It seems he has taken the pains to have them make affidavit in regard to what occurred in the interview between them and me; and like sensible men, as they are, they first declare on oath that my statement is entirely and altogether incorrect as regards what one of them said respecting Mr. Le Couteulx's having been their interpreter, and his having been deceiving them from the commencement,—that is, if my explanation of the meaning of the Pastoral Letter was correct. The public will be painfully amused at the reason which warrants them in declaring, under oath, that my statement is entirely and altogether incorrect. That reason is, that they do not even remember that Mr. Le Couteulx's name was once pronounced during said interview. Now, this only proves on oath that they have had bad memories, but it does not warrant them in stating that a thing did not occur simply because it has escaped their recollections. I made the statement because it was true; because I remember it distinctly. But, considering the position in which Mr. Le Couteulx finds himself, it is singular that he or his associates should deem it necessary to invoke the solemnity of an oath before a Commissioner of Deeds, and that the whole sum and substance of that oath amounts only to a declaration that they do not remember what occurred at the interview. *Non mi ricordo.*

Mr. Le Couteulx reminds me that it was I who drew up the *amende honorable*, signed by the Trustees, and published on the same day in the Buffalo *Commercial Advertiser*. This is true. But I will explain how it happened. The interview occurred on Saturday, after 12 o'clock. It lasted some time. The paper, it was said, was usually published at 2 o'clock. They were exceedingly anxious that I should open, and preach in St. Louis's Church on the following day (Sunday). I, on the other hand, had made known to them my determination never to open that church until they should first ask pardon of their fellow Catholics, of the diocese of New York and of the country, for the scandal which they had given. They attempted to draw up the formulary of a document to that effect. But their very anxietv to have it in time for the afternoon paper, disqualified them from writing it as hastily as they would wish. I witnessed what I considered to be at that moment their good Catholic dispositions, and in order not to disappoint them in their hopes for the following day, I took the pen and drew the form of their apology, making it as little humiliating to them as possible. I saw that they would have signed a card reflecting upon themselves much more seriously for their past conduct; but I felt that it would be ungenerous and uncharitable on my part to take advantage of their disposition, by imposing on them any thing that could be construed into an act of humiliation.

Mr. Le Couteulx is very much surprised that Cardinal Fornari should never have spoken or written to me on the subject of St. Louis Church, in Buffalo. However, the fact is as I have stated No ecclesiastic in the Church, from the Pope downward, has ever spoken or written to me on the subject. What passed between Mr. Le Couteulx and the Nuncio in Paris, I do not know, but when Mr. Le Couteulx stated in his petition to the Legislature, that he had appealed to Cardinal Fornari, as a special deputy from the Trustees of Buffalo, and that he had been "successful in his mission," he placed me under the necessity of showing that he was quite mistaken, and that there was not a word of truth in the pretended success of his mission. He says that he called upon me on his return immediately after his arrival at New York; and that he wrote the next day to Nuncio Fornari, a faithful account of what had taken place between him and me during the brief interview. I should be very curious to see that letter, for I am at a loss to imagine what it could be made up of. I recollect well the substance of what occurred in the interview. I received Mr. Le Couteulx as I would any other gentleman, if not cordially, at least courteously. He never told me that he had been on a mission to Cardinal Fornari, with a view to have my administration impeached or amended. But after the ordinary common-place, he proceeded to express his desire that the difficulties in Buffalo might be brought to an end. I may here observe that, pending those difficulties, I had determined to have no quarrel or controversy with the recusant lay Catholics of St. Louis's Church. And as the best means of carrying out that determination, I had made it a rule to have no conversation with any irresponsible individual or solitary member of that congregation. When Mr. Le Couteulx, therefore, touched on the subject, I signified to him, in language as polite as the occasion would permit, that it was a subject on which I did not allow myself to converse with any unauthorized member of St. Louis's Church, and gave the conversation another turn, by asking what kind of a passage he had had, and whether the weather had been fine during the voyage. He says now that he sent a faithful account, on the following day, of what took place; and since this is the amount of what really did take place, Cardinal Fornari must have found his letter exceedingly interesting.

However, Mr. Le Couteulx seems to have been under some strange hallucination; for he asserts that my Episcopal visitation to Buffalo was just about two months after he had dispatched his letter, and corresponded to a nicety with the time when I should have had a letter from Cardinal Fornari in answer to his. Now such reckoning as to time was fair enough. But the hallucination to which I refer consists in Mr. Le Couteulx's supposing that my visit to Buffalo was in consequence of the Nuncio's admonition; and as proof of this, he says that I went to Buffalo and settled every thing with the Trustees upon the publication of a card, showing that "you (Bishop Hughes) was right, and they (the Trustees) wrong." Mr. Le Couteulx knows that as became my duty, I visited the different congregations of the diocese—that the Catholics of Buffalo were entitled to that visit; and that as to the schismatical Trustees of St. Louis's Church, and their adherents, they were no longer numbered among my flock, except as wayward, self-willed, and erring brethren. I neither sought them out nor spoke of them. And I may say now that as the difficulty then stood, their church would have crumbled into dust, brick by brick, before I should have consented to give them a Priest, or do any other act which should recognize the principle of their stupid resistance to episcopal authority. I did not address myself to the Trustees. They, in language more than sufficiently humble and respectful, addressed themselves to me, begging that I would admit them to an interview. This I declined peremptorily, excepting on condition of their preparedness to come back to the starting point of their schism, and to acknowledge themselves wrong in all their subsequent course. Still, poor Mr. Le Couteulx seems to have imagined that, because it was just two months from the time he wrote a letter to Cardinal Fornari, I must have received from that illustrious Prelate an admonition to proceed to Buffalo and make my peace with the Trustees on the best terms possible. In dealing with such a letter as the one I am now replying to, it is difficult for even pity to triumph over impatience.

It is hardly worth while to be sorry at the ungenerous attack which Mr. Le Couteulx makes on the zealous and amiable Rev. Mr. Pax, the real builder of St. Louis's Church, Buffalo ; for although he could not have built it out of his own funds, yet he wore himself down in toiling to obtain subscriptions for its erection. Nor would he have ever undertaken such a task, if he had not been assured by the venerable Bishop Dubois, that in his mission in Buffalo he would not be under the government of lay Trustees. This assurance was made inasmuch as the respected and venerable father of Mr. Le Couteulx had given a deed of the property on which the church now stands, to the late Bishop Dubois, not dreaming that a number of laymen should, in the mean time, get themselves surreptitiously recognized as Trustees of the same. Their treatment of the Rev. Mr. Pax may be best ascertained from the letters he wrote to me complaining of their conduct, and giving facts and dates regarding what happened. I continued to encourage him, begging of him to bear every thing for the sake of the poor people, assuring him of what was the fact, that if he left them, I had no German clergyman to put in his place. This, however, was long previous to the schism, inaugurated by Mr. Le Couteulx and his colleagues. Even that schism, however, did not authorize me as I thought to remove him ; but when annoyances, and these arising from the rebellious portion of his own flock, as was supposed even by the Buffalo editors at the time, reached a point of endangering his life, such as the hurling of large paving stones through his windows in the darkness of night, I could not in conscience require him to continue longer. Mr. Le Couteulx says that he carried away with him $6,000, which Mr. Le Couteulx describes as "a pretty fair compensation for so short a time of martyrdom." Mr. Le Couteulx must pardon me if I say candidly, that, although it may be true, yet I cannot believe this statement. Will he be pleased to make known his authority that Mr. Pax carried away $6,000! When he shall have stated the authority on which he makes this announcement, I shall take the liberty of examining it, and I have no doubt it will prove as hollow as that on which he has made other statements. Mr. Le Couteulx concludes that in his opinion the great majority of Catholics in this country will rejoice if Hon. Senator Putnam's bill becomes a law. Now, as to the rejoicing of the Catholics, or a majority of them, that is a matter entirely extraneous from the subject in hand. One thing is certain—that neither the great majority, nor the great minority of Catholics in this country, will ever select Mr. Wm. B. Le Couteulx as their spokesman. If they wish the aid of civil legislation in regulating the ecclesiastical matters of their Church, they will make known their desire and express their wants in the language of respect and truthfulness which it becomes those who approach the Legislature of the State to employ. In the mean time, they feel wounded to think that whereas they had not made any complaint to the Legislature, that honorable body should feel itself warranted to thrust upon them a code of discipline which they do not desire, which has been founded on the misrepresentation of the Trustees of St. Louis's Church, Buffalo, and sustained by the illiberal anti-Catholic feeling which now so unhappily prevails throughout the State.

Finally, if Mr. Wm. B. Le Couteulx is now placed in a condition by no means flattering to his own estimate of his character, as possessing "a pure conscience * * * * * and a reputation which he has acquired by the rectitude of his conduct, his manners, and his kind and upright disposition," he must hold himself, not me, responsible for the result. For the last twelve or thirteen years he and his colleagues have lost no opportunity of assailing me, assailing the Bishop of Buffalo, assailing the Prelates of the United States, sometimes directly, sometimes indirectly, by frequent, injurious statements, utterly unfounded in truth. This is the day of reckoning which he and his colleagues have brought upon themselves by the unwarrantable allegation of their petition to the Legislature. Having remained almost silent under such obloquy for these many years past, and having now at length taken my pen in hand, I wish Mr. Le Couteulx and his colleagues to bring out all they have to say, and I pledge myself, founding that pledge on the omnipotence and infallibility of truth, to continue from document to document to oppress them with its crushing weight.

✠ JOHN, *Archbishop of New York.*

NEW YORK, *April* 7, 1855.

To the RIGHT REVEREND JOHN HUGHES, *Catholic Bishop of New York:*

BUFFALO, *Saturday, April* 14, 1855.

RIGHT REVEREND SIR: Your declining to have any direct controversy with me, and your reply to my letter of the 5th inst. containing hardly any thing but denials and sarcasms in bad taste, induces me not to notice your said reply any further than by what follows: That in my opinion, denials against denials being no proofs, would amount to a most miserable pen war, tedious to the public, and likely to augment that scandal for our holy religion of which you complain, although the sole author of it by your first publications. If, after your getting a little more cool about the adoption of the law upon the tenure of Church Property (which by-the-by is only to be attributed to yourself and a few Bishops), you can bring your mind to address me "in that polite language which a French gentleman knows so well how to employ," you will find me always ready to answer you, otherwise not.

Permit me once more to subscribe myself, Right Reverend Sir, respectfully your obedient servant,

W. B. LE COUTEULX

ARCHBISHOP HUGHES IN REVIEW OF SENATOR BROOKS'S SPEECH.

To the Editor of the Courier and Enquirer:

When an individual who never expected much from the favors of fortune, finds himself unexpectedly and all at once the proprietor of immense wealth, it is, I trust, not unbecoming in him to expend a portion of it in promoting the welfare of his countrymen by multiplying the opportunities for acquiring knowledge. Neither should feelings of gratitude be altogether disregarded in such expenditure; and as I am mainly indebted to the Hon. Erastus Brooks for the immense fortune which I now possess, I hope his modesty will permit him to share with me in the immortality which will result to its founder from the magnificence and perpetuity of the monument, "*æra perrenius*," which is to commemorate my princely fortune and his sagacity in finding out its existence. In a speech delivered by Mr. Senator Brooks before that branch of our Legislature which has been so enlightened by the flashing evidences of his erudition, and encouraged to habits of industry by his painstaking search after the titles of property vested in me, he has made known that my property in the city of New York alone is not much short of five millions of dollars. His colleagues must have been as much edified as I have been surprised at this announcement. Still it appears that Mr. Senator Brooks, like an honorable man, who would not deceive, furnished evidences from the records of property in New York to sustain his senatorial statement; for towards the close of his speech he has inserted in brackets the following words:

"To those who were curious in such matters, Mr. Brooks exhibited to the Senate the number, book, and page of those several entries in the city of New York in behalf of John Hughes."

So it seems certain, on the testimony of Mr. Brooks, that my property in this city alone is not much short of five millions of dollars. Out of the city it should be proportionably great, but of its extent Mr. Brooks has not given us any information. Like a strictly conscientious man, he testifies only to what he knows. The amount in his estimate would be five millions; but in order to avoid the possibility of error he leaves a little margin, and declares it not much short of that amount. The paper called the *Presbyterian* sets it down at twenty-five millions of dollars, and I know not by what right Mr. Brooks should have diminished the amount of my property by striking out the surplus twenty millions so generously assigned me by the *Presbyterian*. The reason may be that the *Presbyterian* is not a Senator, and therefore (though I do not admit the validity of the reason) less bound to be truthful in its statements and accurate in its arithmetic than an honorable Senator. Besides, the *Presbyterian* being a religious paper, allowance must be made for its benevolent exaggerations, and its efforts to be *liberal* in dealing with persons of another creed. It seems, then, that I must bid good-bye to the twenty millions, and satisfy myself with what Mr. Brooks allows, —property not much short of five. Let us state it at four millions. And now I have a proposition to make to Mr. Brooks, which will be interesting to him and our fellow-citizens at large. In order to avoid being reduced to want in my old age, I propose to set apart one-half of this amount, and to secure it out of the estate, as a reasonable provision against what is commonly called a "rainy day." I shall reserve to myself the right of expending the other two millions for the public good, according to my own sense of what is likely to be most beneficial.

Much has been already done for the diffusion of knowledge; but the perusal of Mr. Brooks's speech and of other kindred documents, satisfies me that more is still needed. I propose, therefore, to found a Public Library for the use, not of any one profession or class of men, but for all mankind. I think that with the surplus two millions which Mr. Brooks has allowed me, I shall be enabled to erect a suitable building; and I propose to furnish it with the best editions of books that can be found in Europe or America, to the number of five hundred thousand volumes. According to a rough estimate, half a million would be sufficient to put up the building, a million to furnish the books, and another half million to be funded, so that the annual interest may be sufficient to meet current expenses,—such as librarians' salaries, gas lights, provision of Croton water, tables, and the conveniences for writing out any extract which visitors may think proper to make. It is to be open to natives and foreigners, Catholics and Protestants, Jews and Gentiles; in short, a really public library, worthy of this immense city. And as an evidence of my gratitude to our honorable Senator, to whom I am indebted for the discovery of my immense riches, I would have it called—that is, if the gentleman's modesty will permit me—the Erastus Brooks Library. This designation should be engraved in large and gilded letters over its marble portals, and I am sure the honorable gentleman will consent to have the apartment to be allotted as the receptacle of curious pamphlets enriched by a copy of his speech, pronounced in the Senate at Albany on the 6th of March, 1855. Thus posterity will know from the outside of the building not only to whom they are indebted for so important a public institution, but also, from an investigation of its more precious treasures of literature within, what manner of man their benefactor was.

I foresee that there may be a difficulty about the location of the edifice; but without waiting for the formalities which have to be gone through as regards other particulars, we can settle this question immediately. Mr. Brooks, as a gentleman of veracity, assured the Senate of New York, after having examined my property, that "some of the parcels cover whole squares of land, and nearly all of them are of great value." Now this is an extraordinary discovery, and if it had not been asserted on the veracity of an honorable Senator, I could not have believed it. I do not know where any of these squares of land are situated; but, of course, Mr. Brooks knows, and I pledge myself to give him a deed of any one of them he may choose to select, provided he can only find it out—which is more than I can do. This I am ready to do to-morrow, even though it should encroach on that portion of my estate which I would reserve for "pin-money." Mr. Brooks has stated that, within twelve years, fifty-eight entries of as many distinct parcels of property were made in my favor. Now this is more than I am aware of, for, in fact, I never counted such entries. So, also, with regard to the whole squares of land of which I am the owner, if Mr. Brooks has not made a statement at variance with truth. I am not aware of such ownership. I do not know where those squares of land are situated. But, of course, Mr. Brooks knows,—otherwise he would not have made the assertion. It is possible that some persons have made over to me squares of land without giving any intimation of the fact, and I should be much obliged to Mr. Brooks if he would take the pains to consult documents in the Register's office once more, and let me know where those squares of land are. But there are some things which Mr. Brooks has stated with regard to my property which I know to be incorrect and unfounded in truth. He says, for instance, that in the Register's office there are numerous transfers from trustees to me. Now this statement I know to be untrue, inasmuch as I have never received or accepted any transfer of any property whatever from trustees. In this particular, at least, Mr. Brooks allowed himself to be deceived, and contributed his share towards the deception of his fellow Senators and the public. But with regard to the whole squares of land which, he says, are mine, I hereby authorize him to sell any one of them at his option, for cash, pledging myself, as I do hereby, to give to the purchaser such deed as I possess of the same.

You may suppose, gentlemen, that all this is written in playfulness. Now, whether or not will depend on the truth of Mr. Brooks's statements, made in the Senate of New York on the 6th of March. If Mr. Brooks was in earnest, so am I. If Mr. Brooks, on a matter of fact, spoke the truth, taking his assertion as the ground of my hypothesis, I speak the truth also. If my property is not much short of five millions, as Mr. Brooks asserted, I pledge myself solemnly that there is no jest as to the project of the new Library. But, if on the other hand, Mr. Brooks did not speak the truth in the statements which he made, the worse for posterity, and the worse for him. The matter is reduced at present to a question of veracity, and it is for Mr. Brooks to prove his assertion, or occupy the position which his failure to do so has in reserve for him.

In sober seriousness, however, is it not melancholy to witness the multitudinous and mendacious charges which are made from day to day against Catholics as a body, and against individuals professing their religion? If there be an intention among the public men of this country to disfranchise Catholics, to abridge them of their rights, in the name of all that is honorable, I would say let it be done by a manly and noble declaration to that effect. If Protestantism cannot thrive in this country unless it have some one or more denominations to degrade and trample upon, as in Great Britain and Ireland, let it speak out candidly and make known the fact. If defamation in aggregate and in detail can accomplish it, the Catholics of this country will soon be degraded enough in the minds of their fellow-citizens. But even of this we should not have so much reason to complain if the purpose were openly avowed, so that all parties would have fair and timely warning. If that should be done, I have no hesitation in taking on myself to say, that so far as Catholics are concerned, immigration will soon come to a dead stand, and emigration will probably commence.

It is exceedingly painful for me to have to appear in the public press in reference to topics of this kind; but if the trustees of St. Louis's Church, and even an honorable Senator, accuse me of acts which would be dishonorable, and even dishonest, if they were true, have I not a right is it not my duty, both to myself and those who take any interest in my reputation, to hurl back the false accusations in the face of their authors? If Messrs. Brooks and others make charges against me by name which I know to be false, have I not a right to defend myself, and to denounce them as unreliable and false witnesses? If not, I have studied the sense of justice and fair play by which Americans are actuated to very little purpose. If I have no right to defend myself when assailed, personally and by name, by any man, against the accusation, then I have studied the rights of an American citizen and the genius of American institutions to very little purpose indeed. I respect the dignity of a Senator, but when an individual who is invested with that dignity trifles with it at my expense, I claim the right to hold him responsible for the accuracy of his statements.

For these reasons, I request Mr. Erastus Brooks, with all the respect that is due to him, to meet the issue of veracity between him and me, and either to prove his statements, or to retract them under the impulse of those high principles which constitute an honorable man, whether he be a Senator or not.

✠ JOHN, Archbishop of New York.

SENATOR BROOKS TO ARCHBISHOP HUGHES.

To the Editor of the New York Daily Times:

From the pressure of official duties at Albany, up to a late hour on Saturday evening, I have only this moment been able to give a full perusal to the letter signed, "✠ John, Archbishop of New York," in reply to a speech of mine, delivered in the Senate on the 6th of March last. I write now, not to answer the question of veracity between the Archbishop and myself, and not to comment upon the peculiar temper and language of the Archbishop's epistle—but to say that I shall accept and demand, in behalf of the city and the public, and in perfect good faith—if the promise was made in good faith—the offer of that public library, which is tendered in my name, "not for the use of any one profession or class of men but for all mankind."

As a condition of this pledge, I am to show that Archbishop Hughes is, or was, on the 6th of March last, the owner, in his own name, and in this city, of a large amount of real estate; and to show, also, that this property is, or was upon the record, legally his own, to dispose of by assignment, by will, or otherwise, as he may or might direct.

I assume, notwithstanding the reasons for believing otherwise, that in making his offer the Archbishop does not mean to conceal the truth, omit the truth, or to resort to any subterfuge whatever. I assume, too, that he agrees with me that the true definition of a lie is an "intention to deceive," and that he also agrees with the moralist, William Paley, who lays it down as an axiom, that one may state ninety-nine facts, and yet not utter the whole truth, because one truth added would change the basis of the ninety-nine facts.

On this presumption I shall maintain, at my earliest leisure, the spirit, substance, and reality of all that was asserted by me in the speech now in controversy upon the subject of Church Property in this city. And in order that this question may be met fairly, at the start, and in order that the city of New York may be put in possession of the promised public library, I propose, preliminary to all public controversy, that one arbiter shall be named by Archbishop Hughes, one by myself, and that the two thus selected shall jointly elect a third, whose duty it shall be to decide, not merely whether I have stated the truth, or whether Archbishop Hughes has equivocated or omitted the truth, but also the claim of New York city to that public library, in which I shall hereafter feel so deep an interest. I am ready for the arbitration, and shall be ready with my facts.

Very respectfully,

ERASTUS BROOKS.

LETTER FROM ARCHBISHOP HUGHES.

DO CATHOLICS, AS SUCH, MEDDLE IN POLITICS?

To the Editor of the New York Freeman's Journal:—

In the Albany *State Register* there is a long editorial article, headed "*Another Bull from the Vatican,*" purporting to be a review of certain phrases in my letter addressed to your Journal, and published on the 31st ult. In this the editor of the *Register* gives loose rein to the indulgence of strong bigotry, in language hardly remarkable for any thing else than its prosiness and imbecility.

A newspaper is made up of old rags, transformed into adaptation for its use. It receives any impression, true or false, enlightened or stupid, which type have been arranged to impress upon its surface. I can have no direct controversy with a newspaper,—abstractedly from its editor. The editor of the Albany *State Register* is, I perceive, a Mr. S. H. Hammond, a highly respectable man, no doubt, but apparently very credulous, and certainly most inaccurate in his statements. Mr. Hammond must have seen my letter in which I denied the truth of the statement made in the petition of the Trustees in Buffalo, to the effect that I had attempted to compel them to make over the title of their church to me. He must have seen that the correctness of my statement was admitted by Mr. Wm. B. Le Couteulx, one of the signers to the petition, and, as a consequence, he must have seen the falsehood of the charge above referred to. And yet Mr. Hammond does not hesitate to repeat his calumny, as if it had not been denied, and the truth of the denial admitted by one of the parties signing the petition. How is this to be accounted for? It is for Mr. Hammond to answer the question. But not only does he repeat this refuted calumny, but he enlarges on it as if it were true! How is this to be accounted for? I leave Mr. Hammond to answer. I shall not go over the ground again.

But Mr. Hammond has insinuated other charges, to which I think it proper that I should make a suitable reply. He does not state those charges in specific language. He assumes them as matters not to be called into question. He passes from the Catholic individual to the Catholic system, and betrays unmistakable evidences that, whether artificially or naturally, he is under the influence of an anti-Popery mania. Speaking of the Catholic Church and its members in this country, he uses the following language:

> Were the evils of this system confined only to spiritual matters we should have nothing to say. But they reach far beyond this. This despotism seeks a control beyond the mere pale of the Church. It has become ambitious of civil power. It bands its subjects together, and marches them into the arena of politics. It grasps at the control of the political action of the government, and struggles to direct its policy. It favors alliances with political ambition, and joins hands with the demagogues of party. When Governor Seward said "Bishop Hughes is my friend—I honor, respect and confide in him," he was speaking of a political friend and associate; a confederate in securing political influence, a supporter in the exercise of political power. With Bishop Hughes he took the long line of descending Priesthood, and the fettered and bound masses of the Catholic people.

Mr. Hammond is evidently a credulous man. There was a period, when the old-womanism of Protestant London entered into a judical investigation of a reported conspiracy of the Papists, the conspiracy being no more nor less than a plot on the part of the emissaries of Rome to blow up the river Thames, and drown the loyal city of London. If Mr. Hammond had been an editor at the time and place when and where this occurred, the circumstances around him, and the credulous character of his mind, would have been more in harmony with each other than they are at present. If Mr. Hammond knows any fact to prove that the Catholic religion bands its subjects together, and marches them into the arena of politics, he owes it to himself and his country to furnish the evidences. If he knows no such facts, then he is bearing false witness against his neighbor. If he knows any facts going to prove that the Catholic religion or its professors, as such, struggle to direct the policy of this country, he is hardly less than a traitor, if he conceals the proofs of so dangerous a proceeding. If the Catholic religion forms alliances with political ambition, and joins hands with the demagogues of party, Mr. Hammond is more guilty than those he accuses, if he conceals the facts which would substantiate his assertion. If, as he says, Governor Seward did me the honor to call me his friend, and to say that he respected and confided in me, it is more than I ever knew or heard before;—but as to the confidence reposed in me, Governor Seward would not have been disappointed. Mr. Hammond says that Governor Seward was then speaking of a political friend and associate, and I can assure him that in this statement, he has forsaken the path of truth. This I know of my own knowledge, I am not a political friend and associate of Governor Seward; I never was. I am not his confederate in securing political influence. I am not his supporter in the exercise of political power. And yet I am proud to call him my friend, in the only relation that ever existed between us, which has been one of mere social, and, to me, pleasant intercourse. If the people of the United States should think proper to confer on him the highest honor in their gift, I shall not heave a sigh or shed a tear at their choice. But no vote of mine shall aid him. In this, as in all his public acts, he is in the hands of his countrymen, and I am well dispensed from the necessity of either approving or condemning his principles or his conduct. And since this topic has been brought up again, I will say this, that so far from his being a gainer by his friendship towards me, which I highly esteem, he would have been buried under the obloquy which open enemies and deceitful friends have vied with each other in heaping upon him in connection with my name, if he had not been proof against calumny. The long ordeal through which he passed under the calumnious imputations of intrigues with Catholics and foreigners, and his emerging from it with a brighter name than before, is a proof that he needs no individual support, that his is intrinsically the sterling metal of a true man. But he can propel his own bark, as he has hitherto done, without any aid from me or from Catholics.

I will state for the information of Mr. Hammond, who is

probably too young to remember the period when it was necessary for me to state it before, in the face of several editors of New York city and New York State, that in all my life I never voted but once; and in all my life I never advised, publicly or privately, any one as to how he should vote, except once also. That was under very peculiar circumstances. The Catholics of New York city were endeavoring to relieve themselves from the injurious consequences of a system of education for the support of which they had to pay taxes, and the administration and superintendence of which were a monopoly in the hands of a close corporation, known as the Public School Society. At first the Catholics were opposed to me in seeking a change which has since resulted very beneficially to the cause of education. Next, the whole Protestant community were opposed, and sounded the alarm of the dangers of Popery, in a manner just as silly, and just as little true, as the present trumpet notes of the Albany *State Register*. Finally, the truth made its way, the change took place, the facilities for education have been multiplied on every side. The Public School Society is gone, and no persuasion could induce either Catholics or Protestants to return to their old system. To effect the change we had to appeal by petition to the proper authorities; first, to the Common Council, where our petition was denied; next, to the Legislature of the State, where the change took place,—not precisely as we could have desired, but as the Legislature thought proper to make it. Mr. Hammond will be pleased to take particular notice of the fact I am now about to mention, that within a few days previous to the election, the Public School Society, by their agents, waited on the candidates for the Legislature and required a pledge from them, from those of one party as well as those of another, to refuse the petition for a change in the system of Education, in the event of their being elected. This was too much. It was secret. It was insidious. It left the Catholics to vote for one party or the other, concealing from them that no matter which party they voted for, or which candidate, they were elevating into power men who had prejudged their cause, and had bound themselves to reject even a consideration of its merits. In a meeting which they had called in furtherance of their appeal to the Legislature, this discovery of the unworthy trick to deprive them beforehand even of the right of a hearing, was communicated to me, and on that occasion I urged them, with all the zeal and earnestness I was capable of, to refuse their vote to any man, of any party, who had accepted the degrading pledge that if elected he would refuse them even the chance of obtaining justice. If this was meddling with politics, then I did meddle *once*, but I have never regretted it. On the contrary, there is nothing in my life, apart from my sacred ministry, to which I look back with so much satisfaction as to the course I pursued on that occasion. And if by a secret combination among those to be elected by their votes, there should be an attempt to deny them the fair right of petitioning the Legislature as other citizens have a right to do, or to deny the prayer of that petition, however just it might appear in the eyes of an impartial Legislature, I feel that I am yet American citizen enough to do again what I did on that occasion. I did not call it meddling in politics, but only an interference to break up an unworthy combination formed with the view to deny one portion of the people rights to which all are equally entitled.

But in no other case have I ever aided or abetted, or been in connection with any political party, or any individual of any party, since the world began. On the contrary, when I was appointed to take charge of this Diocese, I prescribed for its numerous clergy, as a rule of conduct, to abstain from all interference in politics. I did not deny them the right to vote as other citizens merely in consequence of their being clergymen. That right I believe they have seldom if at all exercised. I myself have not exercised it. I have ever considered that the most appropriate position for a clergyman, whether Catholic or Protestant, to occupy in the midst of political struggles, is one, if not of absolute neutrality, at least of abstinence from all partisanship. There are few congregations in which the members are not divided in their political opinions, and the Catholic clergymen who would take sides on such occasions would be sure to impair the usefulness of his own ministry.

How, then, can Mr. Hammond of the Albany *State Register* call me a political friend and associate of Governor Seward, or of any other man? Is Mr. Hammond at liberty, in violation of a precept of the decalogue, to bear false witness against his neighbor? I defy all men living to point out an act in my life in which I have been connected with any political party, any political caucus, any political individual in the United States or elsewhere. How, then, can Mr. Hammond give circulation to a statement which he knows to be injurious to me, and which is at variance with truth? I tell him the Catholics, as such, have no politics. They are free to vote on all occasions just like their fellow-citizens, that is, as each man chooses. Let them be as free on this subject as Mr. Hammond himself. If they err, they are in the company of immense majorities of Americans and Protestants. If they do not err in their preference or in their party, so much the better for the country. But whether they err or not, they act with large portions of their fellow countrymen.

It is evident that Mr. Hammond is one of the oracles of a new political organization, which hopes to rise into power by depressing Catholics. For myself, I have no great objection to see that party come into power, because once having power in their hands, I think the true American would revive in their breasts, and they would administer it generally just as if they were called by one of the old party names. But I regret that they think it expedient to degrade and depress Catholics as a means to their success. And I am utterly at a loss to understand how a Legislature which evinced so much political virtue and patriotism as was exhibited in the election of Mr. Seward to the Senate, could have found itself capable of passing the anti-Catholic Church Property Bill, but too well calculated to intensify and perpetuate a bitter memory in regard to the influences by which that bill was passed. The Catholics had not asked for such a bill, they did not need it. It was forced upon them under false assertions. It was intended for them alone. It is an act of partial legislation.

They will no doubt submit to it in so far as they are bound to do, but they are not likely to be voluntary parties to its execution.

In conclusion, I request Mr. Hammond, as a particular favor, either to prove that I am a political partisan, a meddler in politics, &c., &c., or else to withdraw so unfounded a charge. I think in doing the one or the other, he will render equally a service to the public and to the undersigned.

✠ JOHN, ARCHBISHOP OF NEW YORK.

NEW YORK, *April 17th*, 1855.

ARCHBISHOP HUGHES' SECOND LETTER.

To the Editor of the New York Freeman's Journal:—

Truth is a great thing. There would be no chance for the protection of innocence or of righteousness without it. Mr. Brooks feels *this*, the force of truth, as if it were his enemy, and he exhibits the instinctive philosophy of poor human nature by shrinking away in dread from its approach, even without waiting until the tribunal at which he stands accused has pronounced him guilty of falsehood. It is the same instinctive philosophy which prompts the man of uncontrolled passions, when he has committed a deed of fatal violence against his fellow-man, to magnify to others, as well as to himself, the great distinction there is between manslaughter and murder, even before his trial has come on. And Mr. Brooks, inheriting this poor human nature like other men, and seeing truth in the distance, but approaching, begins to throw out a remote defence by giving us the moral definition of a lie as necessarily resulting from an intention to deceive. But who has spoken to Mr. Brooks, or even whispered to him, except it be his own conscience, any thing about a lie, or lying? Why then should he anticipate his defence by drawing a distinction between falsehood ignorantly uttered, and deliberate mendacity? Nobody can answer these questions except Mr. Brooks himself. And if Mr. Brooks had not contrived to place himself in the disreputable position which he now occupies, his casuistry about lying would have been altogether superfluous.

However, Senator Brooks, according to the just principles of Anglo-Saxon jurisprudence, is entitled to the benefit of all doubts like any other accused person, whether as regards the facts or the law of the case. I have charged Mr. Brooks with uttering falsehood prejudicial to my reputation, in his speech pronounced on the 6th March, and in presence of his colleagues in the Senate Chamber of New York. I have not enumerated all the falsehoods of that speech, but have taken one or two specimens. The controversy is still pending, as Mr. Brooks has not had time to look after the real state of the case. He has been, to use his own introductory expression, "under the pressure of official duties at Albany."

In that speech Mr. Brooks stated that I was the owner of real estate to the amount of something little short of five million of dollars. This was untrue, and in order to exhibit its author to the public just as he is, I pledged myself solemnly, that after deducting two millions' worth from my supposed enormous estate, I should appropriate the balance to the erection of a library, if Senator Brooks could point out where the property was. This was the first falsehood (Mr. Brooks must pardon me for using the plain term) which I pointed out in his speech. Senator Brooks stated in his place that some of my real estate consisted of whole squares. The Senator did not state how many, and his colleagues, if they believed him at all, may have inferred that these whole squares amounted to fifteen or twenty—at all events, they could not be less than two. This was the second falsehood pointed out and charged on Mr. Brooks, as having been uttered in his speech of the 6th of March. The third was, that many of the conveyances of real estate to me were made by Trustees. Now, I state that any one who asserts either of these three statements, asserts a gross, and towards me, an injurious falsehood.

Senator Brooks thinks he has discovered a way of twisting out of the awkward position into which he rushed with eyes open and malice prepense. He proposes an arbitration, forsooth. He will appoint one, I may appoint another, and these two shall jointly elect a third, whose duty it shall be to decide whether he has stated the truth, or whether Archbishop Hughes has equivocated or omitted the truth. Gentle Senator Brooks! With what a show of artlessness he attempts to evade the direct issue of veracity involved in the controversy. I *know*, of my own knowledge, that in the three statements above referred to, Senator Brooks has taken as great a liberty with truth as if he had said that two and two make seven.

Arbitration is unnecessary. If I am the owner of whole squares of ground, Mr. Brooks can show from the records of the city, or indicate for physical inspection where they are. If he fails to do this, while his proofs, if he has any, are so undeniable, and so within his reach, then the public will not fail to perceive, that Mr. Brooks in his place as Senator has made a statement which is false, and was intended to be injurious. So if I received any conveyance of property from Trustees, the records cited by Mr. Brooks in the Senate will bear him out. If he fail to produce those records, then the public will perceive that his statement is a falsehood, and will not be slow in coming to the conclusion that Senator Brooks is—what he is.

It is, I own, humiliating for me to have to write thus of any of my fellow-citizens, especially with one who has been honored with a confidence large enough to depute him to the Senate of the State. But I have been assailed by so many calumnies from various sources that a test like the present, brought forth in plain and direct language, may be taken as a sample of the power and the advantages which a man cherishing a love of truth, or honor, and of rectitude, will possess over a whole army of such accusers as Mr. Senator Brooks. He cannot prove his statements, and the reason is, because they are untrue. Will it not be better for him, then, to pay homage to truth by acknowledging that he had deceived himself and contributed to the deception of others?

Mr. Wm. B. Le Couteulx comes out with a little card very much in the vein of that instinctive philosophy of poor human nature of which Senator Brooks has given so *naive* a specimen. Mr. Le Couteulx thinks that "denials against denials being no proofs, would amount to a miserable pen war." Mr. Le Couteulx misrepresents the state of the question. It is not denials against denials. I stated that the assertion in Mr. Le Couteulx's petition, namely, that "Bishop Hughes attempted to compel the Trustees to convey the title of this church property to him," was a falsehood. Now, Mr. Le Couteulx did not deny, but acknowledged this in writing, consequently he is my witness, although his testimony is superfluous, to prove that it was a falsehood. And yet he and his colleagues have imposed on the Legislature of the State by having this among other falsehoods believed as the truth. And now Mr. Le Couteulx has come to the conclusion that "denials against denials, being no proofs, would amount to a most miserable pen war." He forgets that he did not deny my statement, that he admitted it, and thereby acknowledged the falsehood of his own. How could he deny the truth, and which he knew to be the truth? For he knew from the beginning, as well as he does now, that I never attempted to compel the Trustees to convey the title of their church property to me. Until Mr. Le Couteulx, therefore, shall find some ground of truth to stand upon, he will do well to give up his "most miserable pen war," and apologize, with Mr. Brooks, for the deception which he, with others, has practised on the Legislature of the State and on his fellow-citizens. Perhaps he makes the distinction about the morality of lying which the Senator has brought forth, namely: That to constitute a lie there must have existed "an intention to deceive." I do not enter into the sanctuary, if it can be called by so sacred a term, of intentions in the breast of either Senator Brooks or Mr. Le Couteulx. I speak of their public acts and of their printed words, leaving others to judge of their intentions as charitably as they may. But even if it were only for the sake of good example to the rising generation, they would do well to retract those false statements, being convinced that the security of the State and the welfare of society are never so well guaranteed as when they rest on the everlasting foundations of truth.

✠ JOHN, ARCHBISHOP OF NEW YORK.

NEW YORK, April 17, 1855.

THE ST. LOUIS CHURCH CONTROVERSY.

To the Right Reverend JOHN HUGHES, *Catholic Archbishop of New York.*

BUFFALO, *April* 21, 1855.

SIR:—I was in the hope that the "little card," which I took the liberty to address you on the 14th instant, in answer to your long letter, would have put an end to all further correspondence between us; but your new attack upon me, jointly with the Hon. Senator Brooks, shows me plainly that I have been mistaken, and that your bile, like the Mount Vesuvius lava, has not completed its irruption. What a wonderful man of war you must be, Right Reverend Sir, to undertake to fight two men at the same time, and by so doing, imitate that other wonderful man, killing two birds at one throw! Indeed, sir, from that great propensity of yours for war, I am brought to the belief that you must have mistaken your vocation, and that the command of a regiment of dragoons would have suited you better than functions requiring a peaceful and conciliatory disposition, which you do not possess. Those military functions, no doubt, in your taste, would have enabled you to go and tender your services to those poor English and French in the Crimea, standing so much in need of help, and afforded you a chance, by spirited charges upon the Russians, of acquiring to yourself a great name, whilst in your present functions, your fiery temper will always be an obstacle to the happiness of that flock confided to your care, or to your making friends and proselytes to our holy religion.

These remarks, rather severe, have been forced out of me by

your repeated provocations; and I fear if you continue your attacks upon those who differ from you in that question of temporalities, as you have done of late, that you will get yourself in a sad mess, and be obliged to hire extra pens to help you to get out of it.

As to that miserable interpretation of what I said about the title to our church property, and which you try to represent as a contradiction, our letters are before the public, and I leave it with them to decide which of us two has been guilty of falsehood. Did I not after "express words," give a relation of all the means which you employed, for two years or more, to bring us to abandon our church property? But, sir, when things are against you, you never have time to notice them.

But, sir, I have not yet done with you, since you have been pleased to provoke me. When, during two successive sessions of the Legislature of this State, you presented, or caused to be presented, a bill whose only object was to enable you and the Bishops of your Archbishoprick to possess all the church and charitable property, and to will it to your successor, what did you mean? When, in your circular letter of March 16, 1852, you confessed that you and the Bishops of your Archbishoprick were then already owners in fee simple of nearly all the religious and charitable property belonging to the Catholic religion in the State of New York, what did you mean? Really, sir, after such public declaration, you must be bold indeed to contest Hon. Senator Brooks' statement of the value of church and charitable property now in your hands and those of the bishops, particularly three years after your said declaration, and when it is presumable that it has considerably increased during that time.

Until now, sir, I have made it a rule to be civil and even respectful towards you; but I am afraid that you have considered that course as the effect of timidity, and that it has emboldened you to be more arch and uncivil towards me, which constrains me to adopt your own language, so as to be upon equal terms with you.

Permit me to give you a last advice previous to my leaving

you—for this is the last letter I intend to write—which is, to keep cool, and bear manfully that law of the State upon the tenure of church property, since you can attribute it but to yoursélf; and to leave off provoking all those who do not agree with your plans, as you have done of late, if you wish to keep that remnant of consideration which your station requires.

WILLIAM B. LE COUTEULX.

REPLY OF ARCHBISHOP HUGHES.

To the Editor of the New York Daily Times:—

Mr. William B. Le Couteulx, George Fisher, Michael Hesmin, John Londrack, by name, and seventeen others without name, were the authors of the falsehood palmed on the Legislature of New York, in their petition on behalf of St. Louis's Church, Buffalo. The Anti-Catholic Church Property Bill, brought in by Mr. Putnam, was founded in great part on the falsehoods thus attested. One of these was, that "Bishop Hughes attempted to compel the trustees of St. Louis church to convey the title of their church property to him." The falsehood of this statement has been already pointed out by me, and reluctantly admitted by Mr. William B. Le Couteulx, who, in his letter published in the New York *Daily Times*, of the 7th instant, admits that I never demanded the title to their church property; but, that after reading my pastoral letter, published in 1842, he and his colleagues were stupid enough to come to the conclusion that, if they acquiesced in the requirements of the pastoral letter, "the whole would have passed under my absolute control and absolute dominion." I have already stated that this consequence need not necessarily follow, and as a proof, which Mr. Le Couteulx and his colleague may be capable of understanding, the trustees of St. Nicholas Church, in Second street, in this city, did acquiesce in the requirements of the pastoral, and yet continued to be legally the owners and administrators of their church property just the same as before. Mr. Le Couteulx, in a letter of his dated Buffalo, April 21, attempts to go over this ground again. That is quite unnecessary. He forgets, indeed, the politeness of a French gentleman, and as showing his consciousness of the fact he says:—

"These remarks, rather severe, have been forced out of me."

The good gentleman may be perfectly easy on this score. He has forfeited the attributes which would have left it in his power to be "*severe*," towards any one, but especially towards me.

As there is still some misapprehension with regard to the history of the unfortunate St. Louis Church in Buffalo, I shall take advantage of this occasion to supply the information I possess on the subject. First of all, Mr. Le Couteulx, senior, gave a deed to Bishop Dubois for a certain piece of ground to be used for the purposes of Catholic worship. Next, Mr. Wm. B. Couteulx and some others, by a surreptitious movement, even while Bishop Dubois was still living, contrived to become a corporate body to take charge of his father's donation to the Bishop. Thirdly, since the Church has been completed, Mr. Wm. B. Le Couteulx has not left any thing undone to defeat the intentions of his venerable father, and drive away Catholic worship from the ground which his parent had given to the late Bishop of New York for religious purposes. Fourth, it is not certain that Mr. Wm. B. Le Couteulx wishes to deprive the Catholic congregation of St. Louis of this property by bringing about its relapse into the residuary estate of his father, from which even something might be added to his own private inheritance; and yet it is difficult to account for the obstinate and schismatic course which Mr. William B. Le Couteulx has adopted in regard to it on any other hypothesis. His generous and pious father made a donation to the city of Buffalo of ground for an orphan asylum. Mr. Wm. B. Le Couteulx must be cognizant of the fact that, when the asylum was built, and Catholic children, among others, admitted, the Protestant bigotry of the managers would not admit the ministry of a Catholic priest towards the poor children of that religion which his father professed, and of which he was an ornament, just as much as his son Wm. B. is the reverse. Here, then, is the result of his father's benevolence. He contrives that the Catholic priest shall be alienated from the ground given by his father for Catholic purposes; and the managers of the orphan asylum contrive to have the same priest repelled from entrance on the ground given for an orphan asylum.

I do not thank Mr. Le Couteulx for admitting the falsehood already pointed out in the petition of which he was one of the signers. He could not have done otherwise. And if he thinks that he is honoring his father's memory by defeating his father's pious intention, let him continue in his unfortunate anti-Catholic course.

As there has been some mistake in regard to the name of Le Couteulx, I think it proper to state that no son or daughter of Mr. William B. Le Couteulx is now in this country. At all events, Mr. Le Couteulx of this city is the son of the truly Catholic and amiable Mr. Le Couteulx who at present resides in Paris, and who so well sustains the honor of his hereditary name. He is only nephew to Mr. Wm. B Le Couteulx, leader of the trustees of St. Louis' Church, Buffalo.

✠ JOHN, Archbishop of New York.

New York April 28, 1855.

TEMPORALITIES.

To the Editor of the New York Daily Times:

I proceed to reply to the letter of "✠ JOHN, Archbishop of New York," in regard to his ownership of real estate property in the City of New York. I have no time to waste in humor, evasion or words, and therefore shall not follow the example of even so illustrious a personage as the Archbishop, in what he has to say upon irrelevant topics. The *Presbyterian* can speak for itself as to the amount of property held by the Archbishop throughout the entire State. What is said of "riches" and "provisions for rainy days," of "pin money" and "mendacity," of "defamation" and "immigration," and even of that public library which the Archbishop now owes the City of New York, if he is a man of his word, has nothing to do with the fact and extent of his ownership of real estate. As the guilty boy at school and the guilty man at Court endeavor to turn teacher and judge, master and Court, from the contemplation of facts certain to lead to their conviction, so my distinguished accuser, slippery as an eel, seems unwilling fairly to meet the facts as I presented them to the Senate. I might rejoin by saying, that when the head of a Church leaves the pulpit and gospel to become personal and political in controversy, he ceases to command that measure of respect which would otherwise be due his religious office.

This is not the first time the Archbishop has volunteered to participate in secular strife, or lost his usual civility in defending what he esteems to be the rights of the Romish Church. The Common School discussion found him alternately at the City Hall and Carroll Hall, addressing, in the latter place, amidst vociferous shouts, and in loud partisan appeals, an excited Irish populace, who, with all other citizens, were directly appealed to, to elect such men only to the Legislature as would oppose the reading of the simple texts of the Bible in the Common Schools of the City. The Common School question then, and the Church Property question now, seem equally to have disturbed the amiability and equanimity of the Archbishop.

Before entering upon the material part of this controversy, let me say, in answer to the Archbishop's sweeping assertion to the contrary, that at no time has any public man or party in this State, attempted "to disfranchise Catholics or abridge them of their rights." The charge is a fiction, unworthy of the high clerical character of the man who makes it. Where—when—by whom—has any such disfranchisement been attempted? The Constitution of the United States, and of this State, knowing no distinction of sects in religion, places the believers of every faith upon that perfect equality, from which no man—certainly no true American citizen—proposes to remove them. When, therefore, the Archbishop talks of "hurling back such false acusations, in the very faces of their authors," I must respectfully advise him to stand from under, if he would not have his own blows fall upon himself.

The Archbishop, in his long epistle to my short rejoinder, is pleased to charge me with "falsehood," "*falsehood*," "FALSEHOOD." A scullion can call names, and use epithets—but names and epithets are not truth. The utterance of such language by an Archbishop, and the bad temper displayed in the two letters to me, will carry conviction with all impartial minds, that I have already made out my case, even though I have but begun the work of exposition. The Prelate, not daring manfully to meet the issue I have raised, finds relief in personality and rage.

I have proposed that upon the issue of veracity between the Archbishop and myself, that he should select one arbiter, I a second, and the two a third, and that these three should decide, upon the legal facts to be presented for their consideration, which of the two uttered the *falsehood*. THE ARCHBISHOP DECLINES THE PROPOSITION, and declares that "*Arbitration is unnecessary*." I feared that it would come to this at the start, and that the promised library was but a "word of promise to the ear, to be broken to the hope."

But if I must lose a library for the City, I do not mean to lose my temper, nor to allow the Archbishop to escape with mere denials of facts, however bitter and angry they may be.

What I meant and mean by the ownership of Real Estate, is what the law means by it, and, therefore, we can have no misunderstanding of ideas. I mean that the legal title is vested in John Hughes. I mean by John Hughes, the Archbishop of New York. I mean by "ownership of Real Estate," the legal right to control, possess and use it, by assignment, by will, or otherwise. I mean, that if the Archbishop, John Hughes, were to die without a will, or to change his faith, or should choose to dispose of his property to his own heirs, or for his personal advantage, that he has the legal power to do so, at his own will and pleasure. I mean that, in fact and in act, by the Baltimore Ordinances of 1849 and of 1852, by prior claim and subsequent determination, he and other Archbishops and Bishops, own, and assume, control and direct the TEMPORALITIES of the Church, its lands, its estates, and its entire property. I mean, speaking now after an examination of legal Records and Indentures, that the conveyances to the Archbishop are "*to him, his heirs, or assigns*," and no others. I mean of course, also, that no trust is specified in the deed, and that the conveyances, without such specifications of trust, would, in case of his death, go to the next akin. I think I am understood, and that no one will accuse me of seeking a loop-hole of escape, or with any desire to occupy an equivocal position.

Now for the record, in part.

In the Archbishop's letter of last week, charging me directly with deception and indirectly with mendacity, I find the following:

> "But there are some things which Mr. Brooks has stated with regard to my property which I know to be incorrect and unfounded in truth. He says, for instance, that in the Register's Office there are numerous transfers from Trustees to me. Now this statement I know to be untrue, inasmuch as I have never received or accepted any transfer of any property whatever from Trustees."

In the Archbishop's letter of this week the following appears:

> "The third falsehood was, that many of the conveyances of real estate to me were made by Trustees. Now I state that any one who asserts either of these three statements, asserts a gross, and towards me, an injurious falsehood."

I now offer PROOFS OF MY STATEMENT, from the legal records of the City, beginning with the conveyance made to John Hughes from the Trustees of St. John's Roman Catholic Church:

CONVEYANCES TO JOHN HUGHES.

NUMBER ONE.

Trustees of St. John's Roman Catholic Church to John Hughes.	Lease. Dated July 17, 1844.—999 years. Consideration one cent a year. Recorded in liber 451, p. 240, July 20, 1844.

All those three certain lots, pieces or parcels of lands, situate in the Sixteenth (late Twelfth) Ward of the City of New York, which taken together are bounded and *contain* as follows, namely: Beginning on the northerly side of Thirtieth street 100 feet from the westerly side of the Seventh-avenue, running thence northerly and parallel with the Seventh-avenue 100 feet, thence westerly and parallel with Thirtieth street, 75 feet thence southerly and parallel to Seventh-avenue 100 feet, to the northerly side of Thirtieth street, thence easterly and along the northerly side of Thirtieth street 75 feet to beginning.

NUMBER TWO.

Patrick Doherty *to* *John Hughes.* } Indenture of Lease dated July 2, 1842. Recorded in liber 448, page 17, April 13, 1844, conveyed to P. Doherty by the Mayor, Aldermen, &c., of the City of New York, and by him conveyed to John Hughes. Consideration, $24, 17-100. Leased for assessment tax. Vide page 15, 20 years.

Lot, piece or parcel of land, known and distinguished on the assessment map for the opening of One Hundred and Seventeenth street, from Fourth-avenue to Harlem River, by the number 5, assessed to St. Paul's Church, situate on the north side of One Hundred and Seventeenth street, between Fourth-avenue and the Old Post Road, being 100 feet front, for which he has paid the sum of $7, 94-100.

NUMBER THREE.

George Wildes, merchant, and Agnes, his wife, by Wm. C. Pickersgill, his Attorney, *to* *John Hughes.* } Date of Deed, February 6, 1845. Recorded in liber 455, p. 446, February 21, 1845. Consideration, $2,000.

All those two certain lots, pieces or parcels of ground situate, lying and being in the City of New York, on the northerly side of Twenty-fifth street, between the Eighth and Ninth-avenues, and known and distinguished on a certain map of ground situated at Greenwich, in the City of New York, belonging to Thomas B. Clark, made by Amos Corning and Uzal W. Freeman, City Surveyor, and filed in the Register's Office, by the numbers 230 and 231, and being taken together, are bounded by the said map as follows, to wit: Beginning at a point on the said northerly side of Twenty-fifth street, 300 feet easterly from the northeast corner of the Ninth-avenue and Twenty-fifth street, thence northerly on line parallel with the Ninth-avenue, along lot distinguished on said map by the number 232, 98 feet 9 inches, thence easterly parallel with Twenty-fifth street, along the rears of lots distinguished on said map by the numbers 206 and 207, 50 feet, thence southerly, parallel with the Ninth-avenue, along lot distinguished on said map by the number 229, 98 feet 9 inches, to Twenty-fifth street, and thence westerly along the northerly side of Twenty-fifth street 50 feet, to the place of beginning.

NUMBER FOUR.

Andrew Byrne to *John Hughes.* } Date, April 30, 1841. Record—liber 456, p. 487. March 29, 1845. Consideration, $5,400. Conveyance of Lease for 18 years and 9 months. No description of premises.

Robert Lane, and Effe Maria, his wife, to *John Hughes.* } Conveyance date, March 5, 1845, Record—liber. 459, p. 125. Consideration, $15,500.

All those three certain lots of land situated in the Sixth Ward of the City of New York, which on a certain map of property, belonging to the estate of George Janeway, in the Sixth Ward of the City of New York, made by Joseph Bridges, City Surveyor, surveyed (as to part lots on said map) in January, 1838, are distinguished by the numbers 17, 18 and 19. Said lot, No. 17, being situated at the corner of City Hall Place and Duane street, and said three lots are bounded as follows, that is to say, beginning at the easterly corner of City Hall Place (late Augusta street) and Duane street, thence running southerly in front along Duane toward Chatham, 75 feet to other ground of the estate of the said George Janeway; thence running northeasterly on the one side along the ground of the estate of the said George Janeway, 67 feet 2 inches, to other ground of estate of said George Janeway, and formerly leased by him to Mrs. Phillips; thence running northwesterly in the rear along the said ground leased to Mrs. Phillips as aforesaid, 73 feet to City Hall Place (formerly Augusta street,) aforesaid; thence running southwesterly on the other side along City Hall Place aforesaid 67 feet to place of beginning.

NUMBER FIVE.

David Dudley Field and Stephen J. Field, Trustees of wife, and Harriet D. Field, wife of D. D. Field, to *John Hughes.* } Date of Conveyance, February 7th, 1845. Record (liber 460, p. 497, Consideration, $2,000,) May 23d, 1845.

All those two certain lots, pieces or parcels of land, situated in the Sixteenth ward of the city of New York, known and distinguished on a map of lands in the Sixteenth ward of the city of New York, the property of the heirs of Mary Clarke, deceased, made by George B. Smith, City Surveyor, and dated April 6th, 1837, (a copy on file in the Register's office,) by numbers 228 and 229, and bounded, taken together, as follows: beginning at a point on the northerly line of Twenty-fifth street, distant 350 feet easterly from north-east corner of Twenty-fifth street and Ninth avenue, running thence easterly along said northerly line 50 feet, thence northerly, parallel with Ninth avenue, ninety-four feet, nine inches, to middle of the block between Twenty-fifth street and Twenty-sixth street, to a point equi-distant from the two ; thence westerly, parallel with Twenty-fifth street, fifty feet ; thence southerly in a straight line to place of beginning.

NUMBER SIX.

William Patton, D. D., and Mary his wife, to John Hughes.	Date of Conveyance, May 8th, 1845. Record (in liber 460, p. 550,) May 31st, 1845. Consideration, $75.

All and singular the equal undivided half part (being the S. part thereof,) of a certain vault or place for the deposit of the dead, situated in and upon the premises formerly owned by the Second avenue Presbyterian Church, on the Easterly side of, and fronting on the Second avenue, between Second and Third streets. (William Patton, liber 460, p. 551, same.)

NUMBER SEVEN.

George Wildes, and Agnes, his wife, to J. Hughes.	Date of Conveyance, February 6, 1845. Record, liber 465, p. 513, September 23, 1845. Consideration, $2,000.

All those two certain lots, pieces or parcels of ground, situate, lying and being in Sixteenth ward of the city of New York, on Northerly side of Twenty-fifth street, between Eighth and Ninth avenues. (Same as other in liber 455, p. 446.)

NUMBER EIGHT.

Bartholomew O'Connor, Trustee to Christ Church, to John Hughes.	Date of Conveyance, Feb. 7, 1845. Record, liber 465, p. 514, Sept. 23, 1845. Consideration, $42,000.

All four lots of ground, situate, &c., in Fourth ward, city of New York, bounded and containing as follows : Westerly by James street, 100 feet ; Southerly, by ground, now or lately belonging to Walter Bowne ; 100 feet Easterly in the rear, partly by ground of John Wood, and partly by ground now or late of —— Gardner, 100 feet ; and Northerly by ground now or late belonging to Samuel Milbank, 100 feet. (Liber 466, p. 422, quit claim for land described in liber 460, p. 497. Consideration, $1,000.

NUMBER NINE.

George Plammann, and Catharine A., his wife ; Thomas Ward, and Margarette, his wife, Nat. P. Bailey and his wife, et al., to Nicholas Dean, of the 2d part, and John Hughes, of the 3d part.	Date of Conveyance, Feb. 6, 1847. Record in liber 487, p. 75, Feb. 19, 1847. Consideration, $50,000.

Rev. Andrew Byrne,
Clergyman,
to
John Hughes, Bishop.
Date of Conveyance, Dec. 6th, 1843. Recorded in liber. p. 178, February 10th, 1844. Consideration, $3,825.

All those three certain lots of land, together with the buildings thereon erected, situate, lying and being in the (now or late) Eleventh Ward of the City of New York, and being part of the estate of Mangle Minthorne, deceased, and are known and described on the map of the said estate now on file in the Register's Office, of the said City of New York, by lots Nos. 71, 72, 73; fronting westwardly on the Second avenue, and are as follows: northwardly by lot No. 74, eastwardly by lot No. 76, and land formerly called the Hilyer estate; southerly by land of the said Hilyer estate, and westwardly by the Second avenue aforesaid. The said three lots being in length on each side 100 feet, and the said lots, Nos. 72 and 73, being each in width in front and rear, 25 feet, and the said lot No. 71 being in width in front 25 feet; and in width on the rear 24 feet and 11½ inches as the said lots are laid down and numbered on the said map. Being the same premises whereon the Church of the Nativity now stands; subject, however, to a mortgage by the party of 1st part to Rev. John Corry, to secure the payment of $5,000 and interest.

NUMBER TEN.

Same
to
Same.
Date of conveyance 6th December, 1844. Recorded Feb. 10, 1844. Consideration $3,825.

All that certain lot, piece or parcel of land, situate, lying, and being in the Seventeenth Ward (late Eleventh), of the City of New York, fronting on the easterly line of Second avenue, between Second and Third streets, beginning at a point distant sixty-four feet seven inches from the northeast corner of said Second avenue and Second street; running thence eastwardly and parallel to Second street seventy-five feet; thence northwardly and parallel to the said Second avenue twenty-one feet and six inches, to the place of beginning; the said lot being part of lots known and distinguished by the letters C and D on a map of property in the Eleventh and Thirteenth Wards of the City of New York, belonging to the estate of Henry Eckford, deceased, filed in office of the Register, and numbered 230. Also, all that certain other lot, piece, or parcel of land, situate, lying and being in the Seventeenth (late Eleventh) Ward of said City of New York, fronting on the northerly line of Second street, between the First and Second avenues. Beginning at a point distant seventy-five feet from the northeast corner of Second avenue and Second street, and running thence northwardly parallel to Second avenue aforesaid eighty-six feet; thence eastwardly parallel to Second street aforesaid twenty-five feet; thence southwardly parallel to Second avenue aforesaid eighty-six feet; thence westwardly along the said line of Second street aforesaid twenty-five feet, to the place of beginning.

This is but the beginning of the end. It is only the basis of my claim to that promised public library which the Archbishop owes to the City of New York, and which for the next fifty years, if he and I should live so long, I shall demand in the name of the people of this City, "for the use, not of any one profession or class, but for all mankind." The amiable Archbishop—and he is *arch* in more senses than one—is pleased to say, if my modesty will permit, that this great library shall bear the name of "the Erastus Brooks' Library, engraven in large and gilded letters over its marble portals." I have no such ambition to have my name handed down to posterity, and grateful at this new display of the Archbishop's new-born zeal for public libraries and letters, for intelligence and history, I prefer that this library, which will exist, I fear, only in the broken promises of an irritable prelate, if ever founded at all, should bear the name, not in "large and gilded letters," but rather in letters of brass, corresponding with the brazen denials of the man, the name of "✠ John, Archbishop of the Province of New York!"

For to-day, I am,

Very respectfully yours,

ERASTUS BROOKS.

New York, *April* 18*th*, 1855.

ARCHBISHOP HUGHES *vs.* SENATOR BROOKS.

To the Editors of the Courier and Enquirer:

I am glad to perceive by his attempted defence in your paper of this date, that Mr. Brooks begins to realize vaguely the position in which he has placed himself. He commences his pitiable defence by misrepresenting the state of the question. He says it is "in regard to my ownership of real estate property in the city of New York." The question is not in regard to any such thing, and this Mr. Brooks knows as well as I do. The question is in regard to the truth or falsehood of certain statements made by him in the Senate of New York, on the 6th of March. In reference to my ownership of *real estate property*, as Mr. Brooks calls it, there is no question. The title of many Catholic Churches in the city of New York is vested in me, and so far I am the owner. My intention, even, is to add to this property by purchasing such additional lots, or accepting the gift of them, as I may find from time to time to be desirable for the purpose of providing religious instruction for the wants of the Catholic flock committed to my charge. If Mr. Brooks will examine the records of the city of New York three months from this time, he will probably find conveyances made to me by parties who have the right to sell or bestow as they think proper.

But I shall waive all controversy regarding matters introduced into Mr. Brooks's reply, in order to direct his wandering attention to the real state of the case. On the 6th of March he asserted that my property in the city of New York alone was not much short of five millions. This was falsehood No. 1. He asserted that of this property, numerous transfers had been made to me by Trustees. This was falsehood No. 2. He asserted that some of the parcels conveyed to me covered whole squares of land. This was falsehood No. 3.

Now, we shall take these falsehoods in their order. Mr. Brooks, in maintaining falsehood No. 1, has copied out ten entries as found in the Register's books of this city. He heads the list with the words—

"CONVEYANCES TO JOHN HUGHES."

The first conveyance is a *lease*, which shows, so far as the ownership of real estate is concerned, that the very heading of the entries is not correct.

The second is also a lease, showing the same thing.

The third is from George Wildes and Agnes his wife, and it remains for Mr. Brooks to show that Mr. Wildes and his wife had been Trustees of a Catholic Church.

The fourth is from Andrew Byrne, and is the conveyance, not of real estate, but of a lease also.

The fifth is from David Dudley Field, and Stephen J. Field, Trustees of Wife and Harriet D. Field, wife of D. D. Field. (I copy from Mr. Brooks's report of these matters in your journal, but I decline all responsibility for their accuracy.) Mr. Brooks does not inform us whether these parties had been Trustees of Catholic Church property or not.

The sixth is from the Rev. Wm. Patton, D. D., and Mary his wife. Mr. Brooks does not say that the Rev. Dr. and his wife had been Trustees of any Catholic Church.

Here Mr. Senator Brooks seems to have become desperate, and gives a duplicate under head No. 7 of the conveyance made by George Wildes, and Agnes his wife, as already recorded under head No. 3. I was not aware that Mr. Wildes had given me two deeds of the same property. But Mr. Senator Brooks is a man of singular enterprise, and he has made the discovery, and attempted to impose upon the public by a falsehood so easily to be detected.

No. 8 is from Mr. Bartholomew O'Connor, who, if Mr. Brooks is to be believed, is named in the record as trustee to Christ's Church—the truth being that Mr. Bartholomew O'Connor in that case was only the Assignee of a bankrupt Board of Trustees.

No. 9 is from George Plammann, and Catharine A. his wife; Thomas Ward, and Margaretta his wife; Nathaniel P. Baily, and his wife, *et al.* to Nicholas Dean, of the second part, and John Hughes, of the third part. Under the same No. 9 we find immediately following, Andrew Byrne, Clergyman, to John Hughes, Bishop.

No. 10 is a specimen of Mr. Brooks's eloquent brevity of style. It is entitled, "*Same to Same.*" Here again Mr. Brooks duplicates the same conveyance, so that in the simple copying from the Registry, by way of defence for older falsehoods, he invents new ones, and in two instances copies the same conveyances—I suppose by way of guarding against mistakes.

I hope the respectable gentlemen and their wives here mentioned, will hold Mr. Brooks, and not me, responsible for having their names paraded in a public newspaper. The extract of all these entries is brought forth by Mr. Brooks, to substantiate what I have taken the liberty to call his falsehood, uttered in the Senate of New York, when he alleged in his official capacity, and as one having taken pains to be well informed on the subject, that the value of my real estate in the city of New York alone was not much short of five millions. We have just seen that Mr. Brooks has counted two conveyances each twice over, and that instead of ten conveyances there are in reality only eight on the very record which he professes to have examined. None of these conveyances of real estate are from Trustees of Catholic Churches.

Is it not lamentable to think that a man who has been Senator of the State of New York, should so misrepresent the records of entries which are open to the inspection of all in the Register's office?

But the question is not whether I am the owner of some portion of real estate, but whether Mr. Brooks did not utter a falsehood when he stated that the value of my property in the city of New York alone, was little short of five millions of dollars. The gentleman attempts to make his extract honest-looking by describing the boundaries of each section of property thus conveyed with a minuteness very uninteresting to the public, but with an exactitude becoming a conveyancer's apprentice. One would suppose that he imagined himself copying a list of the arrivals at the hotels, to be published in that meanest of all printed newspapers, the New York *Express*, of which he is one of the Editors.

Now the difference between the value of the eight conveyances cited by Mr. Brooks, and a little short of five millions of dollars, will be the measure of the difference between the truth of his present defence, and the falsehood of his assertion in the Senate on the 6th of last March. I suppose the gross value of the eight conveyances enumerated, to be two hundred thousand dollars, and deduct two hundred thousand dollars from a sum a little short of five millions—say four millions seven hundred and fifty thousand dollars, there remains a difference between truth and falsehood of four millions five hundred and fifty thousand dollars, which Mr. Brooks has still to account for. In other words, by a strict arithmetical calculation, there is a difference of two thousand two hundred and seventy-five per cent. between the truth, if we can call it so, of Mr. Brooks's defence and the original falsehood of his statement. This is a large per centage, but Senator Brooks may yet have means of reducing it. So far, I think, it is quite clear that the charge of falsehood No. 1 has not been refuted. However, small work is enough for the Senator during one day, and as he signs his letter "for to-day, yours very respectfully," we must wait to see what he has in reserve for to-morrow. I would only beg him not to attempt filling up his schedule by enumerating the same conveyance twice as he has done "for to-day."

Falsehood No. 2, as found in his speech of the 6th of March, is, that among the conveyances there are numerous transfers from trustees to John Hughes. Mr. Brooks has done nothing as yet by way of attempt to sustain this falsehood. He has not shown one single such transfer, and accordingly we may say there is little short of five millions per cent. between his impotent defence and his false assertion on the 6th of March, in the Senate of New York. But, we must be indulgent, and allow him time to examine the records for them.

The statement in his speech which we marked as falsehood No. 3, that some of the parcels of property conveyed to me cover whole squares of land, Mr. Brooks "for to-day" has not had time, I suppose, to indicate, as he has done in other instances, in what part of the city all these certain lots, or whole squares of land lie, and are situate. But we must give him time. He has done pretty well for one day. He has made ten entries for the newspapers out of eight in the Register's books—and to a man who can do this, powers of originality cannot be denied.

On the whole, I think Mr. Brooks has been very unsuccessful in his attempt to substantiate the three propositions which I have indicated as falsehoods Nos. 1, 2, and 3.

In the present melancholy predicament in which Mr. Brooks has contrived to place himself, I think he might dispense with all moralizing as regards proprieties of language. They are out of season for his pen. He is not satisfied at my using the word falsehood in regard to any of his assertions, however injurious to me, or mischievous to others. Now falsehood is the only word that could express my meaning. To gentlemen of more refined sensibility than the Senator, a gentler term would have been sufficient to arouse that quick and honorable resentment, either to prove the assertion advanced, or to apologize manfully for having been betrayed into it. On the other hand, if a stronger expression had been used, it would have implied a direct violation of the courtesies of life, even in regard to one by whom truth had been so outraged. Mr. Brooks is very severe upon me, as he imagines, when he says that "a scullion can call names, and use epithets, but names and epithets," says Mr. Brooks, "are not truth." Pray, where did Mr. Brooks learn this philosophy? I can assure him that names and epithets rightly applied are truth, and oftentimes, truth in its condensed form. Nor do they cease to be truth when they are rightly employed, even by scullions. The only philosophy which would be profitable to Senator Brooks, is that by which in his dealings with his fellow-men, whether in the Senate Chamber or elsewhere, he should take those precautions becoming an honorable gentleman, to see that it should not be in the power of friend or foe, of scullion or prelate, to apply to him any name or epithet which should unfortunately be too well founded in truth.

I confess that it is any thing but pleasant to me to be obliged to employ them. But when Mr. Brooks has so gratuitously gone out of his way to impress upon the minds of his colleagues in the Senate, and of his fellow citizens elsewhere, the belief of statements utterly at variance with truth, he cannot deny me the privilege of calling upon him for the proof of his statements, if he has any, and of stigmatizing them as falsehoods, if he has not.

I do not know that I have any thing more to say until Mr.

Brooks brings out the results of another day's investigation of the records.

✠ JOHN, ARCHBISHOP OF NEW YORK.

NEW YORK, *April* 19, 1855.

SENATOR BROOKS *vs.* ARCHBISHOP HUGHES.

To the Editor of the Courier and Enquirer:

I have no time to bandy words with John Hughes. In personality and vulgarity he has reached an elevation to which I do not aspire, and if he is content with that elevation, and of his position under it, as the Archbishop of a powerful church, I am more than content as his antagonist. I could not see without regret a friend in so bad a position, nor desire to put an enemy in a worse one. I shall therefore leave all that part of the Archbishop's third letter, which is irrelevant to Church Property, and the facts at issue, to answer itself.

My statements in the Senate were .

Firstly:—As to the fact of the property owned by John Hughes,—meaning the Archbishop.

Secondly:—As to the value of the property thus held by John Hughes,—meaning the Archbishop.

Thirdly:—As to the transfer from Trustees to John Hughes,—meaning the Archbishop.

I am charged with FALSEHOOD in these, my several asseverations.

I proposed to settle the question of fact, as to the veracity of the spirit, substance and reality of my statements, and the truth of the denial of his, by reference to an umpire of three persons,—one to be selected by each of us, and one by the umpire. The Archbishop sneered at my proposition, and declined the offer.

The Archbishop conveyed the idea, and meant to convey the idea, and was so understood by the public,—that HE was not the owner of Church Property in this city and elsewhere. Driven from this position by the record transcribed from the Register's Office, showing the actual conveyances of property to him, he now, with more boldness than ever, admits the truth of what I said on this point, and declares that the question between us "*is not in regard to any such thing as his ownership of Real Estate Property in this city!*" He adds to this the following declaration:—

> "In reference to my ownership of *real estate property*, as Mr. Brooks calls it, there is no question. The title of many Catholic Churches in the city of New York is vested in me, and so far I am the owner. My intention is, even, to add to this property by purchasing such additional lots, or accepting the gift of them, as I may find from time to time to be desirable for the purpose of providing religious instruction for the wants of the Catholic flock committed to my charge. If Mr. Brooks will examine the records of the city of New York three months from this time, he will probably find conveyances made to me by parties who have the right to sell or bestow as they think proper."

Truly—"Truth is a great thing."

But I am also charged with falsehood, because I asserted that there were transfers from Trustees to John Hughes, notwithstanding I gave the record of the Transfer of:

"*The Trustees of St. John's Roman Catholic Church to John Hughes. Lease* 999 *years. Consideration*, ONE CENT A YEAR.

The Archbishop answers me, and this record, thus:

> "The first conveyance is a *lease*, which shows, so far as the ownership of real estate is concerned, that the very heading of the entries is not correct.
>
> "The second is also a lease, showing the same thing.
>
> "The third is from George Wildes and Agnes his wife, and it remains for Mr. Brooks to show that Mr. Wildes and his wife had been Trustees of a Catholic Church."

What will lawyers,—what will laymen,—what will Christian men think of such a denial as this? Is not a lease for 999 years at one cent a year, in all true senses, moral and legal, equal to a conveyance in fee? A mortgage of real estate property is a conveyance in a more limited sense, but often results, by foreclosure and otherwise, to a conveyance in fee. How dare the Archbishop assert, in the face of the public record and of all truth—that I "have not shown one single transfer from Trustees to the Bishop?"

Let me add one more extract from his last letter:

"No. 8 is from Mr. Bartholomew O'Connor, who, if Mr. Brooks is to be believed, is named in the record as Trustee to Christ's Church—the truth being that Mr. Bartholomew O'Connor in that case was only the assignee of a *bankrupt Board of Trustees.*"

Here, too, is an unintentional admission that John Hughes received property from Bartholomew O'Connor, "the Assignee of a *Bankrupt Board of Trustees*." It came, by admission, from Trustees, through the Assignee, to John Hughes! Is it not a quibble beneath an Archbishop, or the poorest layman, to say that such property did not come from Trustees?

But let me quote further:

"Under the same No. 9 we find immediately following, Andrew Byrne, Clergyman, to John Hughes, Bishop.

"No. 10. is a specimen of Mr. Brooks's eloquent brevity of style. It is entitled, "*Same to same.*" Here again Mr. Brooks duplicates the same conveyance, so that in the simple copying from the Registry, by way of defence for older falsehoods, he invents new ones, and in two instances copies the same conveyance—I suppose by way of guarding against mistakes."

It is the Archbishop who duplicates,—not I. It is the Archbishop also who misstates the record,—not I. If he will look again, he will see that there were two transfers from him to Andrew Byrne,—that one conveyance covered part of the Mangle Minthorne Estate, and conveyed three lots of property, and that the second conveyance was of two parcels of property, and one of the Henry Eckford Estate.

The Archbishop owes to himself, if not to me and the public, an apology for this erroneous (I will not say false) record, and I owe it to the public to state that a transfer of property was twice cited by me by mistake, because it was so written, and had the conveyance of William C. Pickersgill, recorded February 6th,

1845, and of George Wildes, September 23d, 1845. The one was probably a conveyance by attorney in February, and the other in person in the following September. John Hughes would, therefore, seem to have had two deeds of the same property, even though he does not know it.

But I have not done with my record of property or values. I have only, indeed, given the beginning of the end.

I do not wish to pry unnecessarily into the temporalities of the Archbishop in this city and throughout his Diocese, but his plump denials make it necessary to do so in order to convict him of the want of veracity in his accusations against me. It is no slight thing to charge a man with falsehood, and if the war is carried into Africa, as I intend it shall be, in my prosecutions of this investigation, the Archbishop has himself to thank for compelling an exposure of his affairs, which, but for his denials, might never have come to the light of day.

From the Metropolitan and Catholic Almanac, and Laity's Directory of 1855—published at Baltimore by Lucas, Brothers, and purporting to be "sold by all Catholic Booksellers," I find that in this city, and a few of the River towns, 38 in all, there are 280,000 Roman Catholics, 55 Churches and Chapels, (27 of which are in this city,) 30 stations, 82 Clergymen on the mission, 26 otherwise employed, beside Asylums, Seminaries, Literary Institutions, &c. Among these are:

The Redemptorist Convent, 3d street.
College of St. Francis Xavier, West 15th street.
Community of Brothers, &c., Canal street.
Academy of the Holy Infant Jesus, Manhattanville.
Convent of the Sacred Heart, near Manhattanville.
Sacred Heart Academy, near Harlem.
Convent of Sisters of Mercy, Houston and Mulberry.
Academy of St. Vincent, 107th street.
St. Mary's School, East Broadway.
The Archconfraternity of the Immaculate Heart of Mary.
The Confraternity of the Rosary, &c., &c.

This record, with many other facts appended thereto, the books tells us, was furnished from the Most Reverend the Archbishop.

"The Diocese of Brooklyn" has fifteen churches in the city of Brooklyn, and twenty-four on Long Island, besides eleven stations, thirty clergymen, the School of St. Alphonsus, conducted by the Nuns of the Order of St. Dominic, and other institutions under the care of "the Sisters of Charity" and "Brothers of the Christian Schools."

The diocese of Albany (87 churches), and Buffalo (100 churches), are larger as to the number of churches, some of which are gorgeous and costly edifices. The rule there, as here, is to place the temporalities of the Church in the hands of the Bishops.

I am not complaining of all this, or of the Roman Catholics, or of their faith. I am not even complaining of the numerical force or great riches which make up the temporalities of the Romish power in the City and State, I am showing in whose hands, and under whose control most of these TEMPORALITIES are.

On the matter of values, too, I shall not fall much, if any, short of the amount mentioned in the Senate of New York on the 6th of March last. With such estates as these at Fordham, costing seventy thousand dollars, and now worth four or five hundred thousand dollars,—as the McGowan property on the middle Island Road, and known as McGowan's Pass, the Jacob Lorillard property, of one hundred acres,—the valuable property, commencing on 51st street, opposite the Deaf and Dumb Institution, added to church property, it will be easy to count up millions in present value.

One word just here, of this last piece of property.

When the Directors of the Deaf and Dumb Institution earnestly begged the Common Council of this city, and as a matter of public charity to enable them the better to educate the Deaf and Dumb of the City and State, for a part of the tract of land, at a nominal rent, now occupied by them, *they were refused.* They had to pay $28,000 to the Corporation for the balance of a block between 49th and 50th streets, and the balance of a block between 48th and 49th streets. The Common Council so decreed, and the Mayor so approved. A prayer from Protestants, for a great and noble Christian charity, benefiting all sects, was met by adverse reports and adverse acts, even when the Common Council of the City, *for one dollar*, conveyed to John Hughes, President, and V. O. Donnelly, Secretary, for the Roman Catholic Orphan Asylum, one of the most valuable pieces of land in the city, and on a square quite large enough for that "Erastus Brooks Library," which the Archbishop now owes the City of New York.

The Deaf and Dumb were compelled to pay, for a much smaller piece of ground, $28,000. The Archbishop and the Roman Catholics, for an estate bounded by the Fifth avenue, 51st and 52d streets, paid the sum of one dollar! The particulars of all this may be found in the Book of Deeds, marked A., page 271, and those who are more curious may turn to a Common Council report, where they will find the rejection of the prayer of the Protestants for the deaf and dumb, and the grant of the prayer of the Roman Catholics. The city property thus given for one dollar is worth to-day from $150,000, to $250,000, and in view of its value I cite these not very pleasant facts for those who made the grant in the one case, and declined it in the other.

The Fordham property also is a princely estate, owned by John Hughes. The deeds, I understand are in his name. Negotiations connected with the property are conducted in his name. I have had the copy of one before me, which begins thus:

> "This indenture, made on the 1st of December, 1854, between Most Reverend John Hughes, Archbishop of New York, and the Harlem Railroad Co.," &c.

And a very funny document it is for "John Hughes, *his heirs and assignees.*"

One article covenants that he, his heirs or assignees, shall have a *free pass over the Harlem Railroad, with fifty pounds of baggage daily.* If the Bishop does not choose to avail himself of this liberal grant,—for I learn from all quarters that he is good at driving a bargain,—he is to name the person who shall receive the benefit. The *dead-head* system is thus formally covenanted for over a public highway between Fordham and New York, by the distinguished ✠ John, Archbishop of the Province of New York."

But all this is only preliminary to more important matter which follows, and in continuation of the record I cite the following

CONVEYANCES TO JOHN HUGHES.

NUMBER ELEVEN.

Zacharius Kuntze *to* *John Hughes.*	Date of Conveyance, March 24, 1848. Recorded in liber 500, p. 509, May 10, 1848. Consideration, one dollar.

All and singular those two several lots, pieces or parcels of land situated, lying and being on the north side of Thirty-first street, between Sixth and Seventh avenues, in Sixteenth (late Twelfth) Ward of City of New York, and laid down and distinguished upon a certain map—is annexed to the report of Fred. DePeyster and others, commissioners appointed by order of Court of Chancery of State of New York, in a certain suit before Vice Chancellor of first Circuit, brought by Moulton Bullock, complainant, against Thomas Burlock and other defendants, to make partition of certain lands and premises held in common between the parties, among which were lands and premises laid down in said map—on which map the said two several lots, pieces or parcels of land, hereby intended to be conveyed, are known and distinguished as numbers seven and forty. The lots in dimension, when taken together, are specified on said map to be 159 feet 6¼ inches in depth on the westerly side thereof, and 25 feet width in the rear, and 165 feet and 1 inch in depth on easterly side; said two lots, pieces or parcels of land, lying and being on easterly side of and next adjoining to premises now occupied for a Catholic Church.

NUMBER TWELVE.

James Foster, Contractor, and Emilia his wife, to *John Hughes.*	Date of Conveyance, February, 21, 1848. Recorded in liber 562, p. 244, February 29, 1848. Consideration $4,400.

All those two certain lots of land situate, lying and being in Eleventh Ward of the City of New York, on South-east corner of Eighth street and Avenue B; taken together, bounded and described as follows:—Beginning at the point formed by the intersection of the southerly side of Eighth-street with the easterly side of Avenue B, running thence southerly along the east line of Avenue B, 48 feet and 8 inches, thence east on a line parallel with south side of Eighth street 100 feet, thence northerly in a line parallel with easterly line of Avenue B, 48 feet 8 inches, thence westerly along southerly side of Eighth street 100 feet to place of beginning.

NUMBER THIRTEEN.

Sarah Remsen to *John Hughes.* } Date of Conveyance, May 1, 1848. Recorded in liber. 503, p. 542, May 2, 1848. Consideration, $2,175.

All that certain lot, piece or parcel of land, situate, lying and being in the Eleventh Ward of the City of New York, on the east side of Avenue B, between Seventh and Eighth-streets, in said City, and which is bounded and described as follows, that is to say, beginning at a part on easterly side of Avenue B, distant 73 feet 2 inches southerly from south-east corner of Avenue B and Eighth-street, and running thence easterly and parallel with Eighth-street, 100 feet, thence running southerly and parallel with Avenue B, 24 feet 4 inches, thence running west and parallel with Eighth-street, 100 feet to Avenue B, and thence running north along Avenue B, 24 feet 4 inches, to place of beginning.

NUMBER FOURTEEN.

George W. Hall, of Buffalo, to *John Hughes.* } Date of Conveyance, May, 1, 1848. Record, June 19, 1848, in liber 508, p. 98. Consideration, $10.

All that certain lot, piece or parcel of ground, situate, lying and being in the Eighth Ward of the City of New York, on the west side of Mulberry-street, known and distinguished on a certain map or chart thereof made by Casimer H. Goerch, late City Surveyor, by part of lot No. 82—bounded eastwardly in front on Mulberry-street aforesaid, northerly by lot No. 83, westerly, in rear, by lot No. 168, and southerly by remaining part of said lot No. 82. Containing in width and front 25 feet 2 inches, and in rear 24 feet, and in length 120 feet.

NUMBER FIFTEEN.

James Rea, of Macon, Ga. to *John Hughes.* } Recorded in liber 508 p. 100. June 29, 1848. Consideration, $1.

All and singular, the one equal undivided fifth part of the following lot, piece or parcel of land, with buildings thereon, situate, lying and being in the Fourteenth (formerly Eighth) Ward of the City of New York, and late part or parcel of the estate of Alderman Dickerson, deceased, known and distinguished on a certain map or chart thereof, made by Casimer H. Goerch, late City Surveyor, bearing date February 12, 1795, by lot No. 84, bounded and containing as follows, to wit: Beginning at a point on south side of Houston-street, distant 116 feet 6 inches westerly from southwesterly corner of said Houston and Mulberry-streets, and running thence easterly along said Houston-street, about 40 feet 11 inches, to land formerly belonging to John P. Schermerhorn, thence running easterly along southerly line of said Schermerhorn's land about 75 feet 8 inches to Mulberry-street, aforesaid, thence running southerly along said Mulberry-street, 27 feet 6 inches to northerly line of No. 83 on said Map, thence westerly along northern line of said lot No. 83, 120 feet to westerly line of said lot No. 84, thence northerly along said westerly line of lot No. 84, 20 feet 2 inches to place of beginning.

NUMBER SIXTEEN.

Geo. W. Hall, and Amelia W., his wife, *to* *John Hughes.*	Date of Conveyance, April 1, 1848. Recorded in liber 508, p. 101, June 19, 1848. Consideration $32,700.

All those six certain lots, pieces, parcels of land with the buildings thereon, situated, lying and being in the Fourteenth Ward of the City of New York, on South-west corner of Houston and Mulberry-streets, in the said City, bounded and described as follows:—Beginning at a point forming the intersection of the south-west corner of Houston and Mulberry-streets, aforesaid, running thence south along west side of Mulberry-street, to the land late belonging to Moses Leon, now deceased, 65 feet 9 inches, thence west along said last mentioned land, 120 feet to land formerly belonging to Luke Usher, thence north along said last mentioned land and land of George Heydon, Lessee, to Houston-street, aforesaid, 45 feet, thence easterly along said Houston-street, 116 feet six inches, to place of beginning. *Also*, all those certain pieces or parcels of land beginning at a point on west side of said Mulberry-street, formed by intersection of said west side of Mulberry-street with south line of land late of Leon, deceased, and which point is supposed to be distant south from the south west corner of said Houston and Mulberry-streets, 90 feet and 11 inches, thence along western side of said Mulberry-street, 48 feet 2 inches to along and including the land conveyed by Nathan Bangs, and others, executors, &c., and Elizabeth Sandford, to said George W. Hale, by deed dated April 15, 1836; thence west along said southern boundary of last mentioned land, 125 feet, to land formerly belonging to William Jones; thence north 45 feet and 6 inches to said land late of Moses Leon, deceased; thence east along southern boundary of last mentioned land 120 feet to said Mulberry-street, the place of beginning.

NUMBER SEVENTEEN.

George Washington Costar and *Henry Arnold Costar,* *to* *John Hughes.*	Date of Conveyance, July 19, 1848; Rec. in liber 510, p. 60, July 28, 1848. Consideration, $11, 64-100.

All that certain strip, piece, or parcel of land situate, lying, and being on east side of Avenue B, commencing at a point on east side of said Avenue B, distant 118 feet 8 inches southerly from the south-east corner of Eighth-street and said Avenue B, and running thence east, and parallel with said Eighth-street 100 feet; thence running south and parallel with said Avenue B 2 inches; thence running west and parallel with said Eighth-street 100 feet to said Avenue B; thence running northerly along easterly side of said Avenue B 2 inches to place of beginning.

NUMBER EIGHTEEN.

Mary Ann Gaffney, Bernard Gaffney, and Arthur J. Donnelly, Executors, to John Hughes.	Date of Conveyance, November 9, 1848. Record in liber 510, p. 32, November 14, 1848. Consideration, $10,622, 37-100.

All those certain lots, pieces or parcels of ground, situated, lying and being in the Eighteenth Ward of the City of New York, on the east side of Madison avenue and south side of Twenty-seventh-street, and taken together bounded as follows, viz.: beginning at the point east side Madison avenue, distant 93 feet 9 inches south from the south side of Twenty-seventh-street, thence running east at right angles to Madison avenue, along ground now or late belonging to ——— Sauler. Same as Release of Dower.

NUMBER NINETEEN.

Jno. J. V. Westervelt, Sheriff, to John Hughes.	Date of Conveyance, June 14, 1848. Record in liber 522, p. 444, June 15, 1849. Consideration, $950.

Four certain lots of ground, situate, lying and being in the Twelfth Ward of the City of New York, and known and distinguished on a map of the property of Peter Poillon, made by J. F. Bridges, City Surveyor, bearing date September, 1826, and now on file in Register's office as lots Nos. 541, 542, and 543, and taken together are bounded as follows: North by the central line between One Hundred and Seventeenth and One Hundred and Eighteenth-streets, west by a line parallel to Fourth avenue on the east side thereof 160 feet therefrom, southerly in front by One Hundred and Seventeenth-street, and east by a line drawn parallel to Fourth avenue on the east side thereof at a distance of 260 feet therefrom; each of said lots being 25 feet in width in front and rear and about 100 feet deep on each side, with the church edifice erected thereon.

NUMBER TWENTY.

Richard Kein, Clergyman, to John Hughes.	Date of Conveyance, December 1, 1848. Record in liber 527, p. 279, Sept. 19, 1849. Consideration $2,000.

All that certain lot, piece or parcel of land, situate, lying and being in the Eleventh Ward of the City of New York, and is bounded and described as follows, that is to say—beginning at a point on east side of Avenue B, distant 48 feet 8 inches more or less south from the south line of the Avenue, and running thence east and parallel with Eighth-street 100 feet, thence running south and parallel with Avenue B 24 feet 4 inches, more or less; thence running west and parallel with Eighth-street, 100 feet to Avenue B, and thence running north along Avenue B 24 feet 4 inches, more or less, to place of beginning.

NUMBER TWENTY-ONE.

Gregory Dillon, *to* *John Hughes.*	Date of Conveyance, August 20, 1850. Recorded in liber 551, p. 291, August 21, 1850. Consideration, $10.

All those five certain lots, pieces or parcels of land, together with the buildings thereon, known as St. Peter's Church, situated, &c., in Third Ward of the City of New York, contiguous to each other, being part of the lands commonly called and known by the name of the Church Farm, distinguished on map thereof by numbers 85, 86, 87, 88, 89, bounded north by Barclay-street, west by Church-street, and south and east by the other lots, part of said Church Farm; the whole being in extent towards Barclay-street 100 feet, towards Church-street 125 feet, on south side 100 feet, and on east side 125 feet.

It is to be remembered that the value of property at the time these conveyances were made is very different from its value now. What cost $70,000 a few years ago, is worth $400,000 now, and what cost $10,000 then has sold for $40,000 since. Let the Archbishop possess his soul in patience—before the end he shall hear not only of his dealings with the living, but with the dead in whose decease and burial he profits.

Very respectfully, for to-day,

I am yours, &c.,

ERASTUS BROOKS.

New York, April 20, 1855.

ARCHBISHOP HUGHES *vs.* SENATOR BROOKS.

To the Editors of the Courier and Enquirer:

THERE is a moral of general utility involved and in process of increasing development in the controversy between Senator Brooks and myself, which the public will do well to store away in its memory. If I dare make a suggestion for the benefit of the rising generation who are now receiving instruction in the public schools, I would urge the teachers to impress upon the children the possibility of their giving utterance to some falsehood,—since to err is human,—but to caution them at the same time against the culpability and dangers of attempting to maintain a falsehood, if by any misfortune they should have asserted it. And as an illustration, they might say to the classes—"Just look at the condition of Senator Brooks, who is actually in this predicament." The Senator begins his unfortunate defence in the *Courier and Enquirer* of this morning, by the following assertion:

"My statements in the Senate were:

"*First.*—As to the fact of the property owned by John Hughes—meaning the Archbishop.

"*Secondly.*—As to the value of the property thus held by John Hughes, meaning the Archbishop.

"*Thirdly.*—As to their transfer from Trustees to John Hughes—meaning the Archbishop."

He adds: "I am charged with falsehood in these my several asseverations."

It is not true that these were Mr. Senator Brooks's statements in the Senate. It is not true that Mr. Brooks has been charged with falsehood in these his several statements. Mr. Brooks knows that neither of these assertions of his is true. And Mr. Brooks knows that he shall be my witness to prove that he knows that they are not true.

In his speech in the Senate, after having professed to make himself acquainted with the amount of property held by John

Hughes, in this city, as taken from the Register's office, he goes on to say:

"*I suppose its value to be, in New York alone, not much short of five millions of dollars. So far from this property being held, when in Churches, by Trustees, there are numerous transfers from Trustees to* JOHN HUGHES. *Beginning with February,* 1842, *and continuing through* 1854, *a friend of mine copied fifty-eight entries of as many distinct parcels of property made in the name of land for* JOHN HUGHES, *all in the space of twelve years.—Not to* JOHN HUGHES, *Bishop, not to* JOHN HUGHES, *Arch✠Bishop (Sic).*, *nor to* JOHN HUGHES, *as trustee of the Roman Catholic Church, but to plain* JOHN HUGHES, *in his propria persona. Some of these parcels cover whole squares of land, and nearly all of them are of great value.*"

[Speech of Mr. Brooks delivered in the Senate of New York on the 6th of March, 1855.]

When Mr. Brooks attempts in his letter of this morning to substitute another set of statements instead of these, and declares them to be the statements made by him in the Senate, he does that which an honorable man, with the knowledge which he has, would have shrunk from doing. He furnishes, like a broken-down witness under cross-examination, the very testimony which is fatal to himself.

The charge of falsehood was made against his statements as found in his speech, and not against the silly subterfuge of statements as set down in his letter of this morning. Having disposed of this point in which Mr. Brooks is witness against himself, we must proceed to examine the result of his labors in trying to make up for the two thousand two hundred and seventy-five per ct. which his account, after his first day's investigation of the Records, left as a balance to be still accounted for, between the truth of his defence and the falsehoods of his speech.

I shall endeavor to allow a great many trifling things to pass to the credit of Mr. Brooks, so as to relieve him, if possible, from the weight of the burden under which he labors. He begins by alleging that he is borne out in regard to conveyances from trustees by the fact that the trustees of St. John's Roman Catholic Church gave me a lease of their property. Now one of two things:—A man who has a lease is either the owner of the property or he is not. If he is not the owner, the property has not been conveyed to him in the sense of Mr. Brooks's statement, that numerous transfers of property were made to me by trustees; and, in that event, Mr. Brooks has failed to prove his assertion. He has only proved that I am the tenant of the trustees of St. John's Church; and if he thinks this warrants his statement, then a lease, according to Mr. Brooks, will be equivalent to a deed in fee simple. This is Radicalism, Fourierism, such as has not been put forth before. But besides, it so happens that this St. John's Roman Catholic Church has been always, and now is managed, in its temporal affairs, by lay trustees, and the Archbishop has never meddled with them, except when they attempted, once or twice, to disregard the discipline of the diocese in other respects.

The next pretended trustee is Mr. Bartholomew O'Connor, who became legal assignee of one of our bankrupt boards of lay trustees, and who transferred it according to law, and entirely in his civil capacity, as an agent of the law. The Archbishop purchased it at the highest price it would bring, paid its debts, and preserved it for the uses of religion to the congregation by whose exertions it had been built, and by whose lay trustees it would have been ruined if the Archbishop had not taken it in hand.

Mr. Brooks demurs as to the question of conveyance from Andrew Byrne, and denies that he duplicated. But he corrects his error in a way which surprises me. He says now that the transfers were made, not by Andrew Byrne to me, but by me to Andrew Byrne. His words are:—"If he, the Archbishop, will look again, he will see that there were two transfers *from* him" (the Archbishop) "*to* Andrew Byrne." Now, if this be so, it will tell against Mr. Brooks, and actually increase, instead of diminishing the per-centage of difference between the truth of his defence, and the falsehoods of his speech in the Senate. He acknowledges, however, that in the case of Geo. Wildes, and Agnes his wife, he, Senator Brooks, did duplicate, and counted the same transfer twice, and in reference to this, I am proud to see him acknowledge the truth. He says:

"I owe it to the public to state that a transfer of property was twice cited by me by mistake, because it was so written." Well, well, whether it was so written or not, this little confession will do him no harm.

But, unfortunately, Mr. Brooks shows scanty signs of penitence; for, although he acknowledges that he duplicated, he does not omit to add the false citation to the number of entries. In his preceding letter, the conveyances, according to Mr. Brooks, amounted to ten. Now strike out from ten, one entry which he duplicated, and let us suppose him correct in stating, as he does in his letter of this date, that two other entries which he had adduced as from Andrew Byrne to John Hughes, were in reality from John Hughes to Andrew Byrne, his ten entries of yesterday are reduced to seven "for to-day." Still, after acknowledging these mistakes, Mr. Brooks dashes on, and counts his conveyance for to-day as No. 11 instead of No. 8. This is from Zachariah Kuntz to John Hughes, and is, no doubt, the ground on which the St. Francis Church, in 31st st., now stands.

No. 12, according to Mr. Brooks, but No. 9, according to his corrected statement, is from James Foster and his wife to John Hughes. The Senator does not say that Mr. and Mrs. Foster had been Trustees of a Catholic Church.

No. 13 is Sarah Remsen to John Hughes.

No. 14 is George W. Hall, of Buffalo, to John Hughes.

No. 15 is from James Rae, of Macon, Georgia, to John Hughes.

No. 16. George W. Hall and wife to John Hughes.

No. 17. G. W. and H. A. Costar to John Hughes.

Here I must pause to point out an instance of the exceeding exactness and scrupulosity with which our Senator describes the dimensions of this particular lot. He says it is between 7th and 8th streets, and is "*one hundred feet by two inches.*" See what it is to be exact. A few more discoveries of this kind will mount up towards the five millions. One hundred feet by two inches!

No. 18. Mary Anne Gaffney, B. Gaffney, and A. J. Donnelly to John Hughes.

No. 19. John V. Westervelt, sheriff, to John Hughes.

No. 20. Richard Kein, clergyman, to John Hughes.

No. 21. Gregory Dillon to John Hughes.

Thus closes Senator Brooks's second day's labor in finding out the entries of property conveyed to me. I shall not examine them minutely, but just take them as the Senator has presented them. I shall only claim that he shall strike out three from twenty-one, as mistakes acknowledged by himself—then there will remain eighteen. But in his speech at Albany he asserted that he had "copied FIFTY-EIGHT ENTRIES OF AS MANY DISTINCT PARCELS OF PROPERTY, made in the name of land from John Hughes." Out of these he has discovered, so far, but eighteen; and he has forty more to find out, if he would support the false statement of his speech.—But Mr. Brooks begins to despair of the Recorder's Office, and I shall not trouble him further at present in regard to it, except to say that I shall hold him accountable for the forty other entries which would be necessary to change the statement in his speech from a falsehood into a fact. He hopes to prove, however, from the Catholic Almanac, what the Register's office fails him in. He says the diocese of Brooklyn has fifteen churches, and insinuates that I am the owner of them all. The diocese of Buffalo has a hundred churches, and that of Albany eighty-seven, and Mr. Brooks arranges his defence so as to insinuate that these churches belong to me. I may tell him that all church property in the diocese of Brooklyn, Albany and Buffalo belong to the Catholic people of each.

But Mr. Brooks is determined that I shall be rich whether I will or not, and he enumerates, not as from the Register's office, but as from the Catholic Almanac, among other items of property, "The Confraternity of the Rosary, &c., &c." "The Arch-Confraternity of the Immaculate Heart of Mary."—He does not tell us by whom conveyances were made to us of these parcels of property. We may suppose, however, that they are from John Doe and Richard Roe *and their wives*, as found recorded in Lib. 1,759, page, a little short of 5,000,000.

Our veracious Senator next enumerates as my property:

"The Redemptorist Convent, 3d street.
"College of St. Francis Xavier, West 15th street.
"Community of Brothers, Canal street.
"Academy of the Holy Infant Jesus, Manhattanville.
"Convent of the Sacred Heart, near Manhattanville.
"Sacred Heart Academy, near Harlem.
"Convent of Sisters of Mercy, Houston and Mulberry.
"Academy of St. Vincent, 107th street.
"St. Mary's School, East Broadway."

I must tell Mr. Brooks, that in this long list of institutions I have not the slightest portion of property, as he will find if he takes the trouble to examine the records of the Register's office a little more minutely.

In the Senator's next effort I would suggest to him, if he can do it honestly, to diminish the large per centage of difference between whatever is of truth in his defence and the falsehood of statements made by him in his speech at Albany, by slipping in to my account, towards making up the five millions, a large slice of the real estate, which, it is generally understood, is owned by William B. Astor, Esq.—Of course I have said, if this can be done honestly. It will save the Senator the trouble of going out of this city, either to the diocese of Albany, or Buffalo, or Brooklyn.

Let us now come to the arithmetic of the matter. We allowed him for his first day's labor in the Register's office a discovery of property to the amount of two hundred thousand dollars. For his second, and just to encourage him in making out his five millions, we will allow his discoveries to be worth two hundred thousand more. Let us state it thus:

According to Senator Brooks in the Senate of New York, on the 6th of last March, the property of Archbishop Hughes, in the City of New York alone, was worth		$4,750,000
Mr. Brook's first day's investigation of the Archbishop's real estate, say, . . .	$200,000	
Second day's ditto, ...	200,000	
Deduct		$400,000
Balance between truth and falsehood still to be accounted for by the Senator . . .		$4,350,000

Besides this, Mr. Brooks will have to account for the forty missing entries on the Register's books, which he paraded before the Senate on the day and date above mentioned. And I hope he will not give up the Register's Office for the Catholic *Almanac*, or enumerate any more " Confraternities of the Rosary" among the parcels of my property. But what has become of the whole squares of land which the Senator says were mine? Verily the Senator's case furnishes a moral, and should be held up as a beacon, cautioning youth especially against an attempt to sustain any statement which they know to be untrue. How easy would it have been for Mr. Brooks to have come out at first with the old saw, *humanum est errare?* How much less humiliating than his present position, if he had said that he had been misled by the false statements of the Trustees' Petition from St. Louis's Church, Buffalo; that for a moment the anti-popery mania had taken possession of his will, memory and understanding; that he had been carried away by the passions of the hour, and did not reflect on what he was saying, &c., &c.

His letter of this date shows that in his zeal to make up the difference between truth and falsehood, he does not overlook the smallest things. We have seen already the minuteness with which he has set down that valuable property of mine, which, according to him, is a hundred feet one way by two inches the other. He has discovered, also, that, by a deed in the Recorder's office, I am entitled to a free seat in the Harlem Railroad cars from the City Hall to Fordham, and from Fordham to the City Hall, as often as I choose to ride. It is ungenerous in Mr. Brooks to quote this, because in his speech he asserted that he spoke of my property in the city of New York alone, whereas, if he reflects for a moment, he will perceive that this property of a free seat in the Harlem Railroad cars, is only partly in the city. It is in the city from the Park to Harlem Bridge, and all beyond that is out of the city. This is a small matter, but Mr. Brooks is so nice and scrupulous in his enumerations of my property, that I think he must have overlooked it through inadvertency.

The public will perceive that in all I have hitherto written

I have not embarrassed the question by any explanation of the circumstances under which property has been entered in my name. I reserve to myself the privilege of giving a full and candid account of such matters, for the information of those who may take an interest in the question, so soon as Mr. Brooks shall have accounted for the balance of my property, constituting the difference, if he is to be believed, between $400,000, for which we have given him credit already, and $4,750,000 which he said my property in the city of New York alone was worth, on the 6th of last March. But I cannot close the present communication without again directing the attention of the public to the dangers, not so much of making a false and foolish statement in a senatorial speech, as Mr. Brooks has done, but of persevering, as Mr. Brooks does, in the attempt to sustain it by new subterfuges.

✠ JOHN, ARCHBISHOP OF NEW YORK.

NEW YORK, *April* 21.

SENATOR BROOKS *vs.* ARCHBISHOP HUGHES.

To the Editors of the Courier and Enquirer.

I am still accused by "✠ JOHN, Archbishop of New York," of uttering and maintaining FALSEHOODS. My defence is called *unfortunate*, my statements *false*, *foolish*, and *silly subterfuges*, my position *humiliating*, my testimony, *fatal to myself*, and, to sum up all in a sentence, I have done that which "*an honorable man would shrink from doing*." This is a heavy load for an Archbishop to buckle on the shoulders of an humble layman like myself; but if his Arch Highness is content with the progress of the controversy, so am I. If he is satisfied with his string of epithets, I am content with my record of facts. If I was "in an awkward position," in the beginning, and have multiplied "the awkwardness of that position," in the continuation of this correspondence, so much the worse for me, and so much the better for the Archbishop.

I shall proceed in the debate as I have begun, hoping, for the sake of a good cause, neither to lose my temper nor my manners. The charges of "falsehood" and "folly," of "dishonor" and "humiliation," fall harmless at my feet. They neither disturb my nerves by day, nor my rest at night. Each of us are addressing an intelligent people, who are capable of deciding questions of veraçity between man and man, upon the record which his Grace and myself are furnishing the public. I have but a single regret in all the controversy so far, and that is, that all those whom the Archbishop addresses through the public press, I am not also permitted to speak to in the same way. In that "meanest of all printed newspapers, the *New York Express*,"—as the amiable and gentlemanly Archbishop is pleased to style a journal in which my name is associated with others, he has had a hearing, in full, which I have in vain called for, from the press under his control. This may be deemed fair play at Rome, but fair men in America, whether Catholic or Protestant, will regard it as at least wanting in magnanimity and justice.

I have been trying to find an apology for the irritability and personality of the gentleman who styles himself "✠ JOHN, Archbishop of New York." The Legislature preceding the present were asked to pass a special Act for the benefit of him, his sect and party, not only in violation of the spirit of the State acts of April 6, 1788, March 17, 1795, and all these acts combined in one, and which became the law of the State in 1813, but in violation of the 38th article of the old Constitution, which declared in terms that the People and State were "required by the benevolent principles of rational liberty, not only to expel civil tyranny, but also to guard against that spiritual oppression and intolerance wherewith the ambition of weak and wicked priests and princes have scourged mankind."

The Legislature came near forgetting the old law, the old Constitution, and that equal and exact justice, which is the rock of our existence as a free Republic. But reason prevailed over error. The Legislature not only refused additional power to the Archbishop and his party THEN, but they, the successors of that Legislature, have taken steps to restore to Church Trustees,

Congregations, Corporations and individual worshippers, the power of which they were robbed by the Baltimore Ordinances of 1849 and 1852, and by the demands of the Archbishop himself.

Before I have done with the Archbishop, and his accusations of FALSEHOOD against me, I shall have occasion to show that, immediately after the Baltimore Council of Bishops decreed, in 1849, that all the churches and other ecclesiastical property acquired by gifts, or through the obligations of the faithful, designed to be expended for charitable or religious uses, *belong to the Bishop*, unless it is certified in writing that it was given for some religious order or congregation of priests,—Archbishop Hughes set about securing conveyances of church property TO HIMSELF, in all parts of the State. I have such conveyances from Erie and elsewhere, which will appear all in good season.

My offence is, in the eyes of the Archbishop, that I voted for, and spoke for, the Church Property Bill of Mr. Putnam, so unlike *that* Church Property Bill, for the benefit of him and his, which was before a previous Legislature. I have shown the Archbishop's zeal to possess the *temporalities* of the people of his diocese and of the State. I have pointed to his titles and his deeds, and overhauled a long list of records to him, his heirs and assignees. I have, I think, through these records, made the Archbishop hateful in his own eyes, and certainly a reproach even among many of his own people, whose sympathies and encouragement I have. He reads in the Church Property Bill a law of the State, overthrowing the decrees of his Council of Bishops, and putting an end to those transfers of church property, whether of trustees or persons when conveyed to ✠ John Hughes. That law puts an end to grants, conveyances, devises, and leases to persons in ecclesiastical offices, or to their successors, and it grieves the Archbishop to the quick, to see his enormous accumulations checked by law, and the people whose spiritual leader he is, placed even in control of those walls of brick and mortar, which have been built by the labor of their own hands. He may deny a priest to those who conform to the law, and threaten a hundred churches as he did the St. Louis Church at Buffalo, that he will see their edifices, brick by brick, tumble to pieces before he will grant them a spiritual teacher, or priest. Or, he may fulfil his declared intention of defeating the law of the State, if he can, through those "*professional gentlemen*" who "*may discover some defect in the framing and wording of the enactment which will render it inapplicable!*" But let me whisper to him, thus early, that other Legislatures will fill the chinks and crannies which his crafty mind thus opens in advance, and which skilful lawyers may aid him in keeping open for a season. The law has a spirit as well as a letter, and in this land the rule of conduct with all good citizens is, that the law must be obeyed—even by archbishops.

I begin my additional record to-day with another conveyance "from Trustees to John Hughes," and preface it with the Archbishop's repeated declaration, recorded in the *Express*, recorded in the *Courier*, and recorded in the *Times*, on two different days of two different weeks, that I was guilty of FALSEHOOD, in declaring that church property had been conveyed to him by Trustees:—

LOOK ON THIS PICTURE.	AND NOW ON THIS.
STATEMENT IN THE ARCHBISHOP'S FIRST LETTER. "I have never received or accepted ANY *transfer* of ANY *property* WHATEVER *from Trustees*. * * Mr. Brooks's statement 'I KNOW TO BE UNTRUE.'"	THE ARCHBISHOP AGAINST THE RECORD. See the conveyance of the— TRUSTEES *of St. John's Roman Catholic Church* to John Hughes, dated July 17th, 1844, 999 years. Consideration *one cent a year!*
STATEMENT IN THE ARCHBISHOP'S SECOND LETTER. "Any one who asserts that many of the conveyances of real estate to me were made by *Trustees*, *asserts a gross*, and, *towards me, an injurious* FALSEHOOD!"	I now place— THE ARCHBISHOP *against* HIMSELF.——See his letter April 19th. See by his own comment upon conveyance No. 8, cited by me, where he admits that Mr. Bartholomew O'Connor (in the case of his transfer to John Hughes) "*was only the Assignee* [to him] *of a* BANKRUPT BOARD OF TRUSTEES!"

But the end is not yet, though this might do for a poor layman, like myself, in a controversy with a distinguished Archbishop. But, as I said there were more conveyances than one to John Hughes, from Trustees, I am, perhaps, bound to cite more than the two of this class already named, albeit I could not see the cause of the Archbishop's soreness on this point until the truth flashed upon my mind, that all such conveyances from *Trustees to John Hughes were illegal and void!*

Trustees have no authority to convey church property to archbishop, bishop, or priest, except upon application to the Supreme Court, which, I believe, has in no instance, in the record before me, been done. This is the law, and the Archbishop has, therefore, received and holds property in violation of law, which belongs to the Trustees, or those for whose benefit the trust was held! Will the possessor return this property to the legal owners?

But let me give another of the Archbishop's examples of avoiding issues and facts. He says:

"He (Mr. Brooks) begins by alleging that he is borne out in regard to conveyances from trustees by the fact that the trustees of St. John's Roman Catholic Church gave me a lease of their property. Now one of two things: A man who has a lease is either the owner of the property or he is not. If he is not the owner, the property has not been conveyed to him in the sense of Mr. Brooks's statement, that numerous transfers of property were made to me by trustees; and, in that event, Mr. Brooks has failed to prove his assertion. He has only proved that I am the tenant of the trustees of St. John's Church; and if he thinks this warrants his statement, then a lease, according to Mr. Brooks, will be equivalent to a deed in fee simple. This is Radicalism, Fourierism, such as has not been put forth before."

My answer is, that that is property which the law makes property, and a conveyance for 999 years at one cent a year, to John Hughes, his heirs and assignees, makes the property his, morally, legally, actually. It is in his name, at his disposal, under his control. It is so recorded, and nothing but his will and pleasure can change the record.

If the Archbishop will leave off calling names long enough to refer to the 2d Revised Statutes he will find, pages 162 and

171, last edition, sections 1 and 58, the following to be the law of the case:

> "The term 'conveyance,' as used in this chapter, shall be construed to embrace every instrument in writing by which any estate is created, aliened, mortgaged or assigned, or by which the title to any real estate may be effected in loan or equity, except last wills and testaments, leases for a term not exceeding three years, and executory contracts for the sale or purchase of lands."

The following extract from the Revised Statutes will show that property held in the Bishop's name, is his also, unless thus held in violation of other statutes:

> "Every conveyance of real estate, within this State hereafter made, shall be recorded in the office of the Clerk of the County where such real estate shall be situated, and every such conveyance not so recorded shall be void as against any subsequent purchaser in good faith and for a valuable consideration of the same real estate or any portion thereof, whose conveyance shall first be duly recorded."

The Archbishop, as badly off in law as in fact, must now fly to some other technicality to find means of escape. One cannot but marvel to see His Grace misquote my speech—(as where he twice puts *land* for *and*)—and feel pity for him when he misstates my letter in regard to the conveyance from Andrew Byrne. The record stated that the transfer was *to* John Hughes, and I proved from that record that two distinct conveyances, of two distinct parcels of property, were made to him—John Hughes. He is welcome to the advantages of an obvious typographical error. A resort to such straws shows the weakness of his cause and the desperation of his mind. Dealing with one who uses such weapons, and hides himself behind such a refuge, I almost forget that I am dealing with one who is styled the "Most Rev. John Hughes, D.D., Archbishop of the Province and Archdiocese of New York."

But I have not done with the conveyances of property to John Hughes—meaning the Archbishop—nor with the conveyances of trustees to him. I am called over and over again a *falsifier* on this point, and here is a continuation of my answer to such courteous denunciations.

CONVEYANCES OF TRUSTEES TO JOHN HUGHES.

RECORD NUMBER TWENTY-TWO.

From the Register's Office, City of New York.

The Trustees of Transfiguration Church to John Hughes.	Date of Conveyance, Dec. 9, 1851.—Recorded in liber 591, page 268. Consideration one dollar.

All those two certain lots of ground situate, lying and being on north side of Chambers street, in the City of New York, and which, on a map or survey made by Cassine H. Goerch, City Surveyor, dated May 7, 1795, are known and distinguished by lots numbers 16 and 17, adjoining each other, and are together bounded south by Chambers street, north by lots numbers 36 and 37 on said map, and west by lot number 15, and east by lot number 18 on said map, being together, front and rear, 50 feet in breadth, and in length 75 feet 7½ inches, agreeably to said map; and also, all that certain messuage or dwelling-house, and lot, piece or parcel of ground situate, lying and being in Reade street, in the City of New York, described in a certain Indenture of deed recorded in liber 133 of Conveyances, page 11, as follows: *all* that certain lot, piece or parcel of land situate, lying and being in Reade street, in the Sixth Ward in the City of New York, known and distinguished by number 23, bounded north in front by Reade street aforesaid, south in the rear by land claimed by John Agnew, west by ground belonging to Geo. Brinckerhoff, and east by ground claimed by heirs of Peter Nailor, containing in breadth, in front and rear, 25 feet, and in length, on each side, 75 feet 7 inches.

NUMBER TWENTY-THREE.

Peter Johnston and Martha, his wife, to John Hughes.	Date of Conveyance, March 3, 1853. Recorded in liber 623, p. 498, March 4, 1853. Consideration $3,709.

All those certain two lots, pieces or parcels of ground, situate, lying and being in the Eighteenth Ward of the City of New York, and bounded and described as follows: beginning at a point on the south line of Fifteenth street, at the distance of 250 feet westerly from southwest corner of Fifteenth street and Avenue B, thence running northwest along said south line to Fifteenth street 50 feet, thence running southwest at right angles to said south line and parallel with west line of Avenue B, 103 feet 3 inches, to a line equi-distant from Fourteenth street and Fifteenth street, thence running along said last mentioned line southeast and parallel with said south line of Fifteenth street 50 feet, and thence running northeast and parallel with said west line of Avenue B, 103 feet 3 inches to place of beginning.

NUMBER TWENTY-FOUR.

Michael McKeon and Eliza, his wife, to John Hughes.	Date of Conveyance, June 13, 1853; Recorded in liber 650, p. 324, Nov. 5, 1853. Consideration, $8,000.

All those two certain lots, pieces or parcels of land, situate, lying and being in the Ninth Ward of City of New York, known and distinguished on a map or chart of the property of Trinity Church, called the 3d R. N. Division of the Church farm by the numbers 215 and 216, the said lots lying together, being bounded and described as follows: Beginning on the south side of Le Roy street, at a point distant 100 feet eastwardly from the corner formed by its intersection with the easterly side of Greenwich street; running thence southerly at right angles to Le Roy street 100 feet; thence eastwardly, parallel with Le Roy street 50 feet; thence northwardly at right angles to Le Roy street 100 feet to Le Roy street; and thence westwardly along the south line of Le Roy street 50 feet to place of beginning; each of said lots being 25 feet front and rear, and 100 feet on each side.

NUMBER TWENTY-FIVE.

Thomas E. Davis and Anne, his wife, to John Hughes.	Date of Conveyance, April 27, 1853. Recorded in liber 631, p. 438, May 26, 1853. Consideration, $500.

All that certain lot, piece or parcel of land situate, lying and being on the north side of One Hundred and Seventeenth street, in the Twelfth Ward of the City of New York, and bounded and described as follows, viz.: Commencing at a point on the said north side of One Hundred and Seventeenth street, distant 200 feet east from northeast corner of One Hundred and Seventeenth street and Fourth Avenue; running northerly and parallel with Fourth Avenue 100 feet to the centre line of the block between One Hundred and Seventeenth and One Hundred and Eighteenth streets; thence east and parallel with One Hundred and Seventeenth street 25 feet; thence south and parallel with Fourth Avenue 100 feet to said north side of One Hundred and Seventeenth street; and thence westerly along said north side of One Hundred and Seventeenth street 25 feet to point or place of beginning.

NUMBER TWENTY-SIX.

James R. Bayley and James B. Nicholson to John Hughes.	Assignment of Lease. Recorded in liber 586, p. 486, Dec. 17, 1851. Consideration $3,600.

Trustees appointed by the Supreme Court in place of Charles C. Rice, D. D., Surveying Assignee, &c.

NUMBER TWENTY-SEVEN.

Thomas Lennon to John Hughes.	Date of Conveyance, Aug. 30, 1851. Recorded in liber 582, page 378. Consideration, $1.

All and singular those certain lots, pieces or parcels of land situate, lying and being in the Nineteenth Ward of City of New York, and severally known and distinguished on a certain map drawn Feb. 10,

1851, by D. Ewen, City Surveyor, and filed in Register's Office as Nos. 41, 42, 43 and 44, which said four lots, taken together as one parcel, are in the aggregate described as follows, that is to say: Beginning at a point on the southwest line of Eighty-fourth street, distant 800 feet southeast from intersection of southeast line of the Fifth Avenue with the southeast line of Eighty-fourth street; thence running northwest, but along the southwest line of Eighty-fourth street 100 feet; thence southwest but parallel to Fifth Avenue 102 feet and 2 inches; thence southwest, thence southeast, but parallel to Eighty-third street, 180 feet; thence northeast but parallel to Fifth Avenue 102 feet and 2 inches, to place of beginning.

NUMBER TWENTY-EIGHT.

Henry Grinnell and Sarah M., his wife, to John Hughes.	Date Feb. 1, 1853. Recorded in liber 626, p. 505, March 1, 1853. Consideration, $12,000.

All those certain lots, pieces, or parcels of land, situate, lying, and being on north side of Fourteenth street, in the Eighteenth ward of the city of New York, being part of certain premises conveyed to said Henry Grinnell by Eliphalet Nott and wife, by deed bearing date August 1, 1851, and recorded in Register's Office, in liber 579, page 424, as the same are laid down and designated on the diagram annexed to said deed, by numbers 203, 204, 205, and 206, which taken together, are bounded and described as follows: Beginning at a point on the north side of Fourteenth street, distant 250 feet west from north-west corner of Fourteenth street and Avenue B; running thence west along north side of Fourteenth street 100 feet; thence north, on a line parallel with Avenue B, 103 feet 3 inches, to centre line of block between Fourteenth and Fifteenth streets; thence east along said centre line 100 feet; thence south, and on a parallel with Avenue B, 103 feet 3 inches, to place of beginning.

NUMBER TWENTY-NINE.

George N. Lawrence and Mary Ann, his wife, to John Hughes.	Date of contract, Dec. 10, 1852. Recorded in liber 626, p. 192, Feb. 8, 1853. Consideration, $2,400.

All those six certain lots, pieces, or parcels of ground, situate, lying and being in the Twelfth ward of the city of New York, and known and distinguished on a map of property belonging to Hicks, Lawrence & Co., surveyed Dec. 27, 1853, and on file in the Register's Office, by numbers 61, 62, 63, 64, 65, and 66. Said lots being taken together are bounded and described as follows: Beginning at a point on the north-west corner of One Hundred and Thirty-first street and Bloomingdale road, running thence west along north line of One

Hundred and Thirty-first street, 143 feet; thence north and parallel with Eleventh avenue, 99 feet 10 inches; thence east and parallel with One Hundred and Thirty-first street, 134 feet to Bloomingdale road; and thence south along west side of Bloomingdale road, to place of beginning.

NUMBER THIRTY.

Samuel Newby and Sarah, his wife, to John Hughes.	Date of Conveyance, February 2, 1852. Recorded in liber 594, page 237, Feb. 17, 1852. Consideration, $6,000.

All those four certain lots, pieces, or parcels of land situate, lying, and being on north-east side of Forty-second street, between Eighth and Ninth avenues, in the city of New York, and known and distinguished on a map and file in the Register's Office, by numbers 586, 587, 588, and 589, the said lots containing each 25 feet in width, in front and rear, and 100 feet 4 inches in depth on each side, and bounded south-west by Forty-second street, north-east by lots Nos. 550, 551, 552 and 553, south-east by lot No. 585, north-west by lot No. 590.

The Archbishop will see that while he is abusive in words, I am not idle in facts. He will see that I have proved what I said in the Senate in regard to his large possessions of property in this City. He will see that I have proved what I said in regard to conveyances to him from Trustees. He will see that I am reporting pretty rapid progress, too, in regard to the value of the Church Property held by him in this City. He might see, if he would, the difference in value between property in this City ten and twelve years ago and now,—but as he won't see without my aid, I shall furnish him with a pair of spectacles to do so by and by. He might make a clean breast of the magnitude of his possessions in real estate, if he would, and thus save himself the mortification of seeing his duplicity exposed, and me the trouble of exposing that duplicity. But to quote JOHN HUGHES, *humanum est errare.* I am more in pursuit of a PRINCIPLE than a man, and my object has been, is, and will be, to show how Anti-Republican in a Government like this, it is for any man, and most of all the Archbishop of a great Church, to be engaged as a Broker in Real Estate—to be employed in buying houses and lands, churches and vacant lots, especially when some of those lots, reduced to 4 by 4, and 8 by 8, and 16 by 16, are speculated in as burial places FOR THE DEAD.

For to-day, again, I am,

Very respectfully, yours, &c.,

ERASTUS BROOKS.

NEW YORK, *April* 23, 1855.

ARCHBISHOP HUGHES TO SENATOR BROOKS.

To the Editors of the Courier and Enquirer:

I have charged Senator Brooks with falsehoods, uttered deliberately by him in the Senate Chamber of New York, and calculated, if not intended, to inflict injury on my reputation. I have sustained the charge already to some extent by facts, and pledge myself to the public that other facts shall not be wanting to complete the proof of my charge. In the mean time, Senator Brooks affects to ignore the evidences that brand him as no honorable man would suffer himself to be branded, as nothing more than idle epithets that have no meaning. If I call a man a thief, or the receiver of property stolen from me, he may say (provided he is innocent) that the charge of theft, or the receiving of stolen goods, falls harmless at his feet—that if I am satisfied with my "string of epithets," he is content with his "record of facts." But if I show on his person the very property which has been stolen from me, it is too late for him to say that "my charges fall harmless at his feet."

I use this illustration not as intended to degrade Mr. Brooks in any way, but to point out to him that when I charge him with falsehood, it is because he has been guilty of falsehood, and if he dare deny the charge I am quite prepared to prove it.

Our Senator, therefore, must see the necessity of standing up for his reputation. The matter is too serious for that philosophy which he attempts to put on. He should know that his friends, his constituents, the Legislature of New York, and the people of the State and country at large, have an interest in his reputation which he has no right to trifle with. No man is the absolute owner either of his life or character. Neither the one nor the other is his property in any sense that would authorize him to destroy or damage it. His life is the property of God. His character belongs to his fellow-men. His relation to either is that of a trustee, and society has a right to require that he shall act as a faithful guardian for the preservation of both. Mr. Senator Brooks, therefore, is not at liberty to affect the philosophy of indifference when the charge of falsehood is brought against him on responsible authority. He has no right to let himself down to a position of acknowledged degradation, without making an effort to sustain himself against charges which are damaging to his character only in so far as, unhappily for him, they are too true.

Again, Mr. Brooks may not attempt to throw dust into the eyes of that "intelligent people" whom we both address, by copying out extracts from the Register's Office as regards property conveyed to me. This is not the question. If Mr. Brooks had stated before the Senate that certain conveyances had been made to me in the City of New York, or elsewhere, he would have stated what I myself was the first to proclaim,—what is known to the whole community of New York, and what requires no proof. It is known to all that for the last twelve or fourteen years, property designed for Catholic church purposes has been vested in the Bishop,—said property being in all other respects for its uses, its income, its expenditures, as much the property of the several congregations, as if it had been invested in lay Trustees,—the only difference being that there is no authority whereby such property can be mortgaged and brought into jeopardy by irresponsible laymen without the knowledge and concurrence of the Bishop. By copying extracts from the Register's Office, therefore, Mr. Brooks is attempting to prove what is not in dispute, what is admitted, what is known to all as a general fact.

But even in his undertaking to prove what every body knows as to the general fact, Mr. Brooks is not justified in falsifying the records from which he pretends to give extracts. In this he shows the moral danger of any attempt to sustain a primary falsehood, since every such attempt involves the necessity of having recourse to secondary, and, in maintaining these, to certify falsehoods *ad infinitum nauseam.* The fiat of the Almighty at the Creation, in reference to plants and trees, ordaining that each should bear fruit and seed according to its kind, is perfectly applicable to truth and falsehood. Each bears fruit according to its kind.

To elucidate this principle it will be sufficient to state that in human thought or human language there are but three kinds of propositions possible. First, the proposition which is true and which yields fruit according to its kind, requiring nothing but truth to sustain it. Second, the proposition which is false, and in like manner yields fruit according to *its* kind, making it necessary that other falsehoods should be invented and employed for its support. Third, a mixed proposition, which is partly true and partly false; but which, when it comes to be analyzed, and the portion which is true divided from the portion which is false, will produce distinct corresponding fruits each according to its kind. The portion which is false will require falsehoods for its support, and the portion which is true will rest exclusively for support on the fruits which it bears according to its kind. In other words, falsehood cannot be maintained by truth, nor does truth ever require to be maintained by falsehood.

Having premised these observations, I proceed to say that of the primary falsehoods contained in Mr. Brooks's speech in the Senate of New York, the first I shall notice is the statement that "*The value of Archbishop Hughes's property in the city of New York alone is not much short of five millions of dollars.*" As Mr. Brooks is engaged in an attempt to sustain this falsehood, I shall reserve for another communication the proofs that it has already borne fruits according to its kind.

The second is the statement in his speech that he "had copied from the records fifty-eight entries of as many distinct parcels of property made in the name of and for John Hughes." The Senator's extracts from the Register's Office, are an attempt to sustain this statement, and although he has falsified the entries and counted, at least one entry twice over, as shall be shown more fully hereafter, he has as yet reached only No. 30 out of fifty-eight, leaving twenty-eight distinct entries to be still accounted for. In regard to the fifty-eight entries, we find in his speech the following statement, embodied by way of annotation:—"*To those who were curious in such matters, Mr. Brooks exhibited to the Senate the number, book, and page of these several entries in the city of New York.*" This was on the 6th of last March. He has in his pretended extracts from the Register's Office counted some entries twice; he has falsified others, and yet having arrived, according to his own calculation, at No. 30 out of fifty-eight, for which he had day and date, book and number, and page to flourish in the face of his brother Senators more than seven weeks ago, he now acknowledges himself as *minus habens*, and begs for somebody to help him out of his difficulty. This may be seen from the following advertisement in that meanest of all printed newspapers, which it is unnecessary to mention:

"CONVEYANCES TO ARCHBISHOP HUGHES.

"*The friends of the rights of Church Trustees and the Laity against the usurpations of Archbishop Hughes and his associates, are requested to send abstracts of conveyances of Church Property to him, to the office of the New York Express. Our object is to elicit the truth as to the amount and value of the Church Property owned by the Archbishop and his associates in office.*"

So, then, Senator Brooks is now begging that some body may furnish him with evidences to support a statement made by him on the 6th of March, accompanied with a pretended exhibition of number, book, &c., which contained the official proofs of the statements in his speech. Verily, the Senator's propositions are bearing fruit each according to its kind!

The third of the primary falsehoods of his speech was that "*some of these parcels cover whole squares of land, and nearly all of them are of great value.*" I take it for granted that Senator Brooks admits the falsehood of this statement, inasmuch as hitherto he has made no allusion to it. If, however, he does not admit its falsehood, surely he will not withhold from the public the whereabouts of these whole squares of land.

The fourth primary falsehood which I pointed out in the speech of the Senator is, that "numerous transfers of this property, or parcels of land, were made by trustees to John Hughes."

I have always denied that I ever asked, sought, received, or accepted any property from lay trustees. This denial I repeat to-day with increased emphasis. My words in a public document, published before I had seen the speech of Senator Brooks, were, "that I never recognise in them" (trustees of the Catholic Church property) "the right of ownership; * * * * that "they could not make over to me the title of such property; that it was not theirs in such a sense or for such a purpose; that they could not do it if they would." Mr. Brooks affects to believe that he has invalidated this statement by the fact that the trustees of St. John's Church made to me a lease of their property for 999 years. Now to prove the truth of my statement in this particular, it is only necessary to mention two facts. The one is, that this transfer was that of a lease, and not of property in fee-simple, as the false statement in the Senator's speech implied. The second is, that so far from accepting this property, as giving me any right of ownership, I have never meddled with the management of its temporal affairs, directly or indirectly—that it is now, and always has been, administered by lay trustees, just in the same manner as if no such transfer of lease had ever been made.

I wish it to be understood that every report of extracts which Mr. Brooks has hitherto put forth as from the Register's records, shall be specifically and critically examined by a professional gentleman, with the view of showing, number by number, how the several primary falsehoods of the Senator's speech have borne fruit, each according to its kind, in his attempt to sustain them. The Senator has obtained from "The Trade" a series of opinions extracted from various newspapers favorable to his position. He forgets that the matters in debate between him and me are matters of fact and not of opinion. What if the legislature of New York and the Supreme Court of the United States gave an opinion either in his favor or in mine. It would not be worth a straw, inasmuch as the question is not one of opinion but one of fact. Two and two make four. That is a fact. And if any man were to say that they make five or seven, the endorsements of other men, possibly as blinded as himself, would not alter the state of his case one iota.

Besides, these worthy confreres of Senator Brooks are under a mistaken view of the subject. They seem to suppose that if any property had been conveyed to me, then Senator Brooks is right and I am wrong. They seem to suppose that I denied the ownership of any property. But this pretended ignorance must be a piece of affectation. They do not forget that in my very first letter I admitted the ownership of property, nor was I at all parsimonious in reserving a sufficient amount to myself out of the unexpected fortune of twenty-five millions bestowed on me by *The Presbyterian*, which Mr. Brooks had the cruelty to reduce to a sum barely short of five millions.

They do not forget that taking this diminished appropriation of the Senator as the standard of calculation, I reserved the amount of two millions as a provision against want in my old age, and devoted the surplus, say $2,750,000, to the establishment of a great institution which was to bear the title of "The ERASTUS BROOKS LIBRARY"—that is, on the hypothesis that the Senator should point out where all this immense property was. The Senator has attempted to change the issue, and he writes little squibs himself, or gets others to write them for him, or accepts them if spontaneously offered, to the effect that he has triumphed over me, because he has proved that some conveyances of land have been made in my favor, which was never denied. But let these kind editors help him out in showing the amount of property — the fifty-eight entries — the numerous transfers from trustees—the whole squares of land, which, in his speech at Albany, on the 6th of March, he stated were mine.

If they do not help him in this way they do not help him at all, although their little squibs may fill up a portion of the *New York Express*, and induce its readers to think that Senator Brooks imagines himself to be making great progress.

Having disposed sufficiently of the Senator's last effort, at least till a reliable investigation of the Records shall have been made, I will lose sight of the Senator, and address the remaining portion of this communication to the good sense and candor of my fellow-citizens, Catholics and Protestants, whose esteem I value, and who may have been misled in their judgment on the subject involved.

First.—It has been the practice, especially since the bankruptcy of no less than four boards of Catholic Lay Trustees in this city alone, to invest the title of new churches in the Bishop. This was conformable to the discipline of the Catholic Church as regulated by the Provincial Councils of Baltimore. It was also in conformity with the wishes of the Catholic people, at least in this city, whose temporal interests and reputation as a religious community, had been almost destroyed by the bad management of lay trustees. It is understood among Catholics that whatever may be the form of legal tenure by which church property is held, being once recognized as church property, it belongs not to the Bishop or the trustees, or the parishes, or the people, but that it is to be regarded as the property of God, set apart for religious uses, and enjoyed for the common benefit of all.

Secondly.—Under these circumstances, they look upon the Bishop as the natural guardian of property which has been created, not by any gift or donation of the State, but by their own voluntary contributions of charity. And whatever law the State may pass, there is one thing certain, that nothing less than coersion will induce the Catholics to discontinue or withdraw the confidence which they have in their Bishops as the natural guardians of such property. They never dream that the Bishop is the owner of their church and church property, merely because the deed thereof may be recorded in his name. Neither will less than coercion induce them to put their property, and their reputation as a religious community, at the irresponsible disposal of lay trustees, armed with legal power to mortgage their property and impose upon them, as has been done already, the burden of debts by which their churches may become bankrupt and sold for the benefit of creditors.

Thirdly.—It was in this full understanding on all sides, that they, the Catholics of New York, contributed to redeem no less than four Churches from the disgraceful consequences of bankruptcy, through bad management on the part of lay trustees. These Churches were sold under process of law for the benefit of their creditors. The amount which they brought would not have been more than some thirty or forty cents in the dollar. But when the Bishop consented to put himself at the head of the Catholic body, and accept the title of this property, they rallied around him, and by imposing sacrifices on themselves, they paid not only the thirty cents on the dollar, which the law of the State had secured to the creditors, but they went beyond law, and conformed to justice by paying one hundred cents to the dollar. There is no spirit of repudiation of honest debts among Catholics, but they are not willing that lay trustees shall have the power of mortgaging—I will not say their property only, but also their upright and honorable fame.

Fourthly.—It is in this spirit and with this understanding that the Bishop is invested with the title of whatever church property is recorded in his name, either in the city of New York or throughout the diocese. Each church belongs, practically, to the Catholic congregation worshipping therein. All the churches of the diocese belong in the same way to all the Catholics of the diocese. To suppose that the Bishop should alienate them, mortgage them, or in any other manner abuse his trust for his own use and benefit, is to suppose something that has never entered the minds of the Catholic people. And, for myself, I can say, that my support since I have been appointed Bishop of New York, has been derived from the free and voluntary offerings of the flock committed to my charge. Not so much as one farthing has accrued to me from the nominal ownership of church property.

Fifthly.—It must not be inferred from this that I am not sufficiently provided for, whether as regards my personal expenses or the much weightier expenses incident to my position as Catholic Archbishop of New York. In that respect I feel that I am very rich—rich in the confidence and affections of the people committed to my care—rich in the moderate but sufficient sum which is provided annually for the support of my person and my position—rich in the consolation derived from witnessing the increasing piety, harmony, union, zeal, and mutual charity of the people committed to my care—rich in the consciousness that from the moment I was reluctantly induced to accept the office in the Church of which I then felt and still feel myself so unworthy, I made an offering of my mind and heart, and life, for the glory of God, in promoting the spiritual and temporal welfare of the flock over whom I was placed as Pastor by the great Bishop and Shepherd of our souls.

Sixthly.—Having thus shown how rich a man I am, it is but fair now that I should state how poor. Fortunately the temporal affairs of my diocese are in good order, so that my successor, were I to die to-morrow, will only have to look at the private archives to understand at a glance the actual condition of matters and things. As representative of the diocese, I am personally indebted to the amount of thirty thousand dollars. But by way of assets I have in my personal right an amount of property which I suppose, if its value could be realized, would cover the debt. Mr. Brooks and his associates may feel an interest in knowing of what these assets consist, and I will tell him. They are partly bequests, partly donations, partly the hope of a favorable decision in regard to a suit which was in chancery before chancery was abolished. Besides this property, which I consider as assets against my debts, I am the owner of a library which would be of little use to many of those who take an interest in the question of my property, but which to me is very valuable. I am the owner of a part of the furniture of the house in which I live—but only a part. Let us now sum up. All that is Church property on Manhattan Island, whether the title be invested in me or not, belongs to the

Catholics of Manhattan Island and not to me. When this deduction is made I am left the owner of my library and a part of the furniture in my dwelling. But I am not the owner of one square inch of ground within the city of New York. I am the owner of the bed I sleep on, but not of the roof, or the walls that protect me against the inclemency of the seasons. I do not however complain of my poverty, for I am not poor. I know that any one invested with the office which I hold in the Church of God, is the more honored in proportion as his condition assimilates to that of his Divine Master, who had not whereon to lay his head. And it would be an especial reproach to me to be the successor of the devoted and disinterested Bishop Dubois, who died so poor that the Catholics of his cathedral had to bear the expenses of his funeral, if I disgraced the inheritance of his office by grasping at and appropriating to my own use any thing more of the things of this world than are necessary to provide me with daily food and raiment.

But notwithstanding all this, Senator Brooks will have to give some account of the four millions seven hundred and fifty thousand dollars which he said was the value of my property on the 6th day of last March.

✠ JOHN, *Archbishop of New York.*

NEW YORK, *April 28th.*

SENATOR BROOKS vs. ARCHBISHOP HUGHES.

To the Editors of the Courier and Enquirer:

I congratulate the Archbishop upon that degree of recovery of "a near relative of his," which enables him to resume his pen. I am sorry, however, to see that the Archbishop is neither improved in temper nor refreshed in style by the brief suspension of his labors. He continues to pile up epithets, like a pyramid, and to-day he out-does himself. He charges me now with "*falsehoods, uttered deliberately;*" "*brands me as no honorable man would suffer himself to be branded,*" uses the words "*thief*" and "*theft*," to illustrate the temper of his mind, and heads his letter, like a showman, "*the moral degradation of my position.*" If I had no respect for myself, and none for the truth of the case at issue, I might give lie for "lie," and brand for "brand." But in dealing with an Archbishop I choose rather to remember his high and holy calling than his low example. If it is either good manners, sound logic, or true religion to answer a proven fact with such words as the Archbishop makes so familiar to his lips and pen, he is more than welcome in this controversy to the advantage they give him.

Once upon a time a Scotch Professor of King's College, Cambridge, setting an example which an Archbishop might imitate with honor, was asked what he would do if a man told him he was a liar? "What would I do?" said he; "I would not knock him down, but I would tell him to prove it, *prove it*, PROVE IT. And I would say to him, that if he couldn't prove it, he'd be the liar, and then I should have him!" The Archbishop may make the application, and the public will judge upon the evidence given and coming, whether I have John Hughes, or John Hughes has me.

In vindication of my veracity, and to relieve myself from the charge of FALSEHOOD, I have given from the record the legal conveyance to John Hughes of THIRTY pieces or parcels of property. I add ELEVEN more to-day, and the end is not yet. What I said in the Senate on the 6th of March last, qualified by "a supposition of fact," and from date recorded by the searches of a "friend of mine," as to the main fact,—which the Archbishop twice directly misstates to-day, will turn out to be a soberer reality than the Archbishop or myself ever dreamed of when I called public attention to his possessions, and when he pronounced my statements FALSE. The work of investigation is only fairly commenced, and I shall proceed with it, disregarding all irrelevancy and abuse.

First, now, as to "the parcels of property," and "squares of land." I enumerate the THIRTY-TWO lots of ground on 50th and

51st streets, in two parcels, one 350 feet by 210 feet 10 inches, and the other 105 feet by 85 feet. This would make one or two handsome squares, each sufficiently large for that "Erastus Brooks Library," which the Archbishop now seeks to get rid of by an open plea of poverty. The pretence comes too late, is not warranted by the record, was not denominated in the bond, and I, therefore, claim the fulfilment of a promise so carefully considered and so deliberately made. The Cathedral property also rests upon a very spacious and pretty spot of ground, and upon one quite large enough both for the Cathedral, and in its vacant lots, for the Library. The Archbishop may preside over the one, and, with his permission, some friend of mine over the other. There is also another very pretty square at Manhattanville, which would answer very well for the Library, if it were not so far out of town; and another square, also under the control of his Grace, between the First avenue and Avenue A, which might, by permission, be exchanged for some property more favorably situated for a public institution, designed "for the use, not of any one profession or class of men, but for all mankind."

If the Archbishop is still doubtful about those "squares of land," I will direct his attention to conveyance No. 8, 100 by 100 feet, No. 19, which is quite as large, No. 23, from which a very handsome square can be selected, No. 24, 100 by 100, No. 27, 100 by 102 feet and *two inches.* (The Archbishop will see I am particular now as to the *two inches.*) No. 28, 100 by 103 feet *three inches*, No. 29, 143 feet by 99 feet *ten inches*, one way, and 134 feet the other; No. 30, 100 by 104 feet, &c., &c. It would weary the public, the Archbishop and myself, to cite all those parcels of property recorded in his name, which would answer very well for an edifice so honorable to his promised bounty, and which would perpetuate his name, as well as mine, "in large gilded letters," to the latest posterity.

I have not yet deemed it necessary to enumerate all the Archbishop's church and other possessions in this city and elsewhere. By a confession of his, altogether unexpected, to myself, he admits what it was almost the sole purpose of this branch of my speech in the Senate to show, that HE WAS A LARGE OWNER OF CHURCH PROPERTY. This, I believe, is what the lawyers call the plea of "confession and evidence," or an acknowledgment of the truth, when there was no longer power to evade or avoid the issue. Here is "the confession and evidence:"

"In reference to my ownership of *real estate property*, as Mr. Brooks calls it, *there is no question. The title of many Catholic Churches in the city of New York is vested in me, and so far I am the owner.* My intention, even, is to *add to this property* by purchasing such additional lots, or accepting the gift of them, as I may find from time to time to be desirable for the purpose of providing religious instruction for the wants of the Catholic flock committed to my charge. If Mr. Brooks will examine the records of the city of New York three months from this time, he will probably find conveyances made to me by parties who have the right to sell or bestow as they think proper."

This admission is made still broader in the letter of to-day. The "title of ownership," then, is vested in the bishop. The pulpits are his. The keys are his. Doors are opened and shut at his own good will and pleasure. Priests come and go, speak and act, at his bidding. The congregation are his servants. One may not even say Mass over the souls of the dead, except the dead are buried where the Archbishop prescribes and commands. Greenwood and Cypress Hills, Protestant burial places everywhere, are now all unsanctified and accursed ground. The Archbishop seeks to be the master of the living, and to prescribe just where the dead shall be laid, and what price shall be paid for the privilege of interment. But more of this hereafter. I am dealing with a living man, and his estates, now—and with one who, in the space of a few years, has come into the possession not merely of the honors of an Archbishopric, but of princely possessions, and all as the head of a church, whose office, I had supposed, pledged him to poverty. It is not every minister of the Gospel who can thus suddenly be transformed from extreme poverty to luxury, with country seats, retainers and bountiful provisions for relatives and friends. Good Catholics tell me,—and the fact seems probable enough from the record, however violently denied—that the Archbishop is more attentive to the fleece than to the "flock committed to his care."

I must remind him, too, of that other "confession and evidence" of his—more than two years old—embodied in his Circular Letter of the 16th of March, 1852, and printed in the New York *Freeman's Journal*, wherein, as by public advertisement, he claimed for himself and others, a full legal ownership in even more than the churches of their respective Dioceses. The Archbishop then said:

"That the Catholic Bishops of New York, Albany and Buffalo, ARE NOW OWNERS IN FEE SIMPLE of nearly all religious and charitable property existing within their respective Ecclesiastical jurisdictions!"

When the Archbishop again charges me with *falsehood* he will realize what a compound of accusations he makes against himself. In self-defence I turn him over now to his circular letter, of 1852, and to his recent declaration, above quoted:—

"*The title is vested in me.*"
"I AM THE OWNER," &c. &c.

It is because the title is vested in him, and in others of similar power and state, that Trustees of his own Church have prayed the Legislature for redress. Those who build churches themselves claim the right, having paid for them with their own money, of governing the church temporalities as they please. The Legislature of this State have answered their prayers affirmatively, and hence the anathemas which he has, in his ebullitions of temper, exhausted upon me rather than upon the State.

But I shall continue my record of conveyances to-day, and hereafter, to show how far the Archbishop has been justified in accusing me of falsehood. I hope to be excused for thus furnishing him with small doses at a time. It is a rule of practice with skilful men of the Faculty, I believe, not to kill but to cure, and hence the necessity of continuing these prescriptions from day to day. I may not restore the Archbishop to a sane state of mind, nor to equanimity of bearing, but it is enough for me to know that if I have opened public wounds, so that the community can behold them, as they are, the exposure may lead to a speedier cure of the disease than would have resulted from concealment.

CONVEYANCES TO JOHN HUGHES.

NUMBER THIRTY-ONE.

Thomas Farrell, Clergyman, to John Hughes. Date of Conveyance, June 7, 1854. Record in liber 663, p. 366, June 15, 1854. Consideration one dollar.

All those certain two lots, pieces or parcel's of grounds, situate, lying and being in the Thirteenth Ward of the City of New York, on the east side of Pitt street, between Delancey and Rivington streets, known by the street numbers 54 and 36 Pitt street, said lots being each 24 feet in width in front and rear, and 100 feet in depth, be the said dimensions more or less.

THIRTY-TWO.

Richard Kein, Clergyman, to John Hughes. Date of Conveyance Feb. 10, 1853. Record in liber 687, p. 151, Jan. 17, 1854. Consideration, $1,820 50.

All that certain piece or parcel of land, situate, lying and being on the south side of Eighth street, distant 100 feet southeast from the point of intersection of the east side of Avenue B and the south side of Eighth street, thence running east along Eighth street fifteen feet, thence running south and parallel with Avenue B, ninety-seven feet and four inches to centre of block between Seventh and Eighth streets; thence running west along said centre line of the said block fifteen feet, and thence north and parallel with Avenue B, ninety-seven feet four inches to south side of Eighth street, the place of beginning.

THIRTY-THREE.

Charles Toal, and Ann, his wife, to John Hughes. (April 15, 1855, date of conveyance.) Record in liber 658, p. 669, May 8, 1854. Consideration $20,000.

All that certain lot of land situate, lying, and being in the Fourth Ward of the City of New York, and the building thereon erected, now known as the Mariners' Church, being lot No. 1,067 on the Tax Commissioner's map of Fourth Ward, and bounded and described as follows:—Beginning on W. side of Roosevelt street, at a point distant 157 feet and 11 inches, N. from NW. corner of Roosevelt and Cherry streets, running thence W. and at right angles to Roosevelt street, 61 feet and 4 inches; thence N. and parallel with Roosevelt, 71 feet 4 inches; thence E. 60 feet 10 inches to W. side of Roosevelt street; thence S. along W. side of Roosevelt street 71 feet 4 inches to the point or place of beginning.

THIRTY-FOUR.

Matthew Flynn and Margaret, his wife, to John Hughes. } Date of Conveyance April 6, 1854. Record in liber 661, p. 86, April 7, 1854. Consideration $6,000.

All those two certain lots of land, situate, lying, and being in the Sixteenth Ward of the City of New-York, and bounded, taken together, as follows:—Beginning at a point on the north line of twenty-fifth-street, distant 400 feet east from northeast corner of Ninth-avenue and twenty-fifth-street, running thence east along said northerly line 50 feet, thence north parallel with Ninth-avenue, 93 feet 9 inches to middle of block, between Twenty-fifth and Twenty-sixth-streets, and to a point equi-distant from the two, thence west parallel with Twenty-fifth-street 50 feet, thence south in a straight line to place of beginning.

THIRTY-FIVE.

Jas. D. Oliver and Sarah, his wife, to John Hughes. } Date of Conveyance May 1, 1850. Record in liber 599, p. 700, May 1, 1852. Consideration $3,500.

All that certain lot or parcel of land, situate in City of New-York, on north side of Nineteenth-street, formerly a part of the old Warren-road, which was closed by Corporation of the City of New-York, and known and distinguished on map No. 10, of an atlas made by Edwin Smith, City Surveyor, in the month of April, 1835, and entitled Atlas of that part of the Twelfth Ward of the City of New-York, between Fourteenth and Twenty-first-streets, by the number 2,495, bounded on the south, in front, by Nineteenth-street, on the west by lot number 2,494, on the north, in the rear by lot 2,805 on said map, and on the east by the centre line of the old Warren-road, being about 20 feet wide, more or less, in front and rear, and about 90 feet 1 inch deep, more or less. *Also*, all that certain other lot or parcel of land situate in the City of New-York, adjoining the lot or parcel above described, bounded on the south in front by Nineteenth-street, on the west by lot number 2,493 on the aforesaid map, on the north in the rear by lot belonging now or late to John F. Winslow, and on the east by lot number 2,495, being about 26 feet 7 inches wide (more or less) in front, about 23 feet 4 inches wide on rear, about 90 feet deep on the west side, and about 90 feet 1 inch deep on the east side.

THIRTY-SIX.

Stephen C. Burdett, and Eliza, his wife, to John Hughes.	Date of Conveyance, Nov. 27, 1852. Record in liber 699, p. 305, Dec. 1, 1852. Consideration, $4,800.

All those certain lots, pieces or parcels of land, situate, lying and being in the former Twelfth, late Sixteenth, now Eighteenth Ward of City of New-York, which said lots are bounded and described as follows, to wit:—Beginning at a lot on the southwest side of Twenty-ninth-street, distant 100 feet northwest from southwest corner of Third-avenue and Twenty-ninth-street, running thence southwest on a line parallel with Third-avenue 89 feet and 9 inches to the centre line of the block, between Twenty-Eighth and Twenty-ninth-streets, thence running northwest along said centre line 45 feet, thence northeast on a line parallel with Third-avenue 98 feet 9 inches to Twenty-ninth-street, and thence southwest along Twenty-ninth-street 45 feet, to place of beginning.

THIRTY-SEVEN.

Wm. H. De Groot and Alice, his wife, to John Hughes.	Date of Conveyance, April 15, 1853. Record, in liber 641, p. 79, April 19, 1853. Consideration, $1,400.

All those two certain lots, pieces or parcels of land, situate, lying, and being in the —— Ward of the City, County and State of New-York, bounded and described as follows:—Beginning at a point on the southerly side of Eighty-fourth-street, distant 220 feet westerly from the southwest corner of Eighty-fourth-street and Fourth-avenue, running thence westerly along the south side of Eighty-fourth-street 50 feet, running thence south and parallel with Fourth-avenue 102 feet and 2 inches, running thence east and parallel with Eighty-fourth-street 50 feet, and thence north and parallel with the Fourth-avenue 102 feet and 2 inches to place of beginning.

THIRTY-EIGHT.

Daniel Cumming, silversmith, and Mary, his wife, to John Hughes.	Date of Conveyance, April 28, 1853. Record in liber, 640, p. 383, May, 2, 1853. Consideration, $8,000.

All that certain lot, piece or parcel of land, situate, lying, and being in the Sixth Ward of City of New York, and now known by street number 29 Mott-street, and bounded and described as follows, on a map thereof, made by Edward Ludlam, City Surveyor, dated New-York, December, 1849, and filed in the office of the Register of the City and County of New-York, 24th April, 1850, that is to say:—Easterly in front, by westerly side Mott-street, 19 feet and 9 inches; southerly by land, now or late of Zion Church, 36 feet and 10 inches;

westerly by land, now or late of Luther Baldwin, and lands now or late of the estate of Cornelius Schenck, 26 feet and 2 inches; and northerly by land, now or late of John G. Flammer, 87 feet and 7 inches, as laid down on said map.

THIRTY-NINE.

Henry Heyward and Tefa, his wife, to John Hughes.	Date of Conveyance, Nov. 27, 1852. Record in liber 609, p. 342. Consideration, $8,000.

All those four certain lots, pieces or parcels of land situate, or lying and being on former Twelfth, late Sixteenth, now Eighteenth Ward of City of New-York, which said lots, taken together, are bounded and described as follows, to wit:—Beginning at a point on north side of Twenty-eighth-street, distant 123 feet west from northwest corner of Twenty-eighth-street and Third-avenue, running thence north and parallel with Third-avenue 98 feet and 9 inches, to centre line of block, between Twenty-eighth and Twenty-ninth-streets, thence west along said centre line 25 feet, thence again north and parallel with Third-avenue 98 feet and 9 inches to the south side Twenty-ninth-street, thence again west along south side Twenty-ninth-street 50 feet, thence south parallel with Third-avenue 98 feet 9 inches to the centre line of the block, thence east along said centre line 25 feet, thence again south parallel with the Third-avenue 98 feet and 9 inches, to north side of Twenty-eighth-street aforesaid, and thence again east along Twenty-eighth-street 50 feet to place of beginning; each of said lots being 25 feet in width in front and rear, and 98 feet 9 inches in length on each side.

FORTY.

Watson B. Prentiss to John Hughes.	Date of Conveyance, August, 1st, 1853. Record in liber 645, p. 201, August 31, 1853. Consideration, $4,700.

All that certain lot, piece or parcel of land situate, lying and being on south side of Eighth street, in Eleventh ward of the city of New York, and which is bounded and described as follows, viz.: commencing at a point on said south side of Eighth street, distant 115 feet south-east from the corner formed by the intersection of the east side of Avenue B and the south side of Eighth street, and running thence south-west and in a line parallel with Avenue B, 97 feet 4 inches to centre line of block between Seventh and Eighth streets; thence south-east along said centre line of the said block, and in a line parallel with Eighth street 25 feet, to the line of a lot numbered on the Ward map of the said Eleventh ward, as 2,551: thence north-east along the line of said last-mentioned lot, and in a line parallel with Avenue B, 97 feet 4 inches, to the south line of Eighth street, and thence north-east along said south line of Eighth street, 25 feet to the place of beginning.

FORTY-ONE.

Rector, Wardens and Vestry of Zion Church, to John Hughes.	Date of Conveyance, April 30, 1853. Record in liber 640, p. 380, May 2, 1853. Consideration, $30,000.

All that certain piece or parcel of ground, situate in Mott street, in Sixth ward of the city of New York, with the church edfice and school-house thereon erected, bounded and containing as follows: East in front by Mott street, westerly in rear partly by ground now or late of James Miller, partly by ground now or late James Weller's, and partly by ground now or late of James McKay, south by Cross street, and north by ground now or late of —— Williams, containing together in breadth in front on Mott street 83 feet four inches, in the rear 86 feet, and in length on each side 85 feet.

I have nothing to do with the Archbishop's elaborated charges against the "bankruptcy of less than four Boards of Catholic Lay Trustees in this city alone,"—but I claim much for the extorted admission, that "*it has been the practice*," since this bankruptcy, "*to invest* THE TITLE OF NEW CHURCHES IN THE BISHOP," and that,

"This was conformable to the discipline of the Catholic Church as regulated by the Provincial Councils of Baltimore."

But the Archbishop goes on to threaten nullification or disobedience to the Church Property Law. The other day he told the public that "*professional gentlemen were to discover some defect in the framing and wording of the enactment, which will render it inapplicable.*" Now we are more boldly informed, that nothing—

"*less than coercion will induce them to put their property and their reputation as a religious community at the irresponsible disposal of lay trustees*, armed with legal power to mortgage their property and impose upon them, as had been done already, the burden of debts by which their churches may become bankrupt and sold for the benefit of creditors."

And again:—

"And whatever law the State may pass, there is one thing certain, that nothing less than coercion will induce the Catholics to discontinue or withdraw the confidence which they have in their Bishops as the natural guardians of such property."

We shall see whether the one-man Power of the Archbishop, or the sovereign law of the people of the State of New York will prevail.

Nor do I believe that the Archbishop's churches in this city are so poor in means or in men, that Catholic Lay Trustees cannot be found of sufficient capacity and integrity to administer the dollar and cent Temporalities of the Church, quite as well as one who, towards the end of a letter—beginning with such words as "deliberate falsehoods," "brand," "theft," etc., etc.—tells us in words of meekness that he has "made an offering of his mind and heart and life for the glory of God, in promoting the spiritual and temporal welfare of the flock over whom he (I) was placed as a Pastor by the great Bishop and Shepherd of our souls."

The text and context in the judgment of even worldly men will not harmonize with each other.

But while acknowledging titles in churches and other property, the Archbishop now seeks for sympathy by pleading poverty. He owns, he tells us, "a library, and part of the furniture of the house in which he lives." It almost excites one's commiseration to read such doleful, lamb-like statements as the following:—

> "I am the owner of the bed I sleep on, but not of the roof or the walls that protect me from the inclemency of the seasons. I do not, however, complain of poverty, for I am not poor. I know that any one invested with the office which I hold in the Church of God, is the more honored in proportion as his condition assimilates to that of his Divine Master, who had not whereon to lay his head."

Alas, that one thus invested with the office of Bishop "in the Church of God," should so far forget the precepts and example of "his Divine Master," as to indulge in the foul language I have quoted, and in a denial of the statements I have proved.

The Archbishop in this Diocese has assumed a power over Church Property and Catholics unknown to the Priesthood in many of the Catholic Governments of Europe. The oppression and despotism exercised here would not be tolerated there. It is an arbitrary exercise of power, both over the living and the dead. We exhibit, therefore, in a government eminently Protestant, which separates Church and State, and which forbids all interference in matters of faith, the strange anomally of a Priesthood not only holding property worth millions in value, but ruling the members of its Church with a rod of iron.

But the wolf now clothes himself in lamb's wool, and cries humility, penance and honesty. He who had time and money to visit the island of Cuba, the gem of the seas, to pass a season of delightful luxury amidst tropical fruits and flowers, when thousands of his poor flock are cold and hungry at home,—who spends days and weeks of delightful ease within the walls of Rome,—whose steps are familiar to the interior splendors of the Vatican and the Quirinal,—who has studied Theology from the Laocoon, and Poverty in the summer gardens of the Pope,—to whom the Sistine Chapel, decorated with Raphaels and Michael Angelos, are familiar objects,—who can fly for pleasure from the city to Newfoundland or the Lakes, to the Springs, or to Newport,—who has a town residence and a country seat,—now appears before the people to state, "how poor I am," and to declare that his bed, his books, and his furniture, *in part*, are his only worldly fortune!

But enough, for to-day.

Very respectfully yours,
ERASTUS BROOKS.

NEW YORK, *April* 30.

ARCHBISHOP HUGHES TO SENATOR BROOKS.

To the Editors of the Courier and Enquirer:

Our Senator has a vague idea of respectability, under the influence of which he intimates that falsehoods, with the deliberate utterance of which he is charged, and with which no honorable man would suffer himself to be branded, are by no means complimentary to him. But it is impossible to relieve him from these charges. Falsehood he has been guilty of in almost every paragraph of his speech on the 6th of March, and of his writings in reference to it since.

For the present, I shall only enumerate the last falsehood from his pen. It is found in the following words, viz.:

> "*First now as to the parcels of property and squares of land, I enumerate the thirty-two lots of ground on 50th and 51st streets in two parcels, one three hundred and fifty feet by two hundred and ten feet ten inches, and the other, one hundred and five feet by eighty-five.*"

When Mr. Brooks wrote this, he knew as well as I do that I am not the owner of a solitary square inch of ground on 50th or 51st street, and with this knowledge in his mind, Mr. Erastus Brooks has exhibited himself in the light of a man who has no regard for veracity, and who is, therefore, utterly unworthy of notice. I take him consequently with covered hands, to the nearest open sash of a window, and send him forth with the single mental observation, "Go hence, wretched and vile insect,—the world has space for you as well as for me."

✠ JOHN, ARCHBISHOP OF NEW YORK.

NEW YORK, *May* 1, 1855.

SENATOR BROOKS TO ARCHBISHOP HUGHES.

To the Editors of the Courier and Enquirer:

The Archbishop is as profuse of epithets as ever. To-day he is brief in words and abundant in accusations. In a single paragraph he dismisses me, not for good I hope, in the following laconic and amiable manner:

> "I take him consequently with covered hands, to the nearest open sash of a window, and send him forth with the single mental observation,—Go hence, wretched and vile insect:—the world has space for you as well as me.
>
> ✠ JOHN, *Archbishop of New York.*"

Preliminary to this, are charges that "almost every paragraph of my speech on the 6th of March, and of my writings in reference to it since, are FALSE. I am "*branded*," too, again and again, as "guilty of deliberate falsehood," as "no honorable man," &c. &c. Having sufficiently damned and cursed me with his official ✠, I am taken *with covered hands* to the nearest window and dismissed "*as a wretched and vile insect.*"

But, good Archbishop, I am not to be so dismissed. You commenced the war, and I intend to end it. If the *insect* has stung you, and you have been unable either to heal the wound, or have the sting extracted, it is your fault, not mine. There is something to me even more ludicrous than wicked, if possible, in the bitterness and boldness of your denials of the truth, and in the frequency of your personalities. Early in life I was taught that in controversies and intercourse among men, no gentleman insults another, and nobody else can. I know the advantage I have over you in this respect, and mean to maintain it to the end, by an absence of all foul epithets, and all exhibitions of bad temper. You forced me into this controversy, by reiterated charges of FALSEHOOD. You endeavored to hold me up to contempt by satire and ridicule, and finding that your curses upon me, like chickens, have come home to roost upon yourself, and that your satire and ridicule have rebounded, to the point from whence they started, you now, "with covered hands," would throw the insect from the window into the street,—that is if he would let you. I shall buzz under your window, during my own good time, and, may be, find ingress again within your Grace's quarters.

This controversy commenced in an attempt to show that you were a large owner, lawfully and in your own name, of PROPERTY, and that it was repugnant to the spirit of our Government for Ecclesiastics to be large possessors of Church property. It was incidentally stated by me that you received some of this Property from Trustees. It was also stated that you owned several plats and squares of land, nearly all of them of great value. I named several parcels of this character, in the recorded conveyances of the city, as, for example, Nos. 8, 19, 23, 24, 27, 28, 29, 30, &c. Those more than make good my declaration in the Senate.

I also alluded to the 32 lots opposite the Deaf and Dumb Institution, which, after great trouble, I found, through a friend, recorded not in the Register's office, but in the office of the Comptroller.—[Book A of Deeds, page 271. Date August 1st, 1846.] I found your name acknowledging the gift of this splendid public property from this city, for the benefit of the Roman Catholics over whom you are the Chief. I found a receipt for this property signed "John Hughes," President, and by your Secretary, M. O. Donnelly.

Now, sir, though I was warranted in saying you owned *this* property, after your circular letter of the 16th of March, 1852, declaring that you did own "*in fee simple*," "*nearly all charitable and religious property existing in your Diocese*," and after your admission, in a lettter to the public, that "titles were vested in me,"—John Hughes,—"I," John Hughes,—"am the owner," and "my intention is even to add to this property by purchasing additional lots," &c, I did not, as you very well know, rely upon this rich possession, received by you, to prove your ownership in City Property generally or in squares. The public who read your letters and mine (and it is my highest wish that they should read both sides of the discussion) will condemn you both for the omission of the record of Conveyance, and the parade you make of these 32 lots of ground, which, with the Property made over to you, "your heirs and assignees," you call the "property of God," and thus evade the real, and almost the only points at issue.

It was only on the last Sabbath, when speaking in Brooklyn of the question of temporalities, you declared to the Congregation that it would be "a calamity for them and the sanctuary to have persons placed between them and the sanctuary of this holy temple, *as middle men*, *touching with profane hand the sanctuary of which they should stand in awe*, and sinking your church in debt even though you (they) had freed it from all responsibility."

And again you said:—

"But you, in the meantime should be faithful to Almighty God, and not permit men—*well meaning* men if you please, *but incompetent between the clergy and the faithful laity of the Catholic Church*—between you and the devoted pastor whom you so much respect."

Herein is shown your disrespect for popular intelligence and popular right, and your determination, notwithstanding the law of the State, not to allow Lay Trustees to control the Temporalities of the Church.

But let me compromise with you in regard to the squares on 50th and 51st streets, by substituting, if your prefer it, the property in Manhattanville, adjoining C. W. Lawrence's residence. This property covers four acres of ground, cost $32,500, and has the dwelling and grounds of the Archbishop,—though he would probably call it, "the property of God,"—while making the best possible use of it for himself and friends, as he does with the most beautiful portion of the property at Fordham.

I now add, the Catholic Almanac for the current year being my authority—the following record of Roman Catholic Church property in this city at this time. I take the word of the Archbishop himself, that he is, by the Baltimore Ordinances of '49 and '52,—by his Circular Letter of March 1852, by his Sermon on last Sabbath, against "*middle men touching with profane hands, the sanctuary of which they should stand in awe*,"—the controller, director and practical owner, even where the title does not rest in him, of all this property. Added, to what has not before been enumerated, the reader will be enabled to form some estimate of its value, by the price it would command in market, if offered for sale—I think the value of the whole "is not much short of five millions of dollars," and that the value of the Property, owned or controlled by the Archbishop, even in his territorially very limited Diocese, is worth a great deal more.

Cathedral of St. Patrick, between Prince and Houston streets.
St. Peter's, Barclay street.
St. Mary's, corner of Grand and Ridge streets.

St. Joseph's, 6th avenue, corner West Washington place.
St. James's, James street.
Transfiguration, Mott street.
St. Nicholas, 2d street.
St. Andrew's, Duane street, corner of City Hall Place.
Church of the Nativity, 2d avenue.
St. Vincent-de-Paul, Canal street.
Church of the Most Holy Reedeemer, 3d street.
St. John Baptist, 30th street.
St. Columba's, 25th street.
St. Francis', 31st street.
St. Alphonsus', Thompson street.
St. John's, Evangelist, 50th street.
St. Paul's, Harlem, 117th street.
St. Bridget's, corner of 8th street and avenue B.
St. Stephen's, Madison avenue, corner of 27th street.
St. Francis Xavier's, 16th street, between 5th and 6th avenues.
St. Ann's, 8th street, between Broadway and 4th avenue.
St. Lawrence's, 84th street.
Church of the Holy Cross, 42d street.
Convent of the Sacred Heart, Manhattanville.
St Catharine's Convent of Sisters of Mercy, Houston and Mulberry streets.
Mount St Vincent's Mother House, between 5th and 6th avenues.
Manhattanville Church of the Assumption.

I have now to add the following to the city

CONVEYANCES TO JOHN HUGHES.

NUMBER FORTY-TWO.

Abner Benedict and Hannah Catharine, his wife, to John Hughes.	Date of Conveyance March 8th, 1844; recorded in liber 443, p. 446, March 16th, 1844. Consideration, $1,950.

All and singular those six several lots, pieces, parcels and gores of land, situate, lying and being on north side of Thirty-first street, in the Sixteenth (late Twelfth) Ward, of the city of New York, and laid down and distinguished upon a certain map, made Sept. 18, 1835, by Samuel S. Doughty, City Surveyor, and filed in the office of the Clerk of the Court of Chancery; and upon which said map, the said several lots, pieces, parcels, and gores of land, hereby intended to be conveyed, are known and distinguished as numbers 4, 5, 6, 41, 42, and 43; the dimensions of the several lots, pieces, parcels, and gores of land above mentioned, being laid down and particularly specified on the map above referred to.

NUMBER FORTY-THREE.

Michael Curran, Jr., to John Hughes.	Date of Conveyance Oct. 30, 1849; recorded in liber 529, p. 173, Oct. 30, 1849. Consideration, $1.

All that certain lot, piece, or parcel of land, with the improvements thereon, situate, lying, and being in the Twelfth Ward of the city of New York; beginning at the N. E. corner of Fifth Avenue and Fiftieth street, and running thence N. along the E. side of Fifth Avenue 100 feet and five inches, to a point equi-distant from Fiftieth and Fifty-first streets, thence S. and parallel with Fifth Avenue, 100 feet and 5 inches, to Fiftieth street, thence W. along Fiftieth street 100 feet to place of beginning.

NUMBER FORTY-FOUR.

William Wood and Edward Wood, Executors of John Wood, to John Hughes.	Date of Conveyance May 1, 1850; recorded in liber 378, p. 372, June 12, 1851. Consideration, $700.

All that certain piece or parcel of ground, situate, lying, and being in the Fourth Ward of the city of New York, in the interior of the block, being in the rear of the building now fronting on James street, called Christ Church, and partly in the rear of an alley or passage way leading along the north side of the church, bounded as follows: Beginning at a point distant 100 feet east from James street, and 100 feet north from Madison street, thence east parallel with Madison street 32 feet 6 inches, to ground formerly the Jews' burying ground, now belonging to party of third part, thence north parallel with James street 26 feet 3 inches, to ground late of Robert Brown, thence west parallel with Madison street 32 feet 6 inches, and thence south parallel with James street 26 feet 3 inches, to place of beginning.

NUMBER FORTY-FIVE.

Thomas Smith and Ann, his wife, of Baltimore, Md., Patrick Smith and Mary, his wife, of Ohio, and Peter Smith and Ellen, his wife, of Brooklyn, to John Hughes.	Date of Conveyance Oct. 8, 1850; recorded in liber 553, p. 369, Oct. 9, 1850. Consideration, $5,500.

All that certain house and lot of land, situated on west side of Oliver street, in the Fourth Ward of the city of New York, which said house is now known as No. 23 in said street, and which said lot is designated as lot No. 5, on a map dated Jan 13, 1832, made by Thomas R. Ludlam, City Surveyor, the said lot being on file in the Register's office, in the case No. 57, the said lot being more particularly described, as follows: Beginning on the said west side of Oliver street aforesaid, at a point at the middle or centre of the brick part of the party wall, which divides the said house from the adjoining house, known as No. 25 in said street, said adjoining house being on the lot designated as No. 6 on map aforesaid; running thence north from said point along said west side of Oliver street 21 feet 11 inches, to a point in the centre of the brick part of the party wall which divides the said house hereby conveyed from adjoining house known as No. 21

in said street, said house being on lot designated as No. 4 on said map; thence west in a straight line through the said middle of the said brick part of the said party wall, and the south side of the said lot designated as No. 4, 69 feet and 1 inch, to land now or late of Samuel Milbank; thence south along the said last mentioned land 21 feet 11 inches, to the adjoining lot first above mentioned; thence east in a straight line along north line of said lot, and passing through the middle or centre of said brick part of party wall, first above mentioned, 70 feet 1 inch to place of beginning.

NUMBER FORTY-SIX.

Rev. Felix Varelia, to John Hughes. Date of Conveyance April 23, 1850; recorded in liber 554, p. 486, Nov. 1, 1850. Consideration, $30,000.

All those two certain lots of ground, situated, lying, and being on the north side of Chambers street, in the city of New York, and which on a map or survey made by Cassimer Thos. Goerck, City Surveyor, bearing date May 7, 1795, are known and distinguished by lots Nos. 16 and 17 adjoining each other, and are together bounded south by Chambers street, north by lots numbered 36 and 37 on said map, west by lot No. 15 on said map, and east by lot No. 18 on said map, being together in breadth in front and rear 50 feet, and in length 75 feet 7½ inches, agreeably to said map. Also, all that certain messuage, or dwelling house and lot, piece or parcel of ground, situate, lying and being in Reade street, in the city of New York, and described in a certain indenture of deed, recorded in the Register's office in liber 133 of conveyances, and page 11, as follows, viz.: All that certain lot, piece, or parcel of ground, situate, lying and being in Reade street, in the Sixth Ward of the city of New York, known and distinguished by the No. 23, bounded north in front by Reade street aforesaid; southerly on the rear of ground claimed by John Agnew; westerly by ground belonging to George Brinkerhoff, and easterly by ground claimed by the heirs of Peter Nailor, containing in breadth in front and rear 25 feet, and in length on each side 75 feet 7 inches.

RECAPITULATION IN PART.

Conveyances to John Hughes.	Lots.	Place.
Trustees of St. John's R. C. Church,	3	16th Ward.
Patrick Doherty,	1	117th street.
George Wilds, et als.,	2	25th street.
Ebbe Marie,	3	6th Ward.
D. D. Field, et als.,	2	16th Ward.
William Patton, D. D., et als.,	1	2d avenue.
B. O'Connor, Trustee Christ Church,	4	James street.
George Cammann, et als.,	1	See No. 9.
Andrew Byrne,	3	11th Ward.
Andrew Byrne,	1	17th Ward.
Z. Kuntze,	2	16th Ward.

Conveyances to John Hughes.	Lots.	Place.
James Foster,	2	11th Ward.
Sarah Remsen,	1	11th Ward.
James Rea,	1	14th Ward.
G. W. Hall,	6	14th Ward.
George W. Coster,	1	Avenue B.
Mary Ann Gaffney, et als.,	2	Madison avenue.
Westervelt, Sheriff,	4	117th & 118th sts.
R. Klein,	1	11th Ward.
Gregory Dillon,	5	3d Ward.
Trustees of Transfiguration Church,	2	Chambers street.
Peter Johnson, et als.,	2	18th Ward.
Michael McKean, et als.,	2	9th Ward.
T. E. Davis, et als.,	1	12th Ward.
James R. Bayley,	1	Lease.
Thomas London,	4	19th street.
H. Grinnell,	4	14th street.
G. W. Lawrence,	6	12th Ward.
S. Newby, et als.,	4	42d street.
Thomas Farrell,	2	13th Ward.
William H. De Groot,	2	4th avenue.
D. Cummings, et als.,	1	Mott street.
Zion's Church,	1	6th Ward.
Henry Hayward, et als.,	4	18th Ward.
Walson B. Prentiss,	1	11th Ward.
Charles Toal, et als.,	1	4th Ward.
Walter Flynn, et als.,	2	9th av. & 25th st.
James D. Oliver, et als.,	1	19th street.
Stephen C. Burdett,	2	18th Ward.
Edward C. Richards,	1	3d avenue.
Thomas Smith, et als.,	1	4th Ward.
Rev. Felix Varelia,	2	Chambers street.
Abner Benedict, et als.,	6	16th Ward.
Michael Curran, Jr.,	1 sq're	12th Ward.
William Wood, et als.,	1	4th Ward.
Number,	101	

I am now, gentlemen, in the condition of one who has been an expected heir to a large fortune, from a rich citizen—the expectancy being founded upon conditions on my part, and promises on his. The conditions imposed upon me were three in number, (both agreeing, at the start, that the fortune should go to found a Public Library).

First.—That I would prove the promised donor to be the rich citizen I had previously declared him to be.

Secondly.—That I would show that he had received conveyances of property from trustees. And

Finally.—That I would prove this rich citizen (meaning Archbishop Hughes all the time), had a great fortune in this city.

The promise was, that if I proved all this, the city of our common residence should have a public edifice, to be called "The Erastus Brooks Library."

My records to-day and before, give good evidence that I have offered good proof as to the first, second, and third of my propositions. The only doubt there can be, is as to the second, and I therefore put the Archbishop's statements and my facts side by side:

STATEMENT.	FACT.
"I have always denied that I ever asked, sought, received or accepted any property from lay trustees. This denial I repeat to day with increased emphasis.—[5th letter of John Hughes. "I have never received or accepted ANY transfer of *any* property whatever from trustees."—[1st letter of John Hughes.	"Trustees of St. John's Roman Catholic Church, to John Hughes. Lease 999 years—consideration one cent a year—liber 451—page 249—July 20, 1844." "Trustees of the Transfiguration Church, to John Hughes."—Liber 591, p. 268. "Bartholomew O'Connor," Assignee of a Board of Trustees, to John Hughes."

And now, where are the promises of the Archbishop? Where is the Public Library? What is to become of the people's interest in this controversy, and which, in order that I might win an institution for them, was with me the grand motive for prosecuting it in so much detail, and at so much length?

Encouraged by the hope of seeing this Public Library established, I have resorted, first to the books, to see what is meant by property; and finding it to mean "ownership," "possession in one's own right," "that to which *a person has a legal title, whether in his possession or not*—an estate, whether in lands, goods or money; I have investigated the case, on this basis, and claim the reward.

But have I proved my case? Fortunately, the Depository of the Records of Private Property—in order that every man owning an estate, may record and show his claim—is open for public inspection. I have resorted to the office of the Sworn Register of the City, and among the deeds and conveyances, I find, in the first place, a large number of conveyances of valuable property to John Hughes, his heirs and assignees. They include all kinds of property, ecclesiastical and secular. So far, all is well.

I look further, and find a lease for 999 years, consideration one cent a year, from the Trustees of St. John's Roman Catholic Church. This lease I had called "property," because law and custom so describe it. I look further, and I find a conveyance "from the Trustees of Transfiguration Church," to the same John Hughes; and if I could be mistaken about the fact, that a 999 years' lease, at one cent a year, is property, I am no longer in doubt, for here is no limitation in time. Pursuing my investigation, I also find a conveyance from one Bartholomew O'Connor, who is acknowledged to be the assignee of "a Board of Trustees," to John Hughes.

And I might enumerate almost without limit. But, *Cui Bono?* I claim that the Archbishop shall make good his promise. I demand, for the people of the city, the Public Library. If the Archbishop will not trust me, I renew the offer to leave the case out to arbitration.

I propose again that John Hughes shall name one person, I a second, and the two selected shall elect a third, to decide, not so much upon this question of veracity between us,—for that is a matter more personal than public,—but what is more important, whether I, upon the record, have not made out a good claim to that Public Library, promised, upon certain conditions specified, in the Archbishop's first letter. I rely upon the record and the fact. I know no distinction between John Hughes, and ✠ John Hughes, Archbishop. The record is of property which he claims and acknowledges to be his, or which is in his own name, and that of his heirs and assignees. It is his to give away, will away, sell away, and dispose of as he pleases. The following record of a conveyance *from* him *to others*, will show that he is as prompt to sell as to buy :

DEED MADE THE SIXTH DAY OF JANUARY, 1853.
JOHN HUGHES
TO
HARLEM RAILROAD COMPANY.
Consideration of $46,000.

All those certain lots, pieces or parcels of land, situate, lying and being in the Eighteenth Ward of the city of New York, on the easterly side of Madison avenue, and the southerly side of Twenty-seventh street.

Recorded April 2, 1853, in liber 616, p. 640.

If this, which was Church property, was "property of God," how could John Hughes sell it? If it was not his own property, how could he deed it away in fee to others? Would not the Harlem Railroad Company do well to look to the validity of a title received from a man who sells "the property of God," and conveys away property which he declares he does not own?

Yours respectfully, for to-day,
ERASTUS BROOKS.

NEW YORK, *May 2d.*

A CARD FROM ARCHBISHOP HUGHES.

TO THE PUBLIC.

The citizens of New York, and of the United States, must have seen, and the decent portion of them must have regretted, the progress of what seemed to be a controversy between the undersigned and Mr. Erastus Brooks, Senator of the State of New York. The point involved is a point of veracity, in which Senator Brooks is responsibly charged with falsehood, and although the case would warrant it, the charge has not been extended to a more degrading term. The undersigned, although not born in this country, is far from being insensible or indifferent to the necessity of maintaining an honorable character for those who represent its high functions in the Legislature, the Judiciary, or the Executive. And it is no pleasure to him, but directly the reverse, that Senator Brooks has placed it in his power, and made it of obligation for him to prove, as he is quite prepared to do, that he, the said Senator Brooks, is a man of falsehood.

All this shall appear in less than ten days from the date of this card.

In the mean time, the undersigned feels humbled at the necessity of saying or writing any thing which should bring infamy or disgrace upon his country, even though the falsehoods of a person like Senator Brooks should be the immediate occasion of it.

The physical and material powers of the United States are becoming more and more recognized from day to day by the civilized nations of the world. Unfortunately the moral attributes of our progressive greatness are, in the estimation of the same nations, sinking from day to day. And what with the unfavorable portion that is perhaps true in this unsettled account, and the prejudices of foreign nations who are unprepared to believe any favorable report in our regard, the probability is, that whether we like it or not, our course in the esteem of the civilized world, has at this moment a rather downward tendency.

The undersigned is but a cypher, yet he feels an interest in the reputation, honor, prosperity and progress of the United States, which makes it a very painful duty for him to charge any one who has officiated as a Senator of the country at large, or of a particular State, with falsehood.

But under present circumstances there is no alternative. He charges Senator Brooks with multiplied and deliberate falsehoods, and he only solicits from the rightmindedness and patience of the American public a suspension of judgment for ten days.

In the mean time, it would be unbecoming and perfectly disgusting in the eyes of foreign journalists, and his own countrymen at home. as well as humiliating and painful to his own feelings, to see and read in the American journals, that a Roman Catholic Archbishop, who claims to be an American, and who, if he is not an American, has no right or claim on any other country in the world, should appear as the accuser of an American Senator, whose place of nativity is unquestioned, charging upon the same Senator falsehoods deliberately and repeatedly uttered. This is the issue to which Mr. Erastus Brooks has urged and brought me. I meet it. And while I shield as much as possible the dignity of character which is implied by the word *Senator*, I hope that the justice of American public opinion will give me full liberty to repel and expose the falsehoods of the *man* called Erastus Brooks. I appeal with entire confidence to the patience, as well as justice, of that American public opinion, which has never disappointed me in matters of truth and justice, for a suspense of ten days or two weeks.

✠ JOHN, Archbishop of New York.

New York, *May* 3, 1855.

SENATOR BROOKS *vs.* ARCHBISHOP HUGHES.

To the Editors of the Courier & Enquirer:

The Archbishop is not content to leave "the wretched and vile insect, Senator Brooks," where he thrust him in his letter of Wednesday last,—"outside of the nearest open sash of a window." As I expected, I am again "worthy of the notice" of the Archbishop. I am recalled to his closet to be blessed again with such amiable epithets as "falsehood," "deliberate falsehoods," repeated, and even duplicated, six times, in seven brief paragraphs.

All this has been said so many times, and in so many ways and forms of phrase, that the Archbishop seems to be apprehensive that the public will forget the harsh names he has called me. I admit that he has called me all these things, and that the public may not forget them, I intend to have them stereotyped.

admit their high, official origin,—"✠ John, Archbishop of New York." I have recorded their frequency by quotation, and by the republication of all the Archbishop's epistles,—but I have not been so impressed with their appropriateness, coming from one who so recently formally proclaimed that he was "invested with an office in the Church of God, which assimilated to that of his Divine Master, who had not whereon to lay his head."

It is more than three weeks since the Archbishop addressed his first contemptuous letter to me,—because of a paragraph in my speech of the 6th March last, wherein I ventured to "SUPPOSE,"—that was the word, sir,—that "the value of the amount of property held by John Hughes in this city was worth not much short of five millions of dollars,"—and wherein I stated, as proofs in part, that "A FRIEND OF MINE" had copied 58 entries of as many distinct parcels of property held in this name. I was careful of my statement and of my authority, who, in this case, was a city lawyer, in good standing, a member of a Christian Church, and a gentleman. It was his copies of "the number, book, and page" of the Register's office, that I exhibited, as stated in my speech to the Senate, along with a huge volume, rare with American readers, but familiar to you, I suppose, entitled "Corpus Juris Canonici Academicum," and a book, equally rare among Protestants, known as the "Pontificate Romanum," from both of which I may have something to read to the public by and by.

How I could be justly charged with FALSEHOOD for a *supposition* of fact as to your wealth, founded upon such a record, passed my dull comprehension. If I should *suppose* John Jacob Astor worth $10,000,000, and his property, in value, should turn out to be even greatly less, I could hardly be called, by a Christian or a gentleman, a liar. If I should state the authority and reason for that *supposition*, an intelligent and honest public, or person, would hardly see the justice for reiterating, from day to day, and from week to week,—all the time without any proof to the contrary of the supposed fact,—the cry of "*falsehood.*"

But, as three weeks have not afforded time enough to prove

that "Senator Brooks is a man of falsehood," the Archbishop now, in "A Card to the Public," desires "the citizens of New York and of the United States," to suspend their judgment for "*ten days or two weeks longer.*" By all means. As many days or weeks as you please. Confined to my room and bed for some days past, by an illness contracted in Albany, I shall be better able to meet you then than now, though, God giving me strength, I am ready now, to meet you, step by step, and day by day, as long as you please.

I have two or three letters more in preparation as to your property, and practices in regard to it, in and out of the city, which, as convenience may suit me, I may or may not publish in advance of your promised concentrated labor of "ten days or two weeks" against me.

I am, for to-day, very respectfully yours,

ERASTUS BROOKS.

NEW YORK, *May* 4, 1855.

ARCHBISHOP HUGHES TO THE PUBLIC.

"* * * * MATER VERITATIS DIES NON PERMISSURA SIT LONGUM FRAUDIBUS REGNUM."—GROTIUS, *de Imp. S. P.* 100 *b.* 6.

"* * * * LIGHT, THE MOTHER OF TRUTH, WILL NOT PERMIT DECEPTION TO ENJOY A LONG REIGN."

During the last session of the New York Legislature, a petition was presented by the Trustees of St. Louis Church, Buffalo, complaining of pretended grievances which they had suffered, as they alleged, at the hands of their ecclesiastical superiors, and praying for an act of civil legislation, on the part of the State, by which their religious grievances might be brought to an end, and similar ones henceforth prevented in other congregations. In that petition they averred, among other numerous falsehoods, that "Bishop Hughes had attempted to compel them (the Trustees) to make the title of their church over to him." The Hon. Mr. Putnam drafted a bill of contingent confiscation and penalties against the Catholics of this State, unless their Bishops should henceforth govern and regulate all matters affecting church property, according to the provisions of the Act. The undersigned denied that there was one word, or syllable, or letter of truth in the statement quoted from the petition; and Mr. Wm. B. Le Couteulx has since admitted its entire falsehood, even while attempting to vindicate his own course and that of his fellow-trustees. Notwithstanding the falsehoods of his petition, they are entirely adopted by Mr. Putnam, and the one already mentioned is specially incorporated in his speech in favor of the bill. There is no evidence that Mr. Putnam was then aware of the falsehood which he had adopted from the text of the petition. But he must be aware of it now.

Mr. Senator Brooks of this city, also made a speech on the same side. By him the falsehood or falsehoods of the Buffalo petition adopted by Mr. Senator Putnam, were entirely thrown in the shade by the gigantic scale on which he projected his. According to him, Bishop Hughes was the owner, in his own personal right, of an immense amount of real estate in the city of New York. He supposed its value to be little short of $5,000,000. It consisted, according to him, of no less than fifty-eight distinct parcels of real estate, some of them covering "whole squares of land," and all recorded in the Register's office, to the number of fifty-eight entries. Of this property there were, according to Mr. Brooks, "numerous transfers from Trustees," and, lest any Senator should doubt his veracity, he sported a pretended reference as from the records in the Register's Office, giving book, number, and page, for the correctness of his statements.

One is at a loss whether to be surprised more at the boldness of this man's falsehoods, or at the imbecile credulity of a public, calling itself enlightened, who, nevertheless, seemed to receive his statements as so many gospel truths.

Shortly after my return from Europe, I called the attention of Senator Brooks to the wantonness and extravagance of his assertions. My letter was written in a spirit of playfulness. I intimated that after reserving to myself, against the wants of old age, out of this property little short of five millions, as Mr. Brooks had asserted, the sum of two millions, I should appropriate all the balance, say two millions seven hundred and fifty thousand dollars, to the founding of a magnificent library, which should be worthy of New York, and as I was indebted to the Senator for my immense fortune, it should bear his name and be called "THE ERASTUS BROOKS LIBRARY."

I intimated, however, in a tone sufficiently serious to attract his attention, that his statements were untrue, and I called upon him either to prove or retract them. He chose the alternative of proof, and the public will see how desperate is the condition of a man who undertakes to prove a falsehood:—since truth will ever scorn to be a hand maid in such an enterprise, and will leave him entirely dependent on his ingenuity for the invention of secondary falsehoods in support of those which were primary.

Out of this grew the late controversy between Mr. Brooks and myself. It was not my business to prove that the statements of his speech were false. It was his to prove them true. It was but fair that he should have full scope to accomplish this awful task in his own way, and the public have witnessed the industry with which he has prosecuted the work.

It has been matter of surprise to some that I should not have had at any moment my proofs at hand to refute both the primary and secondary falsehoods of Mr. Brooks. In other words, that I was not prepared to prove a negative, which no man has ever done by direct argument, and which no man can ever do. The proof of a negative must always be by deduction from argument which is positive; and how could I bring my proofs of a negative through the medium of positive facts to a close until Mr. Brooks should have completed his whole winding and tortuous career of mendacity? I believe he has done this, at least. And now it is time for me to bring my positive facts to bear upon his positive falsehoods, scatter them to the winds, and leave him standing before the community a self-degraded, self-ruined man. But before I commence, it is proper to state, that whatever property may be found on the records of the Register's Books in the city of New York, in my name, is in equity and truth, though not in its legal form, the property of the several congregations to be enumerated hereafter; that the management of this property has been, by a rule of the Diocese, dating as far back as 1843, in the hands of the respective pastors of each congregation, who are required to associate with them one or two respectable and competent laymen to assist them in the administration of the temporalities of their church—to keep regular accounts of its income, its expenditures, &c.—to make and publish from time to time, at least once a year, a report of the condition of the church, to be distributed among their pew-holders, and a copy of the same to be forwarded to the archiepiscopal residence, in order to have it inserted in a diocesan register kept for that purpose. The title of their church lots was vested nominally in the Bishop. But he never considered this as giving him any more right to the ownership, in the sense of Mr. Brooks, than he would have to regard as his own an offering of charity handed to him for the benefit of the Orphan Asylum. Neither has he ever received so much as one farthing of revenue, or income, from this property, in consequence of his nominal ownership. Neither has he troubled himself with the management of the temporalities of these congregations, except in so far as to prevent the church property from being mortgaged, or exposed to alienation, as had been the case under the irresponsible management of lay trustees. Whenever the Clergyman and his advisers reported to the Bishop the expediency of their doing something in regard to such property, he acquiesced, as often as his judgment approved of their proposal. In this way, deeds, and titles, and transfers, and mortgages, &c., were brought to him from time to time for signature, and as a matter of course he went through the legal formality of appending his name. So also when new lots were purchased for the erection of new churches, required by the increasing numbers of the faithful, the deed was made out in the Bishop's name,—and the local pastor and his associates managed all the rest.

It is hardly to be wondered at, therefore, that the Bishop himself should have been almost taken by surprise by the display of documents exhibited by Mr. Brooks, purporting to be extracts from the records in the Register's Office. The Archbishop was perfectly aware, in a general way, that Mr. Brooks had entered boldly on a career of falsehood, but he was not prepared to suppose that a Senator of the State of New York, in order to brazen it out against him, would have dared to falsify the public records. This, however, Mr. Brooks has done.

Before proceeding to exhibit the secondary falsehoods of Mr. Brooks more at length, I shall give a statement of all the property recorded in my name in the Register's Office on the day of the Senator's speech. It is the same to-day, as nothing has been added to or taken from it since.

The property, then, which is recorded in my name, is the aggregate of lots on which fifteen different Catholic congregations have their places of worship, their priests' residences, and in some instances their schools. The number of these lots is seventy-seven, (77,) giving a fraction over five lots each for the church edifices of these fifteen congregations. I am told by competent judges, that if these lots were to be sold, the buildings on them, though exceedingly valuable to the Catholics as places for the purposes of Divine public worship, would not add to their value in the estimation of purchasers. I am further told by competent judges, that, scattered as they are at various points, from Barclay street to Manhattanville, they would not fetch more, one with the other, than five thousand dollars each lot. This would produce, as the total value of property recorded in the Register's office, in the name of the Archbishop :

The sum of	$385,000
But in the same Register's office there are recorded as incumbrances on these seventy-seven lots, mortgages to the amount, in the aggregate, of................	245,640
Reducing the net value of property recorded in the name of Archbishop HUGHES, to the alarming sum, (not of a "little short of $5,000,000," but) of........	$139,360

It is to be observed that before the Archbishop realized, even this sum, it would be necessary for him not only to become a dishonest man, but also to go through the process of turning fifteen Catholic congregations, with their respective priests, into the streets of the city.

Such are the length and breadth, and height and depth, of all the real estate recorded in the name of Archbishop Hughes in the books of the Register's office. I trust the Protestant community will breathe more freely in consequence of knowing this fact. I trust also that our Catholic laity will be prepared better to give an answer, when the supposed immense wealth of their Archbishop is made a reproach to them. I may as well add here, that the property of the Cathedral, including Calvary

Cemetery, is managed by the Board of Trustees of St. Patrick's Church; that they receive and expend, and keep an account of all income and all outlay connected with their trust; that the Archbishop's relation to it, is precisely the same as that of his predecessor; that he has no personal income to the amount of one farthing, from these revenues, except what is annually appropriated by the Board for his decent maintenance;—that the sum thus apportioned, though sufficient, is yet moderate enough, and that if it is not more, the reason is that the Archbishop has more than once declined to accept a larger amount.

There was a period during the late controversy between Mr. Brooks and myself, when I almost doubted whether falsehood would not gain the victory over truth. A perfect novice as regards deeds and titles and formalities of law, I should not have known where to commence my refutation of the man of falsehood. Accordingly, I referred the matter to two respectable legal gentlemen, namely, Messrs. T. James Glover and W. C. Wetmore. When I asked the public to suspend their judgment for ten days or two weeks, it was that these gentlemen might have time to examine the records in the Register's office. This they have done. They have followed Mr. Brooks, number by number. They have examined every thing alleged by him as on the authority of the public records, and from their reliable statement now submitted, I shall be able to show that Mr. Brooks has been guilty of numerous, deliberate, and wilful falsehoods, including the daring experiment of perverting and falsifying the very records which he pretended to cite. Here are the letter and Report of Messrs. Glover and Wetmore:

To the Most Rev. Archbishop Hughes.

In compliance with your request, we have examined the various records of conveyances to you, mentioned in the several letters of Senator Brooks, as well as others made by you; and we beg leave to present to you, as the result of such examination, the accompanying report, upon the accuracy of which you may confidently rely.

We have only to observe that the respective deeds are numbered to correspond with the numbers used by Senator Brooks, and that those which are not noticed, are correctly cited by him, except some inaccuracies of reference.

We have the honor to be with great respect,
Your obedient servants,
(Signed) T. JAMES GLOVER.
W. C. WETMORE.

NEW YORK, *May* 11, 1855.

REPORT.

No. I. Is a lease for 999 years, at a nominal rent, but with a covenant on the part of the lessee to maintain a Church according to the rites and discipline of the Roman Catholic Church.

No. II. Is an assignment of a lease affecting the *same premises mentioned in No. XIX.*

The lots belonging to St. Paul's Church at Harlem, were assessed for the opening of 117th street, in 1840. They were sold to P. Doherty, for non-payment of the assessment, and the same not being redeemed were leased to him by the Mayor, &c., of the City of New York, for twenty years. This is the lease assigned by P. Doherty to the Rt. Rev. John Hughes, as stated in No. II. The identical premises were conveyed by the Sheriff in an execution sale against the Trustees of St. Paul's Church, to the Rt. Rev. John Hughes, as set out in No. XIX. The two deeds convey but one and the same piece of property.

No. III. Is between the same parties and for the same premises mentioned in No. VII.

No. VI. Is a deed by Patten and wife of the half part of a vault for burial on the premises mentioned in No. X.

No. VII. Is the same as No. III. as above stated.

No. VIII. is correctly stated, as follows:

Bartholomew O'Connor of the 1st part, to Rt. Rev. John Hughes of the 2d part.	Deed dated 7th Feb., rec. 22 Sept., 1845. lib. 465, p. 415.

This deed cites a conveyance by the Trustees of Christ Church to Bartholomew O'Connor, dated, 5th January, 1843, whereby the Trustees with the consent of the Court of Chancery, assigned their lands, &c., upon trust to sell the same, and out of the proceeds to pay their creditors. It then, in consideration of $42,000, conveys the four lots on James street, and also the vestments, church furniture, and organ. Mr. O'Connor is nowhere styled *Trustee to Christ Church, nor Trustee of Christ Church.* Nor was he such in fact or in law, nor can he with propriety be so styled. He was simply an assignee for the benefit of Creditors, by virtue of an assignment made Jan. 1843, and conveyed the premises in February, 1845, to Rt. Rev. John Hughes in the same manner as he might have done to any other purchaser.

No. IX.—Is a conveyance of the property of the Sacred Heart at Manhattanville, the whole of which was subsequently conveyed by the Rt. Rev. John Hughes to Aloysia Hardy, by deed dated 10 Feb. 1847, recorded on 17th January, 1848, lib. 497, p. 292.

No. XI. The premises mentioned in this deed, executed by Z. Kantze, though separately numbered on the map, really form but one lot, having a front on the street of twenty-five feet by about one hundred and sixty feet deep.

Nos. XIV., XV., and XVI. all relate to the property of the Convent of Mercy. No. XIV. is an assignment of a lease for life of one lot on Mulberry street. No. XV. is a confirmation of a previous deed by the attorney in fact of Mr. Rea, to W. H. Butler—the power of attorney having been lost. No. XIV. is the main source of title to this property.

The whole of it was conveyed by the Most Rev. John Hughes to "The Institution of Mercy," as soon as incorporated, according to law, by deed dated 1st June, 1854; rec. 15th June, 1854, lib. 663, p. 368.

No. XVII. is a conveyance of a "strip of land," *not a lot, being only two inches in width* by 100 feet in depth, adjoining another lot.

No. XVIII. is the conveyance of an irregular piece of land at the corner of 27th st. and Madison avenue; on the preceding page of the record is a release of dower in the same premises in consideration of $3,377 63.

The whole of this piece of land was conveyed by the Most Rev. Archbishop to the Harlem Railroad Company, by deed dated 6th Jan. 1853; recorded 2d April, 1853, lib. 616, p. 640.

No. XIX. is the sheriff's deed mentioned above under the head of No. II., and conveys the same premises.

No. XXII. is a deed of confirmation of the same premises described in No. XLVI. The latter (No. XLVI.) is a deed from Rev. Felix Varela, to the Most Rev. John Hughes, of the property known as Transfiguration Church. It bears date April 23, 1850, and was recorded on the 1st day of November, 1850, in liber 554, page 486. The conveyance No. XXII. bears date December 9th, 1851, and was recorded on ——, in liber 591, page 268. This deed recites upon its face an order of the Supreme Court, dated November 22d, 1851, authorizing the Trustees to execute it *in confirmation of the title* of the grantee.

The whole of these premises mentioned in the above deeds, was conveyed by the Most Rev. Archbishop to L. J. Wyeth, by deed dated May 2d, 1853; recorded the same day, liber 640, page 464.

No. XXVI. is an assignment of a lease for the unexpired portion of a term, having originally three years and six months to run from November 1st, 1850.

No. XLI. is a conveyance from the Corporation of the Protestant Episcopal Church, known as Zion's Church.

No. XLIII. is a conveyance of four lots, on the corner of Fifth avenue and Fiftieth street—being 100 feet 5 inches on the avenue, by

100 feet in depth. It is not a conveyance of "a square of land," in the sense in which the term is used; nor, indeed, in any sense.

But the entire premises described in this deed, were conveyed by the Most Rev. Archbishop Hughes to the Trustees of St. Patrick's Cathedral, by deed dated February 8th, 1853; recorded March 9th, 1853, liber 630, page 337.

No. XLVI. has been already disposed of.

The deed of the Orphan Asylum property is correctly stated as follows: The Mayor, Aldermen, &c., of the city of New York, of the first part, to the Roman Catholic Orphan Asylum Society, in the city of New York, of the second part—deed dated August 1st, 1846; recorded Book A of Deeds, page 271, Comptroller's office—conveys a piece of land on Fifth avenue, between Fifty-first and Fifty-second streets, and extending easterly 450 feet, upon condition that the parties of the second part erect thereon, within three years, a building to be approved by the Mayor, and that they keep the premises for the purposes contemplated by their charter. The counterpart is signed by the President and Secretary of the Board of Trustees of the Asylum.

(Signed) T. James Glover.
W. C. Wetmore.

The foregoing authentic statements, taken from the records, will warrant me in summing up the results of the examination made by Messrs. Glover and Wetmore, as follows:

I. Mr. Brooks has *falsified* the record, by styling Bartholomew O'Connor "Trustee to Christ Church."

II. He falsely cited the deed from the Trustees of Transfiguration Church, executed in 1851. The *falsehood* consisted in suppressing what appears upon the face of that deed—that it was simply in *confirmation* of a title previously vested in the Archbishop. The premises had been, in truth, conveyed to him by Rev. F. Varela, in 1850.

III. He intentionally falsifies, when he declares that the deed of Michael Curran conveyed "a square of land."

IV. He wilfully counts the following premises *twice:*

1st. The property of St. Paul's Church,—first, under the lease from P. Doherty, and again under the deed from Westervelt.

2d. The half part of a vault for burial, under the deed from Patten and wife, the same having been embraced in the premises conveyed by Rev. Andrew Byrne.

3d. The lot described in deed from Mr. Rea,—first, under that deed, and again under the deed from G. W. Hall.

4th. The Transfiguration Church property,—first, under the Varela deed, and again under the deed of confirmation.

V. He includes the following property, though conveyed away by the Archbishop:

1st. The property of the Sacred Heart at Manhattanville.
2d. The property of the Convent of Mercy.
3d. The property at the corner of Madison avenue and Twenty-seventh street. He will not deny that he knew the Archbishop conveyed away this property, for he cites the deed to the Harlem Railroad Company in the very letter in which he falsely attributes to the Archbishop the ownership of it.
4th. The property of the Transfiguration Church. Not content with setting it down as still vested in the name of the Archbishop, though he conveyed it away two years ago, Mr. B. counts it twice.
5th. The four lots at the corner of Fifth avenue and Fiftieth street.

VI. He counts the following as entire lots:

1st. The half of a vault for burial.
2d. The "strip of land," two inches wide, conveyed by Costar's executors.
3d. A piece of land, 15 feet by 97 feet 4 inches, conveyed by R. Kein.
4th. A piece of land, 26 feet 3 inches by 32 feet 6 inches, conveyed by Wood's executors.

VII. He counts the leasehold lot assigned by J. R. Bayley, although the term expired on the 1st of May, 1854.

VIII. He counts the property conveyed by Z. Kantze as two lots—the same forming, in truth, but one.

This reduces the number of deeds of lots now vested in the Archbishop, to 32; and reduces the lots themselves from 101 to 77, as follows:

Whole number of deeds quoted by Mr. Brooks, ...		46
Actual number as taken from the records in the Register's office,		32
Difference, ...		14
Whole number of lots stated by Mr. Brooks, ...		101
Strike out the following	lots.	
1. Lease—St. John's, ...	3	
2. " J. R. Bayley; expired May, 1854, . .	1	

3.	"	P. Doherty; counted twice,	1	
4.	Deed—	Patten, " "	1	
5.	"	James Rea, " "	1	
6.	"	Trustees of Transfiguration Church; counted twice,	2	
7.	"	Commann; conveyed away,	1	
8.	"	G. W. Hall, "	6	
9.	"	M. A. Gafney, "	2	
10.	"	Rev. F. Varela, "	2	
11.	"	Michael Curran, "	1 "square"	
12.	"	Costar's executors; a strip,	1	
13.	"	P. Kein; part of lot,	1	
14.	"	Wood's executors; part of lot,	1	
		Making in all,		24

Which, subtracted from 101, as reported by Mr. Brooks, leaves a balance, as has been elsewhere mentioned, of lots, ... 77

It would require a small volume to develope, at length, all the circumstances of meanness, that characterize the falsehoods of which Mr. Brooks has been guilty. I may say, in general, that all falsehoods range themselves either under one or other of these two heads, namely: the assertion of something that has no existence in reality, or the denial of something which has. It follows, therefore, that falsehood has no real existence, except as the negative of truth; and, consequently, that what is called public opinion, has no power to create truth from falsehood, or to destroy truth and render it false. Public opinion, to be worth any thing as regards things which exist, or things which do not, ought to be the legitimate offspring of truth—its creature, not its creator. A friend of mine has preserved some four columns of scraps, from different newspapers, published for the most part in the interior, as evidence of public opinion in regard to the late controversy between Mr. Brooks and myself. The generality of the press, however, and especially in the large cities, have had the kindness to abstain from pronouncing judgment on the question of veracity, until the evidence should be all in, and the testimony closed on both sides. For this just course of forbearance, pending the controversy, and especially since I solicited a suspension of judgment for ten days or two weeks, I now make my grateful acknowledgments. But I have no such acknowledgments to make to the journals which have pronounced a premature judgment, and whose hasty opinions have been eagerly gathered into the columns of the *Express*. Having indorsed Mr. Brooks, without waiting to know what they were about, it was but consistent that they should vilify Archbishop Hughes, which they have not failed to do. I do not ask them to retract what they have said. I do not ask them to recall or change their opinions on the subject; but I do ask them, as the only reparation which it is in their power to make, to publish this letter in their respective papers. If they are honorable men, they will do so. If I were their enemy, which I am not, I could not desire to inflict on them a more humiliating punishment for their unfair and rash judgment. If they only publish this letter, they may, of course, if they choose, still continue to encourage falsehood, and the falsification of public documents, by their continued indorsement of Senator Brooks.

It is customary throughout nearly all Christendom for a Catholic Bishop to prefix the sign of the Cross to his signature. Most of those editors just now referred to, and who have been fabricating public opinion for the New York *Express*, seem to be too poor in the resources of their printing offices to possess any type which would represent the symbol of Christianity; and, as the next substitute thereto, or rather in ridicule thereof, they substitute the sign of the assassin, the dagger. They imagine apparently that this substitution will make tremendous havoc on the reputation of Archbishop Hughes. But they seem to forget that the sign of the Cross is the sign of man's redemption, and that symbol in which St. Paul glorified, and the symbol which, when represented by a dagger, they are giving over to the scandal of youth, the ridicule of the infidel, and scoffer at all Christianity. And yet our type-founders are not surely so barren of ingenuity, as not to be able to invent something outside the alphabet, which would give a grave and decent idea of the sign of the Cross. Every civilized nation is familiar with symbolic language, nor are we, as a people, at all deficient in this respect, with the single exception I have just mentioned. Outside the alphabet we have our symbolic type to represent, for instance, a section of railway, a steam engine, a tree, a house, a stray horse, or a runaway negro. In fact we have in our printing offices symbolic type for almost every thing except the sign of the Cross. Surely it cannot be that our printers are so excessively American, according to the late and improved sense of that term, that they reject the sign of the Cross, because it symbolizes a *foreign religion.* Alas! if all Americans were like some of our modern legislators, Christianity, the thing symbolized as well as its type, would be foreign enough. Be this, however, as it may, I will forgive those editors if they will only publish this letter, and allow their readers to see and study the melancholy evidences it exhibits of the humiliating position into which their rash, unjust, hasty conclusions, in my regard, and their blind reliance on the veracity of Senator Brooks, have betrayed them. Their readers will perceive that the Honorable Senator has left no species of falsehood unemployed. Being no doubt acquainted with the rules of evidence, they will perceive that Mr. Brooks has perpetrated the falsehood direct, *assertio falsi,* which, if such a term can be applied in such a case, is manly and undisguised falsehood;—as, for example, the "whole squares of land" which in his speech he said were mine. This is the out and out *assertio falsi,* without a shadow of mitigation. The next species is in the insinuation of what is false, *suggestio falsi;*—take, for example, the case in which he intimates, and would have the public believe, that the property given to the Orphan Asylum by the Corporation of the city was given to me, on the plea that my name as President of the Society, and that of its Secretary, were signed to the conditions on which the conveyance had been made. The third species is the suppressing of the truth, *suppressio veri.* This has been exemplified by our Senator;—as, for instance, in the case of the deed, which has on its face, as certified by Messrs. Glover and Wetmore, "*in confirmation*" of a previous title. If the first species of falsehood here alluded to be regarded as at least bold, open, manly and outspoken, the second and third, whenever a question of veracity is involved, are always looked upon as low, sneaking, and base. On the whole, it appears from records and testimony which Mr. Brooks will not dare deny, that he is an expert in every department of falsehood, and that we can say of him, but in a different sense, what the poet said of Sheridan,—he

> * * * "ran
> Through each mode of the *lyre*,
> And was master of all."

Time will not permit me to go into further details on this melancholy subject. I presume the public is disgusted with the exhibition which Senator Brooks has rendered it my painful but imperative duty thus to furnish, on the authority of witnesses and documents which he cannot gainsay. The reader, however, cannot be more disgusted with it than the writer is. And if he will cast his eyes back over the correspondence which has taken place, he will see that I left nothing undone at an earlier stage of its progress to warn and save Mr. Brooks from results which he has determined on realizing to the bitter end. I spoke of the bad example to our youth which would result from his course,—I reminded him that his reputation belonged not to himself, but to his country, and that he was not at liberty to trifle with it. I tried to rouse him to the dangers of his career by language approaching insult, in order to bring him to an issue on some specific question of veracity before he should have accumulated upon his head the mountain which not only hides, but crushes. It was all in vain. If I was content with my "epithets," he said he was content with his "facts." And by this bold but desperate course, Mr. Brooks must have flattered himself that he should carry a large portion of the public with him, or, at all events, that he should so befog the question as to enable him to escape detection and exposure. That mass of "public opinion," so called, which has been gathered from various newspapers into the columns of the Express, shows that for a brief period Mr. Brooks succeeded in his purpose; but should he ever enter on a controversy again, let him not forget the motto prefixed to this letter, in which the great Dutch philosopher proclaims an important principle, namely: "Light, the mother of Truth, will not permit Deception to enjoy a long reign."

Before closing this communication, I must be allowed to say a few words in reference to the style of vituperation employed towards me by those editors whose adverse opinions have been garnered in the columns of the Express. They hold it as an impertinence for a foreigner like myself to adventure on any criticism of the language which a native born American Senator may think proper to employ to his prejudice. They have indorsed the career and position of Mr. Brooks, in reference to the issue of the late controversy, and in opposition to facts and truth. I hold their opinions, therefore, at a very low estimate. Nevertheless, I must tell them that I am not a foreigner: I renounced foreignism on oath nearly forty years ago. I procured from the proper court a certificate of political and civil birthright as an American citizen, and I am not disposed to relinquish one jot of the privileges to which, in the faith of the country, it entitled me. But if I renounced foreignism, I did not renounce humanity. And whilst I hold myself to be as true and loyal an American as ever claimed the protection of our national flag, I would not exchange the bright memories of my early boyhood in another land, and beneath a different sky, for those of any man living, no matter where he was born. Those editors who fabricate public opinion for the N. Y. Express, say that I am not an American. But they are mistaken. If principles and feelings which are theorized, though, perhaps, not always realized in the system of our free government, constitute an American, they were mine from earliest memory—they were innate—they were inherited—they were a portion of my nature. I could not eliminate them from the moral constitution of my nature and being, even if I would. In this sense I was an American from birth. I revered justice and truth, as it were, by instinct. I hated oppression and despised falsehood. I cherished, both for myself, and, as far as practicable, for all mankind, a love of the largest liberty compatible with private rights and public order. Of course, then, when penal laws, enacted on account of my religion, had rendered my native land unfit for a life-long residence, unless I would belong to a degraded class, America, according to its professed principles, was the country for me. But I came not merely to be an inhabitant, but a citizen of the United States. I have, therefore, been an American—I am an American—I will be an American—I *shall* be an American in despite of all the editors that have rushed into the New York Express, with only half the evidence before them, to record judgment in favor of Senator Brooks, and against Archbishop Hughes.

In regard to the recent enactment of our Legislature, forcing an unsolicited bill on the Catholics of New York, out of which the late controversy with Senator Brooks arose, it is not, perhaps, becoming for me to say much. It is, I think, the first statute passed in the Legislature of New York since the Revolution, which has for its object to abridge the religious and encroach on the civil rights of the members of one specific religious denomination. Hitherto when any denomination of Christians in the State desired the modification of its laws affecting Church property, the Legislature waited for their petitions to that effect—took the same into consideration, and when there was no insuperable objection, modified the laws so as to accommodate them to the requirements of the particular sect or denomination by whom the petition had been presented. Thus the law of 1784, though still on the statute book, has become practically antiquated and obsolete. From its odious and oftentimes impracticable requirements, the Episcopalians, the Presbyterians, the Methodists, the Dutch Reformed Church, the Quakers, and perhaps others besides, have at various times solicited exemption at the hands of the Legislature, and obtained special enactments more in accordance with their faith and discipline respectively. Now this antiquated law is the one which is revived, reinvigorated, strengthened by provisions for contingent confiscation of Church property, and forced upon the Catholics of the State of New York as sufficiently good for them. They had not petitioned for it,—they did not desire it,—they will not have it, if they can lawfully dispense with its enactments.

I am indebted to the kindness of a friend, perfectly competent to form a judgment on the subject, for the following synopsis of the hardships, provided for in the different sections of this Church Tenure Bill:

1st.—It makes void a deed of land, if intended for religious worship,—that is to say, it takes from every man (lay or ecclesiastic) the right, either to give to any individual, or to buy a lot, to devote it to the highest purpose to which it can be devoted, the adoration of the living God.

2d.—It avoids a *last will* of any real estate so used. It thus makes it unlawful for any man to leave such property by will to any person, even his own children, and this notwithstanding he may have purchased it and built a church upon it with his own money.

3d.—It attempts to affect lands, held in fee simple absolute with a newly created trust in law,—by a usurpation of judicial functions—which, if tolerated, would destroy the Judiciary, and make the Legislature supreme and despotic.

4th.—It would thus not only impair the validity of a vested title, in violation of the Constitution of the United States, but it would deprive a man of his property without judicial process, in violation of our State Constitution and Bill of Rights.

5th.—By a short, summary sentence,—it would wrest from the individual and from his heirs and devisees all title to such property on his death, (no matter how lawfully acquired,) declaring by a stretch of power, equalled only by the assumed omnipotence of Parliament, that on his death it *shall vest in the State.*

The Constitution declares that the entire and absolute property in lands is vested in the individual owner, subject only to the law of escheat for *defect of heirs.* Yet here we have a statute above the Constitution—a statute of confiscation and of usurpation. Moreover it is the legislation of the strong against the weak,—the legislation of political and religious animosity, forcing, in the 19th century and in this free land, upon *one* religious body a system of church management hostile to their church discipline.

How many are the private rights, hitherto declared sacred and inalienable, which are stricken down by this bold enactment! Surely there is matter in this act to make thinking men pause and wonder that the transition from unrestricted freedom to absolute despotism is so easy and so rapid.

Such is the synopsis of the effects contemplated by what is called the Church Tenure Bill. And the reader who has had the patience to peruse the whole of this communication, will have seen by what means it was introduced, and by what means its enactment has been accomplished.

✠ JOHN, *Archbishop of New York.*

NEW YORK, *May* 14*th*, 1855.

CATALOGUE

OF

NEW & CHEAP

Standard Catholic Publications.

EDWARD DUNIGAN & BROTHER

Invite the attention of the Catholic Hierarchy and Clergy, Colleges, Convents, Religious Institutions, Catholic Institutes, and the public generally, to their extensive assortment of Catholic works in various languages, consisting of BIBLES, PRAYER BOOKS, HISTORICAL and DEVOTIONAL WORKS, and SCHOOL BOOKS.

They ask special attention to their extensive list of superior SCHOOL BOOKS, especially adapted for the use of the Catholic Schools in the United States; all of which are approved by most of the Archbishops and Bishops, as well as Heads of Religious Orders, including the BROTHERS OF THE CHRISTIAN SCHOOLS.

EDWARD DUNIGAN & BROTHER,
151 FULTON STREET, NEAR BROADWAY,
NEW YORK.

Any work in the within Catalogue sent by Mail, free of postage, on receipt of the price annexed.

COPY OF A LETTER,

Accompanying a Gold Medal sent by the Holy Father,

TO EDWARD DUNIGAN & BROTHER.

Most worthy and respected Gentlemen:

Some books, which, as it appeared by your most courteous letter, you wished to offer to our most holy Lord Pope Pius IX., have been lately handed to him. This act on your part could not but please his Holiness, and the zeal you constantly show by the publication of works in defence and protection of the cause of the Catholic Religion, gives him great joy.

The Sovereign Pontiff, therefore, with great pleasure encourages you in your course by this letter, and returns you his thanks for the gift which you offer.

I am, moreover, ordered to transmit a gold medal, which the same benign Pontiff sends, impressed with his august effigy, and with it, as a pledge of his paternal and especial affection towards you, his Apostolic blessing, which, as an auspice of all heavenly good, he lovingly grants you with the most sincere affection of his heart.

I have only to profess my respects to you, Gentlemen, on whom I earnestly implore all that is saving and propitious from our Lord.

Gentlemen,

Your most humble and obedient Servant,

DOMINIC FIORAMONTI,

Rome, July 6th, 1853. *Latin Secretary to his Holiness.*

To E. DUNIGAN & BROTHER, New York.

I.—BIBLES AND TESTAMENTS.

PUBLISHED UNDER THE APPROBATION OF THE

MOST REV. JOHN HUGHES, ARCHBISHOP OF NEW YORK.

DUNIGAN & BROTHER'S

NEW, CHEAP, SUPERBLY ILLUSTRATED, AND UNABRIDGED EDITION OF

Haydock's Catholic Family Bible and Commentary,

The most comprehensive in the English language.

THE HOLY BIBLE, translated from the Latin Vulgate, diligently compared with the Hebrew, Greek, and other editions in various languages. The OLD TESTAMENT, first published by the English College at Douay, A. D. 1609; and the NEW TESTAMENT, first published by the English College at Rheims, A. D. 1582, with useful notes, Critical, Historical, Controversial, and Explanatory, from the most eminent Commentators and able and judicious critics,

By the Rev. Geo. Leo Haydock, D. D.

Splendidly embellished by eminent Artists, after the great Masters. This edition contains in full the many thousand Critical, Explanatory, and Practical Notes illustrative of the Text, with References, Readings, Chronological Tables, and Indexes of the great Original Work, being an exact reprint of the edition approved by the Catholic hierarchy in England and Ireland. It is published under the approbation of the MOST REV. JOHN HUGHES, D. D., Archbishop of New York, and honored with the patronage of most of the Archbishops, Bishops, and Clergy of the United States and the Canadas.

Price—	American morocco, embossed,	$14
	Turkey morocco, gilt edges,	16
	" " super extra gilt edges,	18
	" " " bevelled,	20
	" " " panelled sides,	25

Also in 38 parts, at 25 cents a part.

APPROBATION OF THE ORDINARY.

"This new edition of the English version of the Bible, with the complete notes of Bishop Challoner, Rev. Geo. Leo Haydock, and others, known as Haydock's Catholic Bible, having been duly examined, we hereby approve of its republication by Edward Dunigan & Brother, of this city.

"Given at New York, this 5th day of May, 1852, under our hand and seal.

"✠ John,
Archbishop of New York."

Additional Approbations.

"I most willingly adhere to the approval of this edition of the Holy Bible, given by my Most Rev. Friend and Brother in Christ, the Archbishop of New York; and I shall not fail to recommend its use to the clergy and faithful of the Ecclesiastical province of Quebec.

"✠ P. F.,
Archbishop of Quebec.

"I return you thanks for your splendid edition of the Bible with Haydock's notes. I am happy to find that you have completed your arduous undertaking, and trust that a rapid sale will reward your noble enterprise.

"✠ Francis Patrick Kenrick,
Archb'p Balt."

"I feel proud of adding my approbation to that of your illustrious Archbishop, and unite with all the Prelates and Catholics of this country, in felicitating you on the auspicious consummation of so noble an undertaking. Wishing you a long succession of years distinguished by labors and virtues, such as merited for you the letter and gold medal from the Holy Father with his Apostolic blessing,

"I remain, &c., ✠ J. B. Purcell,
Abp. Cin."

"Please accept my thanks for your new and unabridged edition of Haydock's Catholic Bible, and enlist my name among your subscribers, who, I sincerely hope, will be as numerous as you have unquestionable right to expect, for the unsurpassed care which you have given to this precious publication. I have the honor to remain

Your affect. serv't,

"✠ Ant.,
Abp. of N. Orleans."

Additional Approbations.

"You may place my name among those of the other Prelates, who recommend your edition to the public.

"✠ **Peter Richard,**
"Ab'p of St. Louis."

"I greatly admire and commend your beautifully illustrated edition of the Holy Bible, with Haydock's valuable notes. Your zeal and enterprise are certainly deserving of all praise, and will, I hope, be rewarded by a widely extended patronage.

"✠ **John,**
"Bp. of Albany."

"Of the circulation of your edition of Haydock's Bible in my diocese, I do not merely declare my cordial approval, but my most earnest wish, that it may find a home and readers in every family.

"✠ **Richard Vincent,**
"Bp. of Wheeling."

"The correctness of the edition of which yours is a reprint, and the value of the notes attached to it, are facts which need not now be proved, for they are well known to all who read the Holy Scriptures in English. The testimony of the Most Rev. Archbishop of New York, prefixed to your edition, furnishes sufficient evidence of the accuracy and faithfulness with which you have performed your part in its reproduction. If, however, you think that my approval may be of any benefit, you are free to make use of it.

"Yours respectfully,

"✠ **John B. Fitzpatrick,**
Bp. of Boston."

"I feel extremely anxious to see this splendid edition among the Catholics of my diocese, and I shall do every thing in my power to circulate it—at least to recommend it. It will prove a rich mine to refute the objections and remove the prejudices of the enemies of our holy religion.

"✠ **James Oliver,**
Bp. of Natchez."

Additional Approbations.

"I know not in what terms to express my admiration of your energy, enterprise and success, in producing a work that reflects credit upon our country and religion. I will do all I can to further its circulation.

"Yours, in our Lord,

"✠ **George Aloysius,**

"Bp. of Covington."

"If my approbation be deemed of any service, most cheerfully do I give it. I will also do all in my power to make this new publication known through the diocese of Galveston. Your zeal to enrich the country with useful books, cannot be sufficiently praised. God, I hope, will reward your generous efforts, and prosper your religious undertakings, so favorable to the diffusion of our holy faith.

"✠ **J. M. Odin,**

"Bp. of Galveston."

"I most cheerfully concur with the Most Rev. Archbishop of New York and other prelates of this country in approving of this republication, and do strongly recommend it to the clergy and faithful of the diocese of Detroit.

"✠ **Peter Paul,**

"Bp. Z. C. A. Detroit."

"I take great pleasure in joining with the other prelates in the approbation of your Bible with a sincere desire not only to warrant, but also to encourage the circulation of this splendid work throughout the extent of my diocese.

"✠ **John Martin,**

"Bp. of Milwaukee."

"Your noble edition of Haydock's Bible is far superior to any edition of the Bible heretofore published in the United States, and I cheerfully unite my approbation with those of the prelates that have preceded me

"✠ **Richard Pius Miles,**

"Bp. of Nashville."

Additional Approbations.

"I trust that the Catholic community, not only in the dioceses of Chicago and Quincy, but throughout the Union, will, whilst seeking instruction in the Book of Life, show their appreciation of your enterprise and success, in presenting to them this Holy Volume in so learned, perfect and beautiful a form.

✠ "**Anthony,**
"BISHOP OF CHICAGO."

"The recommendation of the distinguished Bishop Hughes, and the little I have read of the notes, are more than sufficient to induce me to be a patron of your important and useful new edition of Haydock's Bible. I highly approve your bold and holy work. God will reward you.

" ✠ **Joseph Cretin,**
"BISH. OF ST. PAUL."

"The approbation of so many distinguished prelates, without the addition of mine, which I freely give, is more than sufficient to warrant the circulation of that valuable work in my diocese.

" ✠ **Maurice,**
"BP. OF VINCENNES."

"I most heartily concur with so many of my Right Rev. Brethren in the approbation and recommendation of Ed. Dunigan & Brother's most magnificent edition of the Catholic Bible, with Haydock's notes unabridged. There is no apprehension of misunderstanding any text of the Holy Book in this edition, where every difficult passage is so well and faithfully explained.

" ✠ **Frederic Baraga,**
"BISHOP, AND V. A. OF UPPER MICHIGAN."

"The beautiful edition of Haydock's Family Bible, published by Messrs. Dunigan & Brother, of New York, has my approbation, and I cordially recommend its circulation in the diocese of Brooklyn.

" ✠ **John,**
"BP. OF BROOKLYN."

Additional Approbations—CONTINUED.

"At the request of Messrs. Dunigan & Brother I cheerfully join in recommending their new edition of 'Haydock's Catholic Bible,' a work so much esteemed, and now republished with the approbation of the Most Rev. Dr. Hughes, Archbishop of New York.

"✠ **John,**
Bp. of Buffalo."

"I most willingly give my approbation to the useful undertaking of Messrs. Dunigan & Brother in their publication of the Holy Bible.

"✠ **Mathias,**
Bp. of Dubuque."

"Having examined the beautiful new edition of Haydock's Bible, published by E. Dunigan & Brother, I believe it to be a faithful version of the Holy Scriptures, enriched with learned and copious commentaries by approved Catholic writers; and I cheerfully recommend it to the faithful of my Diocese, as a choice family Bible, elegant in appearance and rich in learning.

"✠ **M. J. Spalding,**
Bp. of Louisville."

"The larger will be the circulation of your unparalleled Family Bible in the Diocese of Toronto, the happier will be, &c.,

"✠ **Armandus Fr. Ma.,**
Bp. of Toronto."

"Having examined the new edition of Haydock's Catholic Bible, by E. Dunigan & Brother, I cheerfully unite with the other prelates in recommending it to the faithful of the Diocese of Charleston, and of the United States.

"✠ **J. A. Reynolds,**
Bishop of Charleston.'

"I cordially recommend Messrs. Dunigan & Brother's edition of Haydock's Bible, published under the sanction of Abp. Hughes, to the attention and patronage of the Catholics of the Diocese of Erie.

"✠ **J. M. Young,**
Bp. of Erie."

IV.—CONTROVERSIAL TREATISES.

PUBLISHED UNDER THE APPROBATION OF

THE MOST REV. JOHN HUGHES, D. D.,

ARCHBISHOP OF NEW YORK.

THE EIGHTH EDITION OF

Kirwin Unmasked.

A Review of Kirwin, in Six Letters.

Addressed to the Rev. Nicholas Murray, D. D., of Elizabethtown,

By the Most Rev. John Hughes, D. D.,

ARCHBISHOP OF NEW YORK.

These letters appeared originally in the New York Freeman's Journal, and are now republished in book form.

They are marked by all the clearness of language, felicity of illustration, and closeness of logic, which invariably characterize the productions of the distinguished author, and possess the additional merit of treating the subject in the most easy and familiar style. It is admirably adapted for circulation among all who lack either the time or inclination for reading more extensive volumes.

Price—6¼ cents, or 50 cents per dozen.

NOTICES.

In these letters the Rev. Nicholas Murray is exhibited to the public in a very unenviable light, and is lashed with the power and sarcasm which he well deserves.—*United States Catholic Magazine.*

It is probable that Mr. Murray designed to get into a religious controversy with Bishop Hughes, and from being thus made the champion of his own portion of Protestants, to elevate himself by the controversy. The *American Bossuet* had already annihilated the best champions of the Protestant cause, and could not well stoop to argument on religious matters with one such as these valuable letters show Mr. Murray to have been.—*Truth Teller.*

The Manual of Controversy,

Containing in one volume, 16mo. size, the celebrated works of the

Grounds of the Catholic Doctrine;

The Papist Misrepresented and Truly Represented;

AND

Fifty Reasons why the Roman Catholic Religion ought to be Preferred to all others.

Price—Cloth binding, 63 cents.

The Grounds of the Catholic Doctrine,

Contained in the Profession of Faith published by Pope Pius IV.; to which are added Reasons why a Catholic cannot conform to the Protestant Religion.

An authoritative statement of Catholic Doctrine. Its simplicity and clearness of form, by way of Question and Answer, and its established accuracy, have given it a wide popularity. 18mo.

Price—Neat paper binding, 9 cts. per doz. . $0 75
Cloth, ... 18¾ cts. " . 1 50

Fifty Reasons why the Roman Catholic Religion ought to be Preferred to all others.

By Anthony Ulric,

Duke of Brunswick and Lunenburg, a Convert from Lutheranism.

This little book has long enjoyed the highest reputation as a succinct and useful summary of the most solid and convincing Reasons that should conduct men to the light of Catholic truth. This edition has several valuable papers annexed.

Price—Neat paper binding, . 9 cts. per doz. . $0 75
Cloth, ... 18¾ cts. " . 1 50

Douay Bible.

THE HOLY BIBLE, translated from the Latin Vulgate. Illustrated Family Edition. Imperial octavo. Printed in double columns, with parallel References, being the only octavo edition printed in the United States that contains them, with Illuminated Title, Family Records, from original designs, and many exquisite Engravings, from the great Masters.

Price—Superb Turkey morocco, 15 illustrations, . .	$9 00
American morocco, illuminated, gilt sides and edges, 14 illustrations, ...	5 00
American morocco, gilt edges, 14 illustrations, .	4 50
Embossed morocco, fancy edges, 14 illustrations,	3 00

Douay Bible.

Cheap Edition. Royal octavo.

Price—American morocco, illuminated, gilt sides and edges, 6 illustrations, ...	$4 00
American moroc., full gilt sides and edg., 6 illus.,	3 50
" " gilt edges, 6 illustrations, .	3 00
" " gilt back and sides, fancy edg., 6 illustrations, ...	2 50
Embossed moroc., gilt back, fancy edg., 4 plates,	2 00
Sheep bindings, 1 plate, . . .	1 50

Approbation.

"The present edition of the Douay version of the Old and New Testament, published by Edward Dunigan, New York, having been revised by our direction, we have great pleasure in recommending it to the faithful, to be read with that reverence and respect which are due to the word of God, and with that humility of heart and docility which the Church enjoins upon all who would read the Scriptures with advantage to their souls.

"Given at the Episcopal residence, this 27th day of January, 1844.

✠ "JOHN HUGHES,
"BISHOP OF NEW YORK."

Approved also by the Archbishops and Bishops generally.

The New Testament of our Lord and Saviour Jesus Christ.

Translated from the Latin Vulgate, and first published by the English College at Rheims, A. D. 1582, with Annotations, a Chronological Index, Table of References, &c., &c. Neat 12mo. edition.

Price—Cloth, plain, ... $0 31
Gilt edges, ... 0 75

El Nuevo Testamento de Nuestro Señor i Salvador Jesu Cristo.

Nuevamente traducido por el exmo. Sr. Don Felix Torres Amat, Obispo de Astorga. Lleva algunas notas tomadas del P. Scio i otras calificados interpretes—con la aprobacion del

Ilmo Fr. Jose S. Alemany,
ARZOBISPO DE SAN FRANCISCO.

A cheap and accurate edition of the approved Spanish translation.

Price—Cloth, plain, ... $1 00
American morocco, ... 1 25
Turkey morocco, ... 2 50

The Acts of the Apostles, the Epistles of St. Paul, the Catholic Epistles, & the Apocalypse.

8vo. Uniform with the "Four Gospels." With Notes, Critical and Explanatory.

By the Most Rev. Francis Patrick Kenrick, D. D.,
ARCHBISHOP OF BALTIMORE.

This volume is a supplement to the "Four Gospels," already published by us, and completes Archbishop Kenrick's new version of the New Testament.

It contains a most valuable commentary, and is invaluable to the clergy, and all who study the sacred volume.

Price—Cloth, ... $2 50

NOTICES.

Any work from the pen of Bishop Kenrick must be received with interest and with respect by every Catholic who speaks the English language.—CARDINAL WISEMAN *in Dublin Review.*

This laborious work is highly creditable to the American Church.—*Tablet.*

The Clifton Tracts,

ORIGINALLY PUBLISHED BY THE BROTHERHOOD OF ST. VINCENT OF PAUL, UNDER THE SANCTION OF THE BISHOP OF CLIFTON, AND WITH THE APPROBATION OF CARDINAL WISEMAN, AND ALL THE CATHOLIC BISHOPS OF ENGLAND. 4 vols. 12mo. **Price**—38 cents per volume.

This series of Tracts was originated with the view of supplying a want long and generally felt, of a number of CHEAP single publications, which, at the same time that they afforded useful reading to Catholics, and the numerous converts that from all sides are being gathered into the fold of the Church, might also furnish inquirers with a plain and simple statement of Catholic doctrine, principles, and practice, together with an exposure of Protestant errors, and a refutation of some, at least, among the many absurd and foolish charges brought against the Catholic religion.

Nothing ever written in the English language is so admirably adapted for general distribution, and for spreading a knowledge of the great truths of the Catholic religion, as this series of Tracts, being written with rare ability and care, and in the best possible spirit of charity, zeal, and good taste; and it is hoped they will win ther way into every family, as each tract discusses in a masterly and condensed manner a single subject only. Their diversity, embracing as they do, Historical, Controversial, and Devotional subjects, must render them also highly attractive not only to the Catholic but to the general reader. They are published in a neat and attractive style and form, with beautiful type and good paper, and sold so CHEAP in price, that they can hardly fail to meet with a large circulation.

The success of the English editions induced their reprint here. Catholics need only to know these excellent tracts, to appreciate them and aid in their dissemination.

1.—**Rosary of the Blessed Virgin Mary,** and the Use of the Beads no "vain Repetition." Price, 4 cents.
2.—**The Church, the Guardian of the Scriptures.** Price, 4 cents.
3.—**The Church, the Witness of the Scriptures.** Price, 4 cents.
4.—**The Church, a Kingdom.** Price, 4 cents.
5.—**The Church, the Dispenser of Scripture;** or, Are Catholics Allowed to Read the Bible? Price, 4 cents.
6.—**The Church, the Interpreter of Scripture;** or, How do we Know what the Bible Means? Price, 4 cents.

7.—**Protestantism Weighed in its own Balance and Found Wanting**: The Bible and the Bible only. Price, 4 cents.

8.—**Protestantism Weighed, &c.**: The Church. Price, 4 cents.

9.—**Protestantism Weighed, &c.**: The Sacraments. Price, 6 cents.

10.—**Protestantism Weighed, &c.**: Devotion to Saints and Angels. Price, 4 cents.

11.—**Protestantism Weighed, &c.**: The Supremacy of St. Peter. Price, 4 cents.

12.—**Benediction of the Most Holy Sacrament**; or, What Catholics do when the Candles are Lighted. Price, 3 cents.

13.—**The Catholic Missionary.** The Jesuits in Paraguay. Price, 6¼ cents.

14.—**The Catholic Missionary.** Father Claver in India. Price, 4 cents.

15.—**How did England become Catholic and how did England become Protestant?** Price 6¼ cents.

16.—**Queen Mary and Her People.** The Smithfield Fires. Price, 6¼ cents.

17.—**Queen Mary and Her People.** How Mary Restored the Catholic Religion. Price, 6¼ cents.

18.—**How the Pope became a King.** The People Deserted by their Rulers. Price, 4 cents.

19.—**How the Pope became a King.** The Fall of Pagan Rome Price, 4 cents.

20.—**How the Pope became a King.** The People Choose a Protector. Price, 4 cents.

21.—**Corpus Christi**; or, The Feast of the Most Holy Sacrament. Price, 4 cents.

22.—**Christmas Day**; whose Birthday is it? Price, 4 cents.

23.—**How Anti-Christ Keeps Christmas**; or, A Peep at Christmas in a Catholic Country. Price, 3 cents.

24.—**The Religion of Catholics, the Worship of Jesus.** Price, 4 cents.

25.—**The Feast of the Assumption of the Blessed Virgin Mary.** Price, 4 cents.

26.—**The Litany of the Blessed Virgin**; commonly called the Litany of Loretto. Price, 4 cents.

27.—**Know Popery**; or, Are all these Conversions Nothing to Me? Price, 4 cents.

28.—**The Intention of the Minister**; Necessary to the Valid Administration of the Sacraments. Price, 4 cents.

29.—**The Holy Sacrifice of the Mass**: Sacrifice the Highest Act of Worship. Price, 4 cents.

30.—**The Holy Sacrifice of the Mass**: The Sacrifice of the Altar one and the same with the Sacrifice of the Cross. Price, 4 cents.

31.—**The Holy Sacrifice of the Mass**: Scripture Proofs of the Doctrine. Price, 4 cents.

32.—**Holy Week**: Palm Sunday; or, The Procession. Price, 3 cents.

33.—**Holy Week**: Maundy Thursday: or, The Holy Sepulchre. Price, 3 cents.

34.—**Holy Week**: Good Friday; or, The Adoration of the Cross. Price, 3 cents.

35.—**Reasons for not Worshipping or Communicating in Religion with Non-Catholics.** By the Right Rev. Bishop Hay. Price, 6¼ cents.

Sure Way to find out the True Religion, in a Conversation between a Father and his Son.

By the Rev. T. Baddeley.

This standard little work has long been a favorite with English Catholics. It discusses the chief points at issue in a simple familiar style.

Price—One volume, paper binding, . . . 12½ cents.
Cloth, ... 19 "

Defensa de Algunos Puntos de la Doctrina Catolica o Sea Contestacion a las Nuevas Observaciones, del Sr. Espinosa, contra el Retrato de la Virgen.

Aprobada y recomendada por el

Reverendisimo Fr. Sadoc Alemani,

ARZOBISBO DE SAN FRANCISCO.

A thorough Spanish work of controversy, on the Bible as the rule of Faith, and the Church as the interpreter of Scripture.

Price—Paper, 38 cents.

Das Primat des Apostolischen Stuhls.

The Primacy of the Apostolic See Vindicated.

By the Most Rev. Francis P. Kenrick, D. D.

Translated into the German language by the Rev. Nicholas Steinbacher, S. J. 8vo.

Nearly three large editions of this important work having been sold in the English language, and it being universally acknowledged the best Vindication of the Primacy ever written, and a most triumphant answer to the entire Protestant statement, has induced an eminent clergyman to make a complete Translation into the German language, for the benefit of those that only read the German. It is printed on good paper and type, and bound in handsome cloth.

Price—Cloth, $2.

The Papist Misrepresented, and truly Represented; Or a Twofold Character of Popery.

The first containing a sum of the Superstitions, Idolatries, Cruelties, Treacheries, and Wicked Principles laid to their charge. The other laying open that religion which those termed Papists own and profess; the chief articles of their faith, and the principal grounds and reasons which attach them to it. 18mo.

By the Rev. John Gother.

Gother perfectly understood the calumnies and prejudices which influence men most strongly against the Catholic Church and faith, and how to expose and dispel them. His little book is a perfect controversial magazine in miniature.

Price—Neat paper binding,	9 cts.	per doz.	$0 75
Cloth, ...	18¾ cts.	"	1 50

Milner's End of Religious Controversy.

The End of Religious Controversy, in a Friendly Correspondence between a Religious Society of Protestants and a Catholic Divine,

By the Rt. Rev. John Milner, D. D.

Printed from the last edition, revised by the author. 1 vol., 12mo. With the Apostolical Tree.

This celebrated work, which so many Protestant divines in England and this country—from the period of its first publication down to Bishop Hopkins—have attempted to answer, but which must ever remain unanswerable, is a perfect treasury of texts and facts from Scripture and History. With a view to securing for such a work the most extensive circulation possible, the subscribers have published an edition at the prices stated, which it must be obvious are so very low, that only the widest sales can remunerate them.

Price—Neat paper covers, ... 25 cents.
Sheep and cloth binding, ... 50 "

www.ingramcontent.com/pod-product-compliance
Lightning Source LLC
LaVergne TN
LVHW011206110826
845150LV00006B/1335
* 9 7 8 1 4 2 5 5 1 8 2 4 0 *